CREATIVE
ANTICIPATION

CREATIVE
ANTICIPATION

Narrative Sermon Designs
For Telling The Story

David A. Enyart

All Scripture quotations, unless otherwise indicated, are taken from the HOLY BIBLE, NEW INTERNATIONAL VERSION®. NIV®. Copyright ©1973, 1978, 1984 by International Bible Society. Used by permission of Zondervan. All rights reserved.

This book was printed in the United States of America.

To order additional copies of this book, contact:
Xlibris Corporation
1-888-795-4274
www.Xlibris.com
Orders@Xlibris.com
15418

CONTENTS

I dedicate this book to my wonderful wife, Mary Faith. For thirty-seven years, she has been my wife and soul-mate. Not only has she encouraged me in writing this volume, she has assisted along the way with her gifted editorial skills. I owe her more than I will ever be able to repay. Thank you, Mary Faith.

In Greek mythology, Odysseus and his crew sail near the dangerous "island of sirens" and the seductive music woos them to the shore. To shut out the tempting strains, Odysseus stuffs the ears of his sailors with cotton. Later, Orpheus and his seamen sail by the same enticing island. Orpheus protects his crew in a different manner: He takes out his lyre and *plays sweeter music* than that which wafts from the island.

PROLOGUE:

LOOKING BACK ON SUNDAY'S

SERMON

For the twenty-seven years that Douglas Chadwick has served God in the pastoral ministry, he has kept a private journal in which he reflects back on each particular Sunday. Douglas writes his weekly entry early Monday morning while Sunday is still fresh in his memory. Evaluating Sunday's sermon is his primary concern: How did the congregation respond? How could he improve the sermon? Was he faithful to the biblical text while meeting the personal needs of his congregation? Did the sermon build an adequate "bridge" between the biblical world and the modern world? Has he found a way to "release the Word" into the lives of his listeners? Douglas laughingly calls his journal his "Monday Memoirs." What follows is one Monday's entry in Douglas Chadwick's journal.

Have I really spent twenty-seven years in the ministry? Nineteen of those years I've served the same church. During that period I have hit an occasional grand-slam in the pulpit; I've also struck-out a few times. Some Monday mornings I have felt discouraged; others, just the reverse. That's the ministry, I guess; always riding the roller coaster.

This morning I feel good; I am not low or high, just good. The congregation responded positively to yesterday's sermon. Both during and after the message, my people let me know that I was genuinely communicating.

I marvel at all the different means I've used during my ministry to measure the effectiveness of my preaching. My perspective of a "successful sermon" has certainly changed over the years. *I'm glad that I'm finally getting a handle on how to evaluate a sermon.* It's taken me all of those years to begin acquiring that skill. At first I judged my sermons by the comments of the older ladies in the congregation. They almost always made me feel assured: "You're just the finest preacher this church has had. Today's message was one of your best!" One Sunday we had a guest minister who preached a shallow and inferior sermon. Afterwards, I noticed that these elderly, saintly ladies complimented his preaching just as they did mine. I am not a genius, but it didn't take me long to realize I needed another criterion for measuring my sermons!

During one period I saw myself primarily as God's "prophet." It embarrasses me even to write it, but I often judged the effectiveness of a sermon by the number of people who were too angry to shake my hand after the service. After all, making folks mad was part of my prophetic responsibility. My philosophy was "Tell it like it is; if they can't take the truth, let them find another church!" One of our finest families left the church during that period; they told me, "We just cannot endure any more negative preaching." I finally realized that my preaching wasn't *prophetic*; *pathetic* was a more accurate representation.

I also cycled through a time when I judged my sermons by the number of people who cried. My goal was to stir deep emotions. On one occasion I was shaking hands after the service, when a woman came out of the church dabbing her eyes with a Kleenex. Proudly I thought, "I really touched her with the power of the Gospel!" Did she ever take the wind out of my sails! "Preacher," she exclaimed, "I'm afraid I didn't hear much of your sermon today. Last evening I dropped my wedding ring into the commode and flushed it before I realized what I had done! I've been so upset; I can't seem to get my mind on anything else!" So much for the "Kleenex-and-wet-eye-method" of sermon appraisal! *My present method for evaluating sermons is definitely an improvement.*

After I had been in the ministry a few years, I judged the effectiveness of my sermons by the number of questions asked. "Preacher, what do you mean by that word 'eschatology'?" "What does 'justified by faith' mean?" With questions like these, surely my preaching was stimulating thought. I do believe that mode of sermon evaluation was superior to some of the others. However, now I don't judge of my sermons by *any* of these previous methods; I've landed on a better technique. Yesterday I observed still more evidence that this method works.

Sunday's message was a narrative sermon entitled "A Tale of Two Marriages." The application of the text (Ephesians 5:22-33) came toward the end of the sermon. My primary objective was to help couples recognize the incarnation of Christ as a model for human relationships—especially marriage. I started by quoting Reuel Howe who characterizes marriage as unique among human relationships; no other demands "such depth and constancy of commitment."[1] Writes Howe,

> In what other relationship are the possibilities for repentance and forgiveness any greater? In what other relationship is it possible to find the resources of love to live creatively with disillusionment and heartbreak? Or where else in human relations is there to be found such depth of joy? Nowhere

else is there such exciting dialogue between love
and hate.[2]

At the outset of the sermon I told the stories of two contrasting marriages. The first I described as "unpleasant and unhappy";
the second, as "joyful and satisfying."

Endless cycles of hostility and bitterness scarred the first marriage. There was a scarcity of love in this match; actually, the couple
didn't even *like* each other. Children born in this home were born
on a battlefield, weaned in a foxhole; ballistic missiles, not bottles,
filled their cribs. I explained to the congregation that children
who witness violence between their parents are actually victims of
that violence; such was certainly the case in this first marriage. As
I demonstrated with a couple of examples, this couple constantly
assaulted each other, both physically and psychologically.

Once, at the supper table, the husband exploded in a fit of
anger. He grabbed a large bowl of beans and slammed it against
the wall. Beans and fragments of glass showered everyone at the
table, including the small children; fortunately, there were only
minor cuts. The meal was destroyed, but it didn't matter; no one
felt like eating anyway. On another occasion, the wife physically
attacked her husband as he drove down the highway; he was barely
able to control the car. In the back seat, the children cowered,
petrified with fear.

In this particular home, the children felt torn between mother
and father, as each parent faulted the other. Sometimes the couple
refused to speak directly to each other, forcing the children to
transmit messages between them. The five children in this household lived in constant anxiety and insecurity. Would their parents
divorce each other? Might they kill each other? Could the children
make things right between their parents? These children were "psychologically invisible"; their thoughts and feelings didn't matter.
The parental dysfunction created a spiritual and emotional vacuum
for every member of the family system.

After revealing the story of this family, I asked the congregation: "Do you think the lack of a serious commitment to Christ might have contributed to this dysfunctional home?"

The second marriage in my sermon contrasted the first; the husband and wife in this union were extremely devoted to each other. Though it sounds corny, I characterized this marriage as a "perpetual honeymoon." The two children were the beneficiaries of the deep love between husband and wife. During meals this family shared the day's happenings, laughed, and told stories. The home wasn't perfect; husband and wife sometimes disagreed, but not with the hostility that marked the first marriage. This husband and wife knew how to learn from their conflict, so that it became constructive rather than destructive; they developed the art of creative compromise.

When the family traveled together in the car, they often sang or listened to Christian music. They related funny stories and even discussed serious issues while on vacation or traveling to grandparents. Joyful, spontaneous interaction distinguished this second family.

I informed the congregation that the second couple was actively involved in God's family, the church. I raised the question: "Do you think the presence of a commitment to Christ might have made the difference in this second family?"

After detailing those two stories, I then turned to my text, Ephesians 5:21-33. Paul utilized a remarkable metaphor; he compared the relationship between husband and wife to the relationship that exists between Christ and his church. Paul wrote, "Submit to one another out of reverence for Christ."[3] [4] As I preached this text, I realized how much we were discovering not simply about marriage and family, but also about incarnational theology. I advised the congregation that the incarnation of Christ provides the model for all relationships—especially, the relationship between husband and wife. In the Philippian Epistle, Paul described Jesus as one who " . . . made himself nothing, taking the very nature of a servant, being made in human likeness."[5] Our Lord's identification with us was complete: "And being found in appearance as a man, he humbled himself and became obedient to death—even death on a cross."[6] A husband is commanded to love his wife "just as Christ loved the church and gave himself up for her"[7] Paul implies that the wife is to love her husband *as the church loves Christ.* In Christian marriage we try to imitate the incarnation as we discover how to fully identify with our mate, to see life through his or her eyes. As Lloyd Ogelvie maintains,

> A marriage is most Christian, not when it is free of problems and difficulties, but when two persons open themselves to the Spirit of Christ, surrender their wills to Him, commit their living to Him, and as a conscious dedication, seek to love each other and give themselves to each other as they have been loved and given to by Christ. This is more than making Christ the head of the home. It is the daily, hourly, moment by moment willingness to see Christ in our mates and to serve, love and honor him by what we say, do, give, and forgive.[8]

To close my sermon, I returned momentarily to my two families. I informed my congregation that I knew the particulars of those two homes intimately because both of the homes I described were *my families.* The first example, the pain-filled marriage, was my childhood home; the husband and wife pictured were my parents. The second example was my adult home, composed of my wife and myself, along with our two girls. Compared to my childhood home, my adult home is "heaven on earth."

Did the absence or presence of commitment to Christ make a difference in those two homes? Most assuredly! Christ did and does make a difference in both marriage and the home that develops from that union. As I told the congregation, "I speak from personal experience!"

I'm pleased that *I now more accurately understand how to evalu-*

ate the effectiveness of a sermon. If after the message, someone comes up to me and says, *"Preacher, your sermon made me think of an experience in my own life; let me tell you about it,"* I am almost certain the sermon has connected.[9]

Yesterday a couple told me *their* story. A husband and wife (Bill and Susan) approached me after the sermon. Susan, who is blind, said, "Preacher, we want to tell you our experience; we've not revealed this story to anyone else, but your sermon brought it to mind. A few years ago, I was having trouble with my eyes; my vision was becoming blurry and glasses didn't seem to help. I assumed—we assumed—that I was suffering from cataracts. I went to an ophthalmologist, who ran several tests on my eyes and instructed me to come back in a week for the results. Bill went with me when I returned. The doctor looked somber as he invited us into his office. He was kind, but direct: 'I'm afraid I have some bad news for you. Susan, you have a disease of the optic nerve for which there is no known treatment. Your condition will steadily deteriorate until you lose your sight.' I was devastated; I could hardly comprehend what the doctor was saying; I wept in self-pity and bitterness. I would not allow either my husband or the doctor to comfort me. How could I be a wife and mother with no sight? Would my husband even love me after I had gone blind? I wasn't sure life was worth living if I lost my sight."

"Bill and I were both shaken. He couldn't find the words to comfort me, and I really wasn't prepared to accept anything he had to say. Bill pleaded, 'Susan, we're both so upset; we need to get our minds off this problem for a while; let's go see a movie.' Reluctantly I agreed. When we arrived at the theater, we discovered that it was almost an hour until the movie started. Bill said, 'Susan, close your eyes and take hold of my arm. There's something I want to show you.' I was in no mood for this sort of thing, but when he persisted, I closed my eyes and took hold of his arm. I couldn't imagine what he desired to show me. We walked for several blocks, taking three distinct turns. Finally, Bill spoke, 'Okay, Susan, open your eyes; I want to show you something.' I opened my eyes and I saw *nothing.* 'What do you mean?' I asked; 'I don't see anything particular.' Bill responded, 'Susan, do you see me?' 'Yes, of course I see you.' 'Susan, I love you and I want you to know that blind or not, I will always love you; I'll always be at your side to help you. As you lose your eyesight, I want you to find strength in my continuing love.'"

Then Susan said to me, "Preacher, as you know, I have lost my sight. Without my faith in God and the support of my husband, I don't think I could have adjusted to blindness. Bill's words to me on that day were the beginning of my adjustment. Your sermon this morning reminded us of our story, and we had to share it with you. I do believe," she asserted, "that my husband loves me 'as Christ loves the church.'" I stood and watched as they went down the steps of the church building; Susan held firmly to her husband's arm. This couple's story impressed upon me a new image for understanding the incarnation of Christ.

After twenty-seven years in the ministry, I realize that there is no "perfect" way to judge the effectiveness of pulpit communication. But I feel reasonably confident of my sermons if *my listeners respond with their own stories—their own sermons.* Theirs are frequently better sermons than mine; I say "better" because they have processed the Gospel through their own lives and experiences. If my sermon causes them to reflect on their own spiritual journeys, their own stories, then I have succeeded.[10] Yes, I feel good about yesterday's sermon—or perhaps I should say yesterday's *sermons.*[11]

CHAPTER 1

CREATIVE ANTICIPATION

"When the doctor left the room, I decided to pick up that book; so I did. I flipped through the pages, and then I started reading it, and then I didn't want to stop. I read and I read, and I finished the whole book that night; it was midnight, maybe. The nurse kept coming in to tell me that I should put my light off and go to sleep because I needed my rest. . . . I read, and when I was done with the story, I felt different. It's hard to say what I mean. I can't tell you, I can't explain what happened; I know that my mind changed after I read Huckleberry Finn. I couldn't get my mind off the book. I forgot about myself. . . . Have you ever read a book that really made a difference to you—a book you couldn't get out of your mind. . . ?"[1]

Robert Coles in The Call of Stories

God created us with the ability to anticipate, i.e., "to expect; to look forward." Without this capacity, we would be unable to plan, dream, or even believe, for each of these behaviors presumes some expectation for the future. Admittedly, our power to look forward also exposes us to worry and anxiety. However, even a brief reflection on human experience reveals "anticipation" as more of a positive than negative attribute:

- "I receive my first paycheck this coming Friday, and I can hardly wait."
- "The doctor says our baby is a little girl; just think, in a few months we will be parents!"
- "Mommy, I can't get my eyes to shut. I keep hearing noises like reindeer landing on the roof!"
- "Married. Three days and I will marry the man of my dreams!"
- "One semester to go and I will have a college degree! I am so tired of books and term papers, but I can hang-on for one more semester."

Sometimes anticipation involves a long-term project like earning a degree or trekking through Europe on vacation. Other times, anticipation may focus on short-term goals, like taking our spouse out on a date or completing a good book. Recently an old man said to me, "Preacher, lookin-foward to something is sometimes better than gettin-it!" I am not sure to what he was referring, but I accept his words as generally true. For example, we often experience disappointment after purchasing a long desired material possession. Anticipating the new car generates more delight than owning it (Those payments are painful!). The cabin in the mountains sounds wonderful until we start packing the car and driving the distance. Nonetheless, though we are sometimes disappointed by that which we have hoped for, the ability to anticipate remains a beneficial gift.

Stories and Creative Anticipation

My wife and I enjoy reading. We spend our free evenings, not in front of a television, but in our easy chairs reading novels, occasionally sharing interesting passages from our respective tomes. Good stories provide one of the most enjoyable forms of *creative anticipation*. Stories captivate us because we anticipate their outcome, their ending. Such stories, real or fictional, as found in books or movies, constitute simple pleasures, readily accessible in western societies. A trip to Europe requires a substantial outlay of funds, but curling up with a good library book is an affordable luxury available to most. I delight in good movies or TV programs, but most of the stories I enjoy come from books. Being a professor of preaching, I read many volumes related to my academic responsibilities. However, I find my greatest pleasure in novels, murder mysteries, human interest stories, and classical literature. When I am reading a good book, I find myself relaxed and highly motivated. The same story made into a movie almost always disappoints me; my imagination creates more authentic characters than Hollywood produces.

Good storytellers are adept at prompting the reader or listener to *creatively anticipate*: "I started that book at 7:30 and could not lay it down until I had finished it at 3:00 A.M.!" As E. M. Forster maintains, a story "can only have one merit: that of making the audience want to know what happens next. And conversely it can only have one fault: that of making the audience not want to know what happens next."[2] Creative writers engage the reader in the story. Amos Wilder asserts that "the first axiom of good storytelling is that it should capture and hold our attention."[3] According to Wilder there are several reasons[4] stories appeal to us:

1) We naturally regard *what happened*, "especially if it was something unusual."[5]

2) We are captivated by what may happen *next;* "One is on a road and one wonders what is around the corner and about how the road forks."[6]

3) Stories stimulate our interest not only in the unfamiliar, but also in the *familiar.* "That feature is lifelike; that detail is precisely evoked, exactly right."[7]

4) The opening details constituting the story's *beginning* prompt our curiosity.

5) We find interest in how the story will *conclude*. The central conflict be resolved, but how?
6) We are intrigued by what the story *means*, by what the storyteller is "getting at."
7) And finally, we find interest in the *art of telling*.

Stories Evoke Response

Typically, stories sustain our interest. But compelling stories provide more than entertainment; the reader participates in the *experience* of the story's characters, particularly the central character or "protagonist." This identification with the protagonist causes his or her story to become the reader's story. Writes Amos Wilder:

> In all those features of storytelling, which exert their spell on hearer or reader, we can recognize the bridge between fiction and life itself. . . . The world of story is our own world in a higher register.[8]

An effectively related story summons memories of our own story. Douglas Chadwick, the hypothetical minister mentioned in the Prologue, learned the value of measuring his sermons according to the personal stories generated within his parishioners. The sermon which listener's shape within themselves I call "the second sermon." As Richard F. Ward states, "The sign of effective personal storytelling is that it creates an atmosphere where other stories within the community's memory are evoked, not demanded."[9] The word "evoke" is significant. The storyteller does not announce, "Now I want you to think of your own story to see how it compares with the story I have just told." Rather, the listener naturally forms the connection.

When an author induces us to "creatively anticipate," we are never quite the same; stories that engage us also change us—sometimes even when we are unaware. Because stories capture our attention, we make little effort to resist the messages they infer. This non-resistance, of course, can be either good or bad depending on the messages conveyed; some stories instill truth, others falsehood. For example, violent movies can motivate unacceptable imitations.[10] For this reason, story discrimination is necessary. The nation's storytellers (which includes preachers) must consider how their narratives[11] will affect hearers. The irresponsible telling of stories can do much harm, both to individuals and society.

New books released in the field of homiletics, such as works by Fred Craddock, Thomas Troeger, Eugene Lowry, and other homileticians always perk my interest. I also enjoy writers of fiction like Dorothy Sayers, J. R. R. Tolkien, Mary Stewart, William Golding, C. S. Lewis, and a host of others. These authors demonstrate *how* to tell a story. As a matter of fact, the books preachers read for pleasure may ultimately have more impact on their preaching than volumes dealing with homiletical methodology; that is certainly the case with me. Reading literature improves our ability to identify with the differing peoples to whom we preach. Consider Pat Conroy's novel *The Prince Of Tides*, which relates the story of a dysfunctional family (the Wingos), who live on an island off the coast of South Carolina. Tom Wingo, the central character, reflects on his own life:

> And each year, I lose a little bit more of what made me special as a kid. I don't think as much or question as much. I dare nothing. I put nothing on the line. Even my passions are now frayed and pathetic. Once I dreamed I'd be a great man. . . . Now, the best I can hope for is that I can fight my way back to being a mediocre man.[12]

I cannot hear the words of this fictional character without looking inside my own family, my own soul. Conroy's story *evokes* mine, and in the process, increases my sensitivity; I become more attuned to both myself and my parishioners. Forced to examine my own roots, my own insecurities and disappointments with life, I become more whole as a person. In the process I become a better communicator and a more perceptive pastor-teacher.

Deduction and Induction

I attended seminary in the 1960's. The homiletics classes drilled future preachers in "deductive" or "discursive" methods, which borrow their pattern from classical Greek rhetoric. Our homiletical emphasis focused mostly on what I call "logical argumentation." Deductive sermons were divided into three categories: 1) expository; 2) topical; and 3) textual. Our professors saturated us with information on directive approaches, often focusing on what we called "three-points-and-a-poem-sermons." In minute detail, we studied the thesis, transitional statement, key word, introduction, points, transitions, conclusions, and, of course, illustrations.[13] The form employed for these three styles was mechanical and, for the most part, beyond question. An established "thesis," which the preacher derived from personal study, constituted the heart of the sermon. It was assumed that the congregation would accept this thesis without any substantial disagreement. After announcing the "thesis" or "proposition," the preacher presented a discourse built around an extensive use of logic and/or argumentation. Listeners, we were taught, would be persuaded by the force and clarity of our arguments. "Metaphors of illustration," woven throughout the message, helped the listeners understand our well-ordered reasoning. With this approach, the congregation was viewed as a receptacle into which we poured the truth, as you might pour water into a glass.[14] Eugene Lowry appropriately states,

> the art of communication consisted primarily of transmitting a set of complete ideas from one location to another via the 'conveyor belt' called speech. A formal speech essentially was a conveyor belt moving in one direction.[15]

John Broadus was a preeminent authority on preaching from 1870 to the mid-twentieth century. Broadus operated on this presupposition: "will is the obedient servant of reason."[16] Broadus assumed that if one's powers of logic and persuasion were sufficiently developed, effective pulpit communication was all but guaranteed. That assumption may have been true in Broadus' time, but I am quite certain it is not accurate today. My bookshelves still hold many of the textbooks by which we future preachers were instructed in deductive sermon methodology: *On the Preparation and Delivery of Sermons* (John A. Broadus); *Expository Preaching Without Notes*, (Charles W. Koller); *Expository Preaching for Today*, (Andrew Blackwood). Our skills in "alliteration" were honed to a razor sharp edge. If David slew Goliath with five smooth stones, we preachers would defeat the forces of evil with three alliterative points. "In this passage we see, the Fearful One, the Foolish One, and the Faithful One." Of this type of preaching, David Buttrick writes:

> What's wrong with categorical point-making sermons? Well, they are intrinsically tedious. They are static and didactic at the same time. Though a minister can jot down categorical points with ease, 1-2-3, people in the pews find such sermons impossible to hear.[17]

Narrative preaching, the focus of this volume, is much more "indirect" or "inductive" in design, and is built around "creative anticipation" rather than "logical argumentation." With induction, the listener reasons alongside the preacher, moving simultaneously toward conclusions. The narrative sermon *arrives at* a universal thesis toward the end of the message, rather than asserting it at the beginning. In many instances, the listener shapes this universal truth herself as she responds to the sermon. Furthermore, narrative or inductive models are less rigid in format, more concerned with *movement* than *points*. As we shall discuss in some detail later, narrative sermons are "plotted," rather than outlined. Deduction *pushes* the listener along by powerful reasoning; induction creatively *pulls* the hearer onward with an unresolved conflict or unanswered question. With inductive sermon designs, speaker and listener walk side by side in search of God's answer to a specific problem or conflict.

A *question*, a *quest*, and a *discovery (Discovery)* constitute the heart of narrative sermons. Most often these three elements are set in a narrative context. I say "most often" because I fully recognize that a sermon can be built around plot, even without story or stories. Thomas Long claims,

> Sermons cannot always be stories; they sometimes do not even include stories, but they must always have plots, patterns of dynamic sequential elements. In this sense, the sermon is storylike, even when it includes no stories per se.[18]

Eugene Lowry makes a distinction between what he calls "narrative content" and "narrative form."[19] For Lowry, sermons may be labeled as "narrative" even though they are not based upon story or stories; that is, they have narrative form even when lacking narrative content. Lowry describes narrative form as moving "from opening disequilibrium through escalation of conflict to surprising reversal to closing denouement (in which the table of life gets set for us in a new way by the gospel)."[20] I believe in the viability of sermons that have narrative form, but lack in story or stories.[21] Why, however, call them "narrative"?[22] Why not simply label them as "inductive"? In any case, my interest is with both narrative form *and* narrative content. The sermon designs examined in this book make use of concrete stories, but not necessarily stories that stand alone.

As I have indicated, movies and novels develop inductively; the viewer or reader often becomes so enraptured by the story-line that her natural defenses are lowered, allowing the message to influence her at a much deeper level than if she were simply advised to believe something. With a good book or movie, a person does not just see or hear the message—he experiences it. Any ingredient that enhances *experience* and fosters *anticipation* is important to the inductive process. Such ingredients might include: an unanswered question/questions, an unresolved narrative/narratives, irritation, dialogue, a partial truth, an unexpected complication or twist, mystery, ambiguity, an intellectual impasse, a contradiction, or a parable. To preach in this mode requires a refined sense of creativity and a keen feel for story. The purpose of this book is to help the preacher grasp the "nuances of narrative" and thereby be able to shape a variety of narrative sermon designs. I believe that the skillful use of sermonic narrative—which I am here calling "creative anticipation"—will inevitably improve pulpit communication.

Preaching and Story

One of my definitions of preaching is "the integrating of your story, their story, and God's Story in such a way that souls are saved, wounds are healed, and Christ is exalted." Effective narrative preaching then revolves around three stories: 1) God's Story; 2) the congregation's story; and 3) the preacher's story.

God's Story as revealed in the life, death, and resurrection of Jesus Christ, is the foundation of all proclamation. The Apostle Paul asserts: "God was pleased through the foolishness of what was preached to save those who believe."[23] Jesus is "the power of God and the wisdom of God."[24] In the person of Jesus Christ, believers learn that good wins over evil, and life overcomes death. As Edmund Steimle expresses it,

> . . . the resurrection means that evil does not have
> the last word. God and his will of love have the
> last word. When evil has done its worst, in and

through me as well as in and through others, there
is always the possibility of a new beginning. 'Behold, I make all things new.'[25]

The gospel of Christ is the Grand Narrative that stands at the
heart of the universe. Apart from God's Story, preaching has no
authority.

Western culture is trapped between the *modern* world and an
emerging *postmodern* world. The modern world, which was shaped
by that historical period called the Enlightenment or the "Age of
Reason," was built around a "rational world paradigm." Diogenes
Allen defines the pillars of that world as "self-sufficiency, reason,
progress, and optimism."[26] Beyond any question, those pillars are
collapsing. In a postmodern world, no commodity will be in shorter
supply than *hope*, a hope which only the gospel can provide. Writes
Robert G. Duffett, "We communicate to a different audience, on
their court, and without help from social structures. The contemporary situation calls for a major reassessment of how the Christian message is communicated."[27] My emphasis on narrative communication addresses that concern.

Ordinary secular men and women continue to love stories, as
reflected in the popularity of television, cinema, and novels. Yet,
many of these secularists express deep skepticism toward any narrative that acknowledges the "transcendent"; they doubt that God
shapes the outcome of anyone's story. Intellectuals also appreciate
cultural narratives, but reject what might be called
"metanarratives"—stories which presume to bring *"closure, certainty,*
or *control."*[28] While no one can precisely describe the world of the
twenty-first century, we can be fairly certain of the continued en-
croachment of an increasingly skeptical postmodern consciousness.
As the new world order evolves, pervasive questions hang in the
air: "Where will postmodern men and women find the meaning
and hope necessary to tell their stories? Can *any story* survive in a
world that rejects *the Grand Story*?" The Church of Jesus Christ
must seize the opportunity and confidently answer these ques-

tions. Contends Robert Jenson: "If there is no God, or indeed if there is some other God than the God of the Bible, there is no narratable world."[29] Jensen continues, ". . . if the church does not *find* her hearers antecedently inhabiting a narratable world, then the church must herself *be* that world."[30]

As members of the Body of Christ, we are "a people of the Story." Like the first century believers, we define ourselves as an "eschatological people"—a people drawn toward a future shaped by God.[31] We live, as did first century Christians, "between the times—that is, between the beginning and the consummation of the end."[32] The gospel, therefore, is the *ultimate form of creative anticipation*, a model for all our stories—*and sermons*. Asserts Steimle, "The kingdom of God is forever appearing, however obliquely, in which 'the mighty acts of the Lord' are taking place."[33] Although we have already tasted the new wine of the incarnated Christ, including the promised Holy Spirit,[34] the consummation of the kingdom awaits the Lord's return.[35] Our days on earth are framed by *creative anticipation*. As believers, we live in this *hope*, even as we long "for his appearing."[36]

In addition to the gospel story, listeners have "their story." An elderly lady in one of my congregations discovered she had cancer; the doctors could only make her reasonably comfortable as she approached death. I visited her in the hospital shortly after the detection of her disease. I should have known that her deep faith would see her through this crisis as it had so many others, but for some reason I expected to find her depressed; such was not the case. "Martha," I commented, "You seem in good spirits. Have you spoken with your doctor?" "Of course, I have," she responded. "I know exactly what my future holds and I am prepared for it. Haven't you told us for years, preacher, that if we trust the Lord we can look forward to 'a city whose builder and maker is God?' Why should I let a little thing like death keep me from the joy I've always known?" I could only answer, somewhat sheepishly, "Martha, how right you are." Martha had learned to "anticipate creatively"; in her time of crisis, she was able to defend herself with the "shield of faith."[37] She had internalized God's Story and woven it like a seamless garment into her own story.

That brings us to the preacher's story. Unless we ministers allow God to speak *to* us, He will not speak *through* us. Referring to the theological education of perspective ministers, Richard Ward states, "The hope is that the student will learn to be open to his or her own story as it unfolds, will learn how that story can become more fully available to the church, and by telling that story, will become a more attentive listener to other stories."[38] Multiple narratives fill the lives of preachers; these revolve around faith and fear, trust and doubt, humility and pride. A given preacher may live on a spiritual mountain top for weeks, enjoying a radiant and vital faith in Christ. Then occurs a season of spiritual drought, when prayer is a struggle and Bible reading an ill-fitted discipline. This "roller-coaster" experience is common to all believers. Repeatedly, we come to God requesting his forgiveness and renewing our vows to him.[39] Behind each of our victories and defeats is a story that connects with the stories of our listeners; effective preaching finds that vital connection. Admitting our humanness, our falleness, our need for spiritual renewal brings authenticity to our pulpit communication.

"God's Story" gives the sermon authority; "their story" gives the sermon relevance; and "my story" gives it passion and genuineness. Our goal in preaching is the integration of these three stories so that "souls are saved, wounds are healed, and Christ is exalted." That integration takes place naturally in the narrative sermon designs we will examine. This book is intended as a ringing endorsement of what I have called "creative anticipation." Of course, "logical argumentation," as I shall demonstrate in my sermon examples, continues to be important in narrative preaching. The *creative interplay* between creative anticipation and logical argumentation is fundamental to preaching.

Specifically, this volume focuses on six narrative styles or designs: 1) Simulating the biblical narrative; 2) Sustaining the narrative; 3) Supplementing the narrative; 4) Segmenting the narrative; 5) Sequencing the narratives; and 6) Suspending the narrative. Each of these sermon designs uses stories as "metaphors of participation," as opposed to "metaphors of illustration."[40] This distinction will be carefully explained in future chapters. We will examine the "nuts-and-bolts" of constructing narrative sermons, focusing on these designs; a sermon example will be given with each design. I make no claim that the narrative forms discussed are the *only* ways to shape story sermons. Nor am I suggesting rigid models which must be used with every text or every sermon. My goal in this book is not to "fill your bucket," but to "prime your pump." Admittedly, I am interested in the preacher's sermon laboratory; I want to encourage some sermonic experimentation.

I believe that the skillful handling of "creative anticipation" can facilitate the process of releasing the Living Word; that is my chief interest. Preaching is an intellectual and spiritual endeavor; it is also an artistic endeavor. Frequently, the artistic capacities of preachers are numbed through their college and seminary experiences; ministerial students often lose their love for narrative (or never develop it). That is a serious loss for preaching, because stories hone imagination and sharpen sensitivity to life; life is story and story is life. Merril Abbey writes, "Nurtured long in schools, a companion of books, [the preacher] is lured away from the action-filled speech of living men."[41] Frequently, creativity and imaginativeness are casualties of ministerial education. Ministers start to mistrust or ignore their own creative impulses; they come to view imagination as a child's *play toy* rather than *an essential tool* for vibrant communication. I say this in the full awareness that some readers may be suspicious of the word "imagination" as having cultic or New Age implications. Certainly imagination has been, and can be, used for evil purposes. But creative imagination rightly used enhances communication and underscores the authority of Scripture.

Taking the Risk

Although from my present perspective, I appreciate narrative sermons as powerful vehicles for delivering the message of the gospel, my confidence in these styles evolved slowly. The traditional approaches drilled into me in seminary seemed so comfortable, so right. I knew, of course, that neither Jesus or Paul used "three-points-and-a-poem-sermons," but this truth did not take hold. If anything, I left seminary with a suspicion of inductive approaches; i.e., doubtful that narrative sermons could speak with the authority necessary to carry the weight of the gospel. For me, the transition into narrative preaching almost felt like *apostasy*—like turning away from some fundamental doctrine of the church. Wasn't it best to preach with a clear, authoritative deductive message? Would the congregation think I was "soft-pedaling" the gospel? Could I do justice to the Scriptures with narrative sermons? Would church members weaned on deductive preaching respond to narrative movement, as opposed to points? Of course, I was not completely abandoning deduction (and I am not advocating that here), but still, I felt apprehensive.

In many respects, a trip I made several years ago to Poland, parallels my experimentation with narrative sermons. A Polish friend invited me to make a preaching and lecture tour of his country. At that time, the Communists still firmly controlled Poland. Though excited with this opportunity, I also felt uneasy. The trip would require me to teach and preach through an interpreter, a form of communication I had seldom practiced. I also questioned my ability to bridge the cultural gap between the people of Eastern Europe and myself. My friend assured me that with his assistance as interpreter I would be able to communicate effectively. But I was not easily convinced; the trip was definitely outside my "comfort zone." What if my friend was wrong? Perhaps I could not communicate with people who held such a different world perspective. In the end, because of the potential benefits of such a trip for both the Polish Christians and myself, I accepted the risks.

I remember my insecurity as the British Airways flight made its landing in Warsaw. The skies were gray; the airport buildings, drab and colorless. Stern-looking soldiers greeted our flight. Before I could meet my Polish friend, I had to wait in long lines to have my luggage, passport, and other papers approved. The gruff soldier who examined my papers reminded me of an unhappy bear; he appeared none too pleased to have this alien visiting his country. Finally, I proceeded through the lines and met my friend Michael and several members of a Polish church; such relief! As is the Polish custom, they welcomed me with a bouquet of flowers.

I traveled and spoke for three enjoyable weeks in Poland. I found the Polish Christians warm and generous beyond my greatest expectations; their hospitality was almost overwhelming. Though not wealthy people, they fed me as if I were royalty. In spite of the language and cultural barriers, I formed many friendships. Preaching and teaching through an interpreter was difficult, but as my colleague had predicted, I made the adjustment. I am convinced that God used me on this trip to exalt his name and advance his Kingdom. I was glad I had taken the risk and learned to communicate in this unfamiliar, yet adventurous fashion.

Similarly, my first full-fledged narrative sermon involved taking risks. Inspired by the writings of Fred Craddock and others, I decided it was time to try my "inductive wings." I put lots of time in that first story sermon. When Sunday morning came, I moved to the pulpit almost like a fearful Peter stepping out on the Sea of Galilee. I can not say that I walked on water, but at least I did not sink! Once into the message, my confidence increased; I found satisfaction in preaching a sermon built on *movement* rather than *points.* That morning I "felt it happening"; preachers will understand my meaning. Some sermons soar like eagles; others flap their wings, but never leave the ground. My listeners responded positively. They did not declare it the greatest sermon I had ever preached, but neither did they criticize this sermonic effort. After the service, a woman stopped to tell me a story which the sermon evoked. Even the more traditional church members seemed to appreciate the narrative approach. Everything considered, this first experience with narrative communication gave me courage to try "creative anticipation" again.

I keep on my office door this statement by John Chido: "It is the process of risk-taking, experimentation, failure, reflection and continued exploration that is the hallmark of creativity, inventiveness, and even successful teaching [preaching]."[42] How easily we become stagnant, saying the same things in the same tired ways. Lifeless preaching is intolerable, boring not only the people who hear, but also the one who preaches. Mark Twain captured the agony of a steady diet of pulpit deduction when he pictured Tom Sawyer in a church service: "The minister gave out his text and droned along monotonously through an argument that was so prosy that many a head by and by began to nod. . . ."[43] Do we wonder that Tom gave his attention that Sunday morning to a "pinch bug," which he carried in a percussion box in his pocket?

Since discovering narrative sermons, preaching has become a more creative enterprise for me. More importantly, I have encountered dynamic, fresh ways to declare the gospel of Christ. In his lectures at Yale, James Broadus offered this advice to preachers, "If only you could manage to drive us sometimes over a different road, even if much less smooth, even if you don't know it well. I am so tired of this!"[44] Well, Mr. Broadus, we have packed a picnic basket and loaded everyone in the old car. Not only that, we have our road map out, and we are looking for a different route! We are not sure where our trip will take us or what obstacles we might encounter; the ride may be a bit bumpy exploring these unfamiliar roads, but how refreshing it will be to discover new sights along the way!

CHAPTER 2

RELEASING THE WORD

"I did not understand the sermon, and I feel sure it was lost on the congregation; it was the most peculiar mixture of erudition and inspiration imaginable. . . . No one had the faintest notion of what he was talking about most of the time."[1]

Barbara Michaels in Greygallows

While deductive preaching still has a place in the contemporary church, I believe its value continues to diminish as a tool for reaching a postmodern word. In my opinion, the day of "the thundering voice from the pulpit" is all but over. Whether we like it or not, the preacher's words no longer *automatically* carry authority. Modern listeners have absorbed the prevailing skepticism of our age; they *will not be commanded* to believe or behave in a certain way. Narrative or inductive sermons communicate best in the contemporary world because they allow the listener to become *a participant* in the process. This style of communication fits the emerging postmodern consciousness. Induction allows the preacher to walk *beside* listeners rather than to *stand over them.*

The Apostle Paul wrote, "I have become all things to all men so that by all possible means I might save some."[2] Like Paul, we must adapt if we are to reach our culture. Of course, we must exercise care that we do not compromise the gospel. In the words of Marsha Witten, we can go too far in "pursuing the route of accommodation."[3] I respect her warning and assert with conviction that the gospel never changes; however, the *form* by which the gospel is transported must be adjusted to *fit the culture.* This fact has been recognized by successful preachers throughout the history of the church. Failure to adapt will create *the appearance* of an irrelevant gospel; as a result, we will preach to empty pews.

Communicating is a *dynamic process*; to reach our culture, we must be "in the flow." This metaphor comes from Donald Smith who compares communication to a flowing river. He states,

> Enter the flowing river of communication, and it changes—perhaps only slightly. Greater change can be caused as it is understood that the flow comes from somewhere outside one person's experience and flows onward beyond that experience. Having learned the course of the river, one can enter its currents with greater effect. [4]

As I see it, the problem with traditional deductive sermons built around "logical argumentation" is that the preacher stands *outside the flow of the river;* these sermons fail to identify with the *temporality* of human existence. As a result, the communicator *walks along the shore (or sits in a lawn chair!)* while the *real* communication happens "in the flow." Rationalistic and propositional sermons strike the listeners as unnatural or out of touch with the world around them. These sermons do not connect with their *ex-*

perience of day to day reality. As a result, listeners simply tune out (or stay away from church altogether).

The Difficulty of Pulpit Communication

Anyone who has spent much time in the pulpit understands the difficulty of "releasing the Word." In no other context of Western societies does a speaker address such a diverse audience as a preacher encounters on a typical Sunday morning. Consider the range of listeners: children, adults, men, women, toddlers, teenagers; educated, illiterate; married, single; professionals, blue-collar workers; homemakers, career women; etc. This list does not begin to take into account individual differences among congregants. Listener diversity partially explains the contrasting opinions given by parishioners toward the same sermon. All hearers process the sermon through their personalities, their own mental filters, their distinctive listening and learning styles. Dean Inge described preaching as "trying to fill rows of narrow necked vessels by throwing buckets of cold water over them."[5] Harry Emerson Fosdick applied a slightly different metaphor. He said it was like a person on a tall building "letting go of a drop of medicine in the hope that it would land in the eye of an ailing person in the crowd below."[6]

The goal of every sermon is to discover the best possible way to *release the Living Word of God into the lives of listeners.* In his Yale Lectures, Phillips Brooks defined preaching as the communication of "truth through personality."[7] According to Brooks, both "truth" and "personality" are essential for preaching: "Neither of these two elements can it spare and still be preaching."[8] The preacher's method and/or personality sometimes interferes with the release of the Word. A harsh, scolding, or moralistic sermon, for example, may prevent listeners from hearing because of the communicator's judgmental attitude. Sermons using the same format month after month may become dull and predictable. Preachers who perpetually rehearse a few pet themes in the same monotonous fashion may put their listeners to sleep with what Clyde Kilby calls the "anesthesia of cliché."[9] As the old quip asserts, "Heresy has slain its thousands, but dullness its tens of thousands!" Dry and pedantic sermons are uninteresting—which is bad; even worse, they *block the release* of the Living Word into the community of believers. As a result, God is not glorified, Christ is not exalted, and the gospel appears irrelevant.

We who preach confront an awesome responsibility; through our preaching listeners experience either the *presence* or the *absence* of God. Other factors, of course, also affect our people's spiritual lives, but we must not minimize the importance of preaching. People come to church with hollow places in their hearts. Their questions are numerous: "Is God real? Does he care about my hopes, fears, or frustrations? Is there any contact between heaven and earth? Is there some Word from God that speaks specifically to my situation? Does the Bible have an authoritative, relevant message that relates to my daily experiences? Does God have anything to advise about my job? my marriage? my family? my illness? my eternal destiny?" We ministers answer these inquiries with a resounding, "Yes! God is real; he knows and cares about our daily lives; our eternal destiny is in his hands. God's revelation of himself to us in Christ makes a profound difference in both the here and the hereafter." Nevertheless, even as we affirm these truths, we acknowledge the difficulty of conveying the reality and power of the gospel.

Variety in Preaching

How then can we best release God's Word into the lives of our listeners? Are narrative sermons effective in discharging that Word? I am aware that any book on preaching methodology must guard against the insinuation that if we could just discover *the way* to preach, then we could easily "release the Word." In the present volume the assumption might go like this: "Narrative preaching is *the answer!* I have discovered Preaching's Promise Land; hear what

I have to say and I guarantee powerful preaching." Such a claim would be absurdly arrogant; story preaching is not a cure-all. While asserting the value of narrative sermons, I do not claim to have contrived some "secret" method of designing sermons which will forever end the preacher's communication struggles. Preaching is not that simple, nor am I so naive.

Narrative sermon patterns are not *the only* legitimate way to communicate from the pulpit. Deductive preaching, with its emphasis on "logical argumentation," still has its role in contemporary pulpits. Some people respond *more positively* to deduction than induction (though I believe they are the minority). Certain biblical texts need to be proclaimed in a more direct manner. After all, Scripture passages should have a voice in not just the *content* of the sermon but also its ultimate *form*. Just as some biblical texts are parabolic or narrative in genre, some are quite propositional in both content *and* form. This hermeneutical fact in itself argues for the occasional use of pulpit deduction. Of course, the sermon form does not *always* imitate the form of the text, though frequently this will be the choice. As Thomas Long explains it, "The preacher's task . . . is not to replicate the text but to regenerate the impact of some portion of that text."[10] In future chapters, we will examine more carefully the connection between the form of the text and the design of the sermon.

Richard Lischer has written a provocative article which he entitles the "The Limits of Story."[11] Lischer calls narrative approaches to preaching the "aesthetic" modes of pulpit communication. While acknowledging a place for this kind of communication, Lischer reminds us of the importance of variety in preaching: "More is needed for the effective proclamation of the faith than simply telling a story or even *the* story."[12] Lischer poses some significant questions for those who might think that story-preaching is the *only* way to preach. He reminds us that: "Stories set the tone for principled action. . . . Each story is incomplete as a vehicle for change until it is *interpreted*. . . . story unmediated by symbol and principle does not effect transformation."[13] Stories, Lischer points out, often will not stand alone; they need explanation, even interpretation. Sometimes the listener needs for the truth of the narrative to be asserted and explained. Listeners, however, are much more capable of sorting out the message of a story sermon than we sometimes assume. Nevertheless, I appreciate the cautions given by Lischer. While stressing the importance of narrative preaching, I also recognize that stories have their limitations. We must not rely too heavily on *any one* method of proclamation.[14]

Having given this caveat, I must add that I am convinced direct (deductive) sermons are *less* effective than we have assumed, and narrative approaches are *more* effective than sometimes assumed. I also endorse "hybrid" sermons that *integrate* induction and deduction. Greg and Ralph Lewis remind us that induction and deduction can function effectively within the same sermon.[15] As I indicated in the last chapter, communicating God's Word through preaching involves the creative interplay between *logical argumentation* and *creative anticipation*. In future chapters, we will discuss "hybrid" sermon designs that combine direct and indirect approaches. However, I still label these hybrids as "narrative sermons" because of the role *creative anticipation* plays; the story provides the core around which the sermon is *plotted*.

Because people are unique, variety in sermonic styles is necessary. The wise and effective herald of the Word has a full arsenal of "deductive" and "inductive" approaches. My wife and I have two married daughters. When our girls were young, we often experimented with modes of disciplining. At one stage we used "naughty chairs" to teach proper behavior. We positioned these chairs in corners at opposite ends of the parsonage. When the girls fussed or engaged in other unruly behavior, we exiled them for a short time to the specified "naughty chairs." Hopefully, in these "penalty boxes" they would ponder their misconduct and come to repentance. Unfortunately, it did not always operate that way. Our four-year-old sat in her chair and wept tears of regret. Our three-year-old on the other hand, thought the naughty chair fun; in her corner, she created imaginary friends; pondering her behavior was the farthest thing from her mind. Needless to say, our youngest daughter required other forms of discipline.

In my present role as a college professor, I observe a variety of learning styles among my students. Some want me to lecture; some hate lecture. A selective group of students is motivated by vigorous discussion; a few become inhibited and unwilling to express their ideas. Field trips fascinate certain ones, while others moan, "Does *everyone* have to go on this field trip?" As a teacher, I am compelled to use multiple methods to reach the varied cognitive styles of my students. If I fail to do so, some will not learn.

Wise parents adjust the discipline to fit the personality of each child; effective teachers use a variety of pedagogical approaches. Even as I emphasize narrative sermons as powerful vehicles for communicating biblical truth, I stress the need for diversity in sermonic forms. To reach our listeners, both deductive and inductive styles should be employed. Some people will be influenced with very direct sermons; others require indirect messages. Stories reflect the nature of reality; they connect with most people. However, one man told me: "As far as I am concerned, preachers could just leave out the stories. Forget the fluff and give me the meat of the Word!" Make no mistake though, this fellow is an exception; most church folk want and need the stories. But the point is, people are different; God did not stamp out clones with a heavenly cookie-cutter. The content *as well as* the form of the sermon should adapt to the particular audience. Teenagers, for example may require a different approach than adults. Further, congregations as whole entities have varying personalities which must be respected. Asserts William Willimon,

> Good preaching communicates the gospel with scandalous particularity so that it hits home to people in such a way that they have little doubt that the truth is addressed to *this* people, living in *this* place at this time. Only the one who knows the particulars of this people can proclaim the gospel in its particularity.[16]

Overhearing the Gospel

While acknowledging that directive and/or deductive approaches to preaching have a role in the contemporary pulpit, I think deduction has been used excessively and over-valued. Fred Craddock's book, *Overhearing the Gospel*,[17] has helped me understand pulpit communication. Craddock describes indirect or inductive transmission of biblical truth as "overhearing." He indicates that direct communication often raises forces of resistance within the listener.[18] This opposition is especially present when the preacher "leaves the hearer no room for lateral movement."[19] As a result, writes Craddock, the listener launches "a silent but effective counter attack . . ."[20] which successfully shuts-out the preacher's directives. I have discovered that preaching and golf have some similarities; the harder you attempt to swing the club, the shorter the distance the ball will travel. Swinging hard tenses the muscles and slows down the speed of the club head, which in turn reduces distance. The same principle works in preaching. More direct, forceful approaches give rise to resistance; as a result, these techniques sometimes have less impact on the listener. In many deductive sermons the only "releasing" taking place is the releasing of angry defiance within the listeners, which effectively blocks communication.

At this point I am not denying the preacher's prophetic role in the pulpit; "telling it straight" is sometimes necessary. But we must not confuse prophetic proclamation with ranting, raving, and scolding. As indicated in the prologue, such raging is not *prophetic*, but *pathetic*. I raise this question: Do plotted sermons, built around a narrative model, have any value *as a prophetic mode* of communication? Do not deductive sermons, which are clear and direct, do a better job of calling men and women to repentance? After all, one might argue, Jesus told parables but he also looked the Pharisees in the eye and said, "Woe to you, teachers of the law and Pharisees, you hypocrites! You travel over land and sea to win a single convert, and when he becomes one, you make him twice as much a son of hell as you are."[21] That's pretty straightforward! Of course, it can always be said that we are not Jesus and our congregations are not the Pharisees, but that does not fully resolve the issue. My response to this question is two-fold.

First, I have already stated that narrative preaching is not the *only* way to preach. As much as I value narrative styles, they should be balanced with sermons that are more forthright and didactic in nature. Second, narrative sermons can themselves be powerful tools for delivering a prophetic word. At times Jesus directly reprimanded the Jewish religious leaders; but he also told them parables. Many of Jesus' parables were used for prophetic purposes; C. J. Cadoux defines parables as "art harnessed for service and conflict. . . ."[22] We also have an excellent example of story as prophetic tool in Nathan's story to David after his adultery with Bathsheba.[23] After Nathan told his story, David pronounced judgment on the rich man who took the poor man's only lamb.[24] In so doing, David spoke a powerful prophetic word *against himself. He* was then prepared to hear the prophet's charge: "Thou art the man!"[25] Stories have their way of drawing us in; we are engaged before we realize that the story is *about us.*

Narrative preaching allows people to "overhear the gospel"; the listener does not feel threatened. She perceives herself as a respected person, and therefore senses no need to "put up her shields." As a result, the message of the narrative penetrates deeply, with lasting impact. This indirect approach demands that we trust both listener and message. As Craddock writes,

> To deliver a message for overhearing, the speaker will need to trust fully in the message to create its own effect, trust the listener to exercise his freedom responsibly, and trust the process, however fragile and accidental it may appear, to be powerful. Voice, hands, posture, and face will testify to the presence of this trust.[26]

Even if the preacher becomes more direct at the conclusion of an inductive sermon, the listener feels less need to resist the message. The soil of the heart has been prepared for the seed of the gospel. With the able assistance of the Holy Spirit, God's Word will do its work within his people.

Translating the Living Word

Any sermon must pass one supreme test: *Does the sermon connect the listeners to the living God through his Living Word?* In the first chapter I proposed this definition of preaching: "the integrating of your story, their story, and God's Story in such a way that souls are saved, wounds are healed, and Christ is exalted." At this time I add another: "Preaching is communication wherein an authentic and dedicated believer translates the Living Word into language that is fresh, clear, interesting, relevant, and life-changing." I will now expand on this second meaning and relate it to the use of creative anticipation (narrative preaching).

In my definition of preaching I use the word "translates." This represents a slightly different metaphor than I used previously when I indicated that we must be "in the flow," but it conveys the same concept. When someone speaks to us in a language we do not understand (or do not fully understand), we need a translator, i.e., someone who can assimilate the foreign words and express them in our language. Without a competent translator, we will never fully grasp the other person's intent. Notice the steps in this process: 1) Interpret what one person is saying in a particular language; 2) Put that meaning into words that accurately communicate in another language. Is this not similar to what happens in preaching? The minister takes a language that people do not understand—or do not fully understand—and, with the direction of the Holy Spirit, puts that message into words that communicate. This process implies that the preacher *diligently studies* the words (and meanings) of Scripture, and having arrived at an interpretation, *attempts* to communicate that understanding with the congregation. I say "attempts" because I recognize the complexity in this procedure; frequently we think we are *translating* when no actual communication is taking place. Of course, if the communicative process is to succeed, the listeners must also assume responsibility. In a sense, they must participate as "co-creators" of the sermon. Narrative approaches, especially, require full participation from the listeners; story sermons are designed to *evoke* personal sermons (stories). We measure effectiveness in proportion to the response evoked— the "second sermon."

In the last chapter I referred to my preaching tour of Poland. At the beginning of that trip, I spoke several times using a gifted Polish interpreter; it took him only a few seconds to understand my meaning and translate into Polish. My audiences were listening; I could tell I was communicating. Then I had to switch to a less capable interpreter. Due to his mediocre understanding of English, he had difficulty selecting Polish words to correlate with the English. This deficiency frustrated both my listeners and me. Had I not already preached successfully through an interpreter, I would have thought the problem mine. This perplexing experience made me appreciate the frustration that listeners endure when they hear inferior preaching. The congregants gather, ready to receive the message of Scripture, but they are stuck with a poor *translator*, who either is unable to grasp the Scriptural message, or inadequately conveys that understanding. In one way or the other, the communication of the gospel is inhibited.

I have a preacher friend who loves the Lord and is a serious student of Scripture. He carefully attends to original languages and is skilled at exegesis. But his sermons do not connect; the Living Word is simply *not* released. In spite of having good things to say, he cannot find the appropriate words or images. My friend seems powerless to make the message concrete; he ineffectively uses metaphor, analogy, and narrative. I don't think it coincidental that he views preaching as simply "conveying information." Many preachers find themselves in similar situations; they know the meaning and message of Scripture, but they are poor translators.[27]

They do not understand how to *involve* their audience in the process so that listeners become what I have called "co-creators" of the sermon. Once again I laud narrative sermons as powerful instruments for promoting congregational involvement .

An Authentic Believer

My second definition presumes that the Living Word is translated by an "authentic and dedicated believer." Helmet Thielicke addresses the issue of ministers and credibility in his classic book, *The Trouble with the Church*. Thielicke indicates that one of the deepest longings of our age is for "credible witnesses." [28] He contends that in all areas of contemporary society, we are exposed to the pretentious:

> We are surrounded by legions of 'functionaries,' propagandists, and paid purveyors of opinion, and nobody knows what they think in their personal and private lives—whether they be political or economic propagandists. One always has the rather macabre impression of being exposed, not to a real conviction, but to a skillfully practiced method of influencing people. [29]

Thielicke then raises a series of prophetic questions: [30] What does it mean to be convinced of something and to advocate it as the 'truth'? Do those who preach of Christ speak of him in their daily conversations? Do they quench their own thirst with the Bible? Do they live what they preach? Thielicke underscores the importance of genuineness and dedication. In both words and actions, the preacher must flesh-out the gospel of Christ; in the biblical sense of the word, the preacher should be a "saint." Saints are a people set apart; they are overwhelmed by the reality of God's grace; they are unashamedly in love with God; their hearts burn with a desire to do his will. Spirit-filled preaching flows from Spirit-filled people; personal conviction is a prelude to powerful preaching.

In preparing each sermon, the flame of faith is kindled in the preacher's own heart which, in turn, lights a fire in those who listen. Richard Jensen explains, "When I pause before a text to let it do me good I am looking for a sense of participation in the gospel which I may pass along to my hearers."[31] If in the second quarter of a given year, I am going to preach from the Gospel of Matthew, I will spend the first quarter of the year using this gospel for my devotions. I keep a daily journal which reflects my own spiritual pilgrimage through this portion of Scripture. Later, while preaching from Matthew, I continue to meditate on the specific passage from which a sermon will be developed. I know that God must speak *to* me if he is to speak *through* me. As William Willimon explains,

> Preaching—Christian preaching—compels only when a compelling message grasps the preacher. When a message grasps the messenger, the sermon lives and breathes and soars. Otherwise the sermon quickly degenerates into a set of moral platitudes or a painfully amateurish attempt at group therapy. . . . .[32]

The Living Word

In my second definition of preaching, I use the phrase "Living Word." Scripture should be regarded as God's Living Agent, released by and through the mediating presence of the Holy Spirit. The author of Hebrews wrote, "For the word of God is living and active. Sharper than any double-edged sword, it penetrates even to dividing soul and spirit, joints and marrow; it judges the thoughts and attitudes of the heart."[33] James Daane describes Scripture as "evocative, dynamic, creative, saving, sin-annulling, death-defeating, healing, [and] life-giving. . . ."[34] Affirms Eugene Peterson,

"Scripture is revelation. When a living God reveals himself the result is a living truth."[35] Peterson argues that the pastor must prevent *revelation* from becoming *information*. Revelation, he explains, "always involves personal histories and personal responses," while information "involves impersonal facts and abstract ideas."[36] Intrinsically, effective pulpit communication demands the highest respect for the organic quality of Scripture—it is a Word alive.

The Hebrews believed that to speak words was to release energy—"a powerful, personal force that could not be called back."[37] As Fran Ferder observes, in the Hebrew culture, a word (*dabar*) spoken and its corresponding reality were almost the same; to say it was to do it.[38] [39] The Old Testament story of the brothers Jacob and Esau illustrates this fact.[40] Remember that Jacob tricked Isaac into giving him the blessing that rightly belonged to Esau because he was the firstborn. Why did Isaac not simply retract his blessing? "A mistake has been made here and I will not have it!" Isaac did not do so because words had power, and once that power was released, it could not be called back.[41] Isaac respected the integrity of the words he had spoken, even if he had been deceived into addressing those words to the wrong son. Words possessed a potency that could not be revoked.[42] This is all the more true with Scripture; to preach is to dispense God's lightning and thunder; the Word is powerful stuff. Releasing the Living Word of God into the community of believers sets God's Spirit to work among his people; as a result, transformation *will* take place. Recall what was said through the prophet Isaiah:

> As the rain and the snow come down from heaven, and do not return to it without watering the earth and making it bud and flourish, so that it yields seed for the sower and bread for the eater, so is my word that goes out from my mouth: It will not return to me empty, but will accomplish what I desire and achieve the purpose for which I sent it.[43]

Life-changing

Ultimately, preaching is about the business of changing lives, including the life of the one delivering the message. My definition of effective preaching uses these adjectives: "fresh, clear, interesting, relevant, and *life-changing*." Although it may sound audacious to suggest that preaching should be "life-changing," that term characterizes the purpose of proclamation. In Romans, Paul asserts that through conversion believers identify with Christ ("united with him"[44]), and receive a new identity: "the old self [is] crucified with him so that the body of sin might be done away with."[45] Writes David Buttrick, preaching "can transform our stories and, thus, our identities."[46] For many contemporary Americans, the gospel is anything but life-transforming; a more accurate description would be *irrelevant*. As Elizabeth Achtemeier maintains,

> There is a rumor abroad in our land that the Christian life is impossible to live and that the sacred story is a fairy tale, comforting for our elder citizens and good ethical guidance for children, but having little relevance to the hard realities of life in consumer America. It is science and technology which reveal and handle the shape of reality in the twentieth century. . . . [47]

For many secular Americans, the gospel is not "good news" but "bad news." Does contemporary preaching contribute to this secular perception of the gospel? We can be certain that a drowsy mind and an inner yawn greet lifeless preaching. If the power and relevance of the gospel are to be conveyed, ministers must become more skilled in translating this Dynamic Word. I contend that appreciating story will help us turn lifeless preaching into a vehicle for life-transformation. Then, in the words of Achtemeier, we will be better prepared to "reveal and handle the shape of reality in the twentieth century."[48]

Not only the *churched* but also the *unchurched* respond to the power of story. In fact, people not accustomed to listening to sermons, are often profoundly affected by narrative sermons. Narrative is the language of this generation via movies, TV shows, novels, etc. Further, narrative sermons connect with the *experience* of listeners so that the spotlight of God's transforming Word shines its penetrating light into darkness of our world. Narrative unobtrusively softens the heart and *evokes* a personal response in the listener; consequently, God's Word begins to do its transforming work. As we preach, we become what Henry Mitchell calls "homiletical coworkers with the Spirit."[49] Our goal, then, is to "let the Word happen" among us.

CHAPTER 3

NARRATIVE AND "INNER

APPROPRIATION"

"In many traditional cultures a person becomes an adult by hearing the secret stories of the community that have been handed down over generations. Elders give instructions, teaching the elements of ritual and art. Black Elk describes this process in detail in his memoirs of growing up in the Oglala Sioux. Sometimes the neophyte has to endure ordeals designed to draw out the adult. The point is to stir the young person so deeply that he or she experiences a major transformation of character."[1]

Thomas Moore in Care of the Soul

The sweet smell of alfalfa mixes with the pungent odor of hogs. The evening is mellow and mild; the sun is about to set on another day. Two old men and three teenage boys relax outside the barn sipping lemonade and talking after a hot, dirty day in the fields; it's time to swap stories. "Have you heard that Henry Erfurt wrecked his pick-up truck? After spending the day hunting deer and not seeing a one, his truck hit a six-point buck one-half mile from his farm." "Well, I hear that Mrs. Branson is mad at her husband. Seems she had just finished scrubbing the kitchen floor when her husband blundered again. To save a few steps, Mr. Branson cut through the house with a bucket of fish he was cleaning; it slipped from his hand, drenching the kitchen." The stories tumble on like stones cascading down a hillside in an avalanche: "When Mr. Wilkins carried out the trash, he found a possum in the trash can." "The new preacher at the Baptist church has an unusual habit; he mows grass while wearing a suit and tie!" Even as darkness engulfs the tellers, the stories continue to bubble-up, each reminding of another; no one wants the story-magic to end.

Stories are the fingerprint of the soul; we are a story-shaped people living in a storied-world. Writes Daniel Taylor, "We live in stories the way fish live in water, breathing them in and out, buoyed up by them, taking from them our sustenance, but rarely conscious of this element in which we exist."[2] Stephen Crites tells us that "the formal quality of experience through time is inherently narrative."[3] Crites declares that narrative, like music, is a kind of universal language;[4] I might add that for many people, it is *the only language* they speak. The nature of the tales change from country to city, from ball field to church parking lot—but the stories never stop. As Sam Keen, Joseph Campbell and others inform us, we process reality through our stories—the ones we hear, or tell, or live. In our tales we define ourselves, our families, our enemies, our beliefs; if we forget our stories, we lose our identities. William Bausch gives an accurate portrayal when he writes, "A person without a story is a person with amnesia. A country without its story has ceased to exist. A humanity without its story has lost its soul."[5]

Our intent thus far in this volume has been to establish a rationale for narrative preaching. I have attempted to persuade the reader that story-preaching is a powerful tool for communicating the gospel of Christ. We have established that our goal is to release the Living Word of God into the lives of our listeners by means of creative anticipation (story). Earlier I defined narrative preaching as "integrating your story, their story, and God's story in such a way that souls are saved, wounds are healed, and Christ is exalted." Our focus in this chapter centers around a basic assumption which will stand behind all the work we will do in future chapters: *Narrative sermons come into existence at the point where the message of the text, the preacher's experience of the text, and the congregation's need overlap.* Discovering that *overlap* is fundamental to story-preaching. To do so requires that we live in a "receptive mode," connected with ourselves, the people to whom we preach, and, most importantly, with God and his Word. Narrative sermons demand this rich, fertile soil; they will not even sprout if one lives in a desert—detached from God, self, and humankind.

Learning to Listen

In this chapter I want to develop the concept which I call "inner appropriation." There can be no effective communication without this in-depth listening to the text, to the congregation, to the surrounding culture, and to material from the preacher's own heart. Many authors and homileticians propose the same idea, though they may label it differently; some call it "listening," others, "seeing." Author Frederick Buechner defines it as "a kind of traveling, of seeing the sights."[6] Writes Buechner, "And the more sights you see, the more feelings and thoughts those sights call up in you, the more alive you become to what is going on in both the world around you and inside you. . . ."[7] Those who have cultivated the skill of "inner appropriation" refuse to live superficially. Their eyes and ears are tuned-in to the richness, the mystery, the complexity, and the majesty of life. Henri Nouwen adds a transcendent element to inner appropriation. He speaks of the one "who can articulate the movements of his inner life, who can give names to his varied experiences. . . ." [8] He is able, continues Nouwen, "to create space for Him whose heart is greater than his, whose eyes see more than his, and whose hands can heal more than his."[9] The preacher who has refined this art lives in the *receptive mode*, open to the penetrating efficacy of both Scripture and human experience.

Make no mistake, competent narrative preaching depends on patient listening; the preacher's ear is at least as important as his mouth. Charles Rice advises, "Preaching is at least two-thirds listening: listening to the text, to the congregation, to the surrounding culture, to oneself."[10] Leander Keck characterizes the pastor as a "priestly listener."[11] By this portrayal, I infer he means hearing God, listening to and trusting our own inner voices, and identifying with the crucial needs of our people. "Inner appropriation," as I shall describe it, is more than a sermon technique; it is a way of living, a manner of seeing and experiencing the world. If we do not cultivate these skills, we will remain fundamentally detached from ourselves, from others, from God, and from life itself.

The preacher who has never learned the art of "inner appropriation" will appear to listeners as inauthentic, lacking in what I shall call *alongsideness*. Of her minister, one woman told me, "He is very well educated, but when he preaches, he seems phony; he just doesn't understand us. Sometimes I wonder if he lives on the same planet." I cannot shake the image of a particular preacher as rendered by Ralph Waldo Emerson:

> He had lived in vain. He had no word intimating that he laughed or wept, was married or in love, had been commended or cheated or chagrined. If he had ever lived and acted, we were none the wiser for it. The capital secret of his profession, namely, to convert life into truth, he had not learned.[12]

Preachers "convert life into truth"; or perhaps, more accurately, they convert "Truth into life." Without this ability, releasing the Living Word through preaching becomes most difficult, if not impossible.

Effective preaching, especially narrative communication, requires the preacher to move *alongside* the listeners. This relationship only happens when congregants view the preacher as one of them—as a person who is human, who laughs and cries, fails and falters, hurts and grieves. Honest and simple stories reveal the person behind the ministerial mask. Chevis Horne states that the first thing he looks for in a sermon, is not the preacher's theology, his scholarship, or his eloquence:

> I listen for pain. Is there a personal cross in his preaching? Has he been too sheltered to know the agony of his world? Or has he exposed himself to the brokenness and hurt of his world so that he knows and experiences its pain? Are his words too glib and easy or have they been chastened by suffering? Has his faith been refined by agony and have his manners been made gentle by pain?[13]

The preacher must possess not only the language of pain, but also that of grace, of joy, of confusion, and of a hundred other emotions which define our humanity. Listen to Charles Rice: "if preaching is to affect human lives, it will clearly have to be done by someone who lives and preaches from a clearly human life—or it will not finally be heard except as entertainment or diversion."[14]

Inner Appropriation: "Moments of Epiphany"

Our sermonic goal in narrative communication is to trigger "inner appropriation" within our listeners; our sermons evoke theirs; our stories link the listeners with their *own personal experience*: "Image evokes image. Story calls forth story. Life speaks to life."[15]

But we can only hope to stimulate this inner response in our listeners if we have cultivated it ourselves. Frederick Buechner maintains, "We are commissioned by God to speak in Christ, and to speak in Christ is to speak truth, and there is no story whose truth we are closer to than our own, than the story of what it's like to live inside ourselves."[16] Each of us looks out on life from our own "frame of reference"; in one sense, our view of the world is unlike any other; in another sense, we share a commonality with every other person. But the point is, we preachers will never be sensitive to the needs of others unless we are aware of what is happening inside of ourselves. If we are to be increasingly perceptive to the inner movements of others, we must be in contact with our own experience, our personal narratives.

John Shea reflects on the normal process whereby we appropriate our personal stories.[17] As a particular life event touches us deeply, we are alive to "the time of its happening."[18] Particular moments take on larger meaning; they "have a lasting impact; they cut through to something deeper; they demand a hearing."[19] I sometimes refer to these times as "moments of epiphany." Donald English, borrowing the language of Ian Ramsey, calls them "disclosure situations."[20] English emphasizes their spiritual nature: "Something—more precisely Someone—is being disclosed to us, if we can but perceive what is happening. We touch the very center of the universe and its meaning."[21] These moments may be negative or positive; they might include the death of a parent or a friend, a wedding, a betrayal, or even a picnic with the grandchildren. Not just monumental happenings, but common experiences acquire added significance; they affect our innermost being.

In order to fully appropriate these occurrences, we must find the courage to reveal them; we know ourselves as we share our stories with others. As Shea states, "So we tell our experiences in story form. But since there is more in our experience than in our appreciation of it, we do not 'get it right' the first time."[22] We continue to reflect upon our experiences so that their value is expanded and clarified. In this manner, surface events secure added meanings that provide personal insight. Our stories become a symbolic map by which we navigate the twists and turns of our earthly pilgrimage. Thomas Moore reflects on this process:

> In memory we never tire of reflecting on the same events. I spent many summers in my childhood on a farm with an uncle who told stories endlessly. This, I now see, was his method of working the raw material of his life, his way of turning his experience round and round in the rotation that stories provide. Out of that incessant storytelling I know he found added depths of meaning.[23]

In the process of repeating our stories, we gain an in depth understanding, not only of ourselves, but also of others. As Shea explains, in the retelling, "the experience, while remaining a specific event, 'leaps out of its particularity' and becomes a clue to the twists and turns of the mystery of life which all people have to deal with. In theological language, the experience has revelatory power."[24] "Revelatory" in this context does not infer that our stories become *inspired* like Scripture; rather, it means that over time we embrace life *events* and integrate them into our faith-shaped view of the world. In the cycles of telling and retelling, our values are clarified; our sensitivity to the needs of others sharpened. These "inner appropriations" are then made available for the wholeness and healing of our parishioners. This occurs both in the pulpit and in the faithful rendering of pastoral service. Henri Nouwen describes ministry as "a deep human encounter" in which a person is willing to put personal faith and doubt, hope and despair, light and darkness "at the disposal of others who want to find a way through their confusion and touch the solid core of life."[25] Touching *the core of life*—that makes for vibrant preaching.

Inner Appropriation and Scripture

We return to our basic assumption: *Narrative sermons come into existence at the point where the message of the text, the preacher's experience of the text, and the congregation's need overlap.* For me, a narrative sermon sometimes originates from a biblical passage; other times an actual experience is the starting point. From my perspective, it makes no difference whether the story or the text comes first, as long as the message of the text, the preacher's appropriation of its message, and the congregation's need become fused with one another. In preparing a narrative sermon, we must discover the point of convergence; text and story, like sperm and egg, must come together before the sermon can be conceived.

I want to stress that "inner appropriation" holds true not simply for life events but *also for Scripture.* Given any biblical text, "God's story" connects with the communicator's story at an *experiential* level. By "experiential" I mean that the preacher personally encounters, identifies with, and *experiences* the message of the passage; "God has spoken to me." Henry Mitchell labels this encounter with the text, preaching in an "eyewitness mode."[26] This individual application of the text to one's life is both *cognitive* and *affective*; it is both an intellectual *and* an emotional response. I mentioned earlier Leander Keck's call for "priestly listening." When that happens, writes Keck, "The text will then not become a selected weapon against the congregation . . . rather, [it] will be a listening-post where pastor and people together hear a word [from God]."[27] Failure to appropriate the text in this manner will hinder our ability to preach sermons which call forth a fervent response from our listeners. The tendency, warns Charles Rice, is to "begin talking too soon, to impose ready-to-hand ideas, 'points,' slogans, a sermon title, Barclay's outlines, tips from sermon aids . . . we do not do the kind of listening that enables form to spring from what is experienced."[28] Patient listening always precedes powerful speaking.

How do we know when we have appropriated the text *experi-*

entially? For me this occurs when I am able to associate the text with my stories, my own "moments of epiphany." That is, I am able to take the message of the passage and connect it to some "disclosure situation" in my life which *I have lived* or I *might live.* In certain instances I *remember* the text into my own experience; in other cases, I *imagine* the text into my life. In other words, if I cannot identify with the text through an actual experience, I may need to *imagine* such an event. Unfortunately, every biblical text does not connect with a personal experience or story; for that reason, *imagination* is often necessary for inner appropriation. I will demonstrate in future chapters exactly what I mean by this use of imagination. For now, I only want to stress that the message of the text *and* my *experience* of that message must unite with my personal *narratives.* If these elements do not interact, I will not be profoundly influenced by the text, nor will I inspire my listeners, evoking their own "moments of epiphany."

When I allow the text to evoke a response in me, my own "revelatory" story/stories surface. John Shea pictures this process as reentering "the time of its happening."[29] Once I have allowed the biblical text to connect with my own story, I then re-experience those stories.[30] In other words, *the thoughts and feelings* that were present at the time my story/stories occurred (though perhaps in diminished form) engulf me. Notice that the text summons not just "my story," but also the fear, frustration, excitement, anger and/or other *emotions* that accompanied my life-events. Being in touch with these feelings is essential for the development of the narrative sermon because I want to communicate the deep emotions that have been evoked in me by the text. I may or may not want to recount my own story/stories in the sermon, but I certainly hope to stay close to the feelings and insights stirred in me by those stories. If my work with the text proceeds as I have described it, I will have engaged in "inner appropriation." Having *appropriated* the text, I am now prepared to connect its message with the lives and stories of my listeners. J. Howard Grant describes the process vividly:

> Effective preaching . . . takes place when the truth
> of the text works its way into the preacher, roam-
> ing through the corridors of his mind and heart,
> and then like a spring run-off after a winter of
> deep snow, it bursts over the spillway of his own
> life and plunges down into the minds and hearts
> of the congregation.[31]

Please notice, I am not reducing the sermon to the one person's spiritual autobiography. The preacher may, on occasion, choose to speak out of the context of personal experience, but the process I have described has merit even if the communicator's specific stories are not detailed. The *feelings and insights* evoked in the preacher will connect with the life experiences of those who hear. This remembering or imagining the message of the text into the preacher's life will help shape a powerfully relevant sermon—even when the choice is made not to communicate personal stories. Living continuously in this receptive mode leads to identification with the needs of others. To quote Thomas Troeger, We "[have located] the thread of revelation that pulls us into the circle of the whole human family."[32]

Examples of Inner Appropriation

I close this chapter with three examples of "inner appropriation." The first two instances come from sermons and the third, from literature. As we examine these models, notice the manner in which stories have taken on a "revelatory" power, i.e., life events have sparked insight and been integrated into a faith-shaped worldview.

Our first example comes from a sermon by the German theologian, Helmut Thielicke; his message was entitled simply "The Parable of the Mustard Seed."[33] The text reads as follows:

> The kingdom of heaven is like a mustard seed,
> which a man took and planted in his field. Though
> it is the smallest of all your seeds, yet when it
> grows, it is the largest of garden plants and be-
> comes a tree, so that the birds of the air come and
> perch in its branches.[34]

In his sermon, Thielicke describes the disappointment Jesus' disciples were experiencing at the time he spoke this parable. The
results of Jesus' ministry were meager; the kingdom of God was
not advancing the way anticipated. If this was an invasion of a
kingdom, it was an invasion of ants. In addition to the disciples,
the followers of Jesus were limited to a few dirty children who ran
after him, "the beggars, and the few hangers-on from the outskirts
of society. . . ."[35] As Thielicke appropriates this parable, he connects it with his own experience. He reflects on the time when he
conducted his first Bible study as a new pastor in Hitler's Ger-
many. Only three people attended; two were old ladies and the
third, a still older man with palsied fingers, who was the organist.
Outside the church building, marching in goose-step were thousands in Hitler's youth battalions. As Thielicke tells the story, one
can almost hear the jack-booted battalions marching; something
of the evil power of the Third German Reich can be *felt*. By comparison, reflects Thielicke, the church appeared almost nonexist-
ent. As he approached this sparsely attended prayer meeting,
Thielicke repeated to himself over and over the words of Jesus: "All
authority in heaven and on earth has been given to me."[36] An
inner voice seemed to bring him assurance: ". . . with me everything begins in a very small way. Seen from the outside, my work
and I myself look minuscule."[37] But, writes Thielicke, we must
not be deceived by appearances: "Hitler . . . and his dreadful power
machine [are] merely puppets hanging by strings in the hands of
this mighty Lord."[38] What a powerful use of appropriated story
transported into a dynamic sermon.

My second example comes from a sermon preached by a friend.

His text came from Hebrews: "For this reason he had to be made like his brothers in every way, in order that he might become a merciful and faithful high priest in service to God"[39] My friend wanted his congregation to comprehend the reality of the incarnation, to know that in and through Jesus Christ, God identifies with his suffering people; in the death of his Son, God gave us the gift of his own brokenness. No one can ever say, "God just doesn't understand!" As he appropriated the profound meanings of this passage, my friend recalled a difficult time in his own life. His grandfather, to whom he was especially close, had just died. The night following the funeral he was unable to sleep; he got out of bed and went outside to sit in a lawn chair. He wept and prayed: "Dear God, I hurt; I loved my grandfather so very much. If I only knew, Lord, that you hurt with me, that I do not cry alone." As he spoke those words, a gentle rain began falling from the heavens and mixed with his tears; to my friend these were the tears of God, and this was a "revelatory experience." It was as though God said to him: "I do know how you feel; I cry with you." When my friend's experience connected with this particular text, a potent sermon was conceived.

We have noted that narrative sermons evoke within the listeners a response which leads them to personal "inner appropriation." As we come to the end of this chapter, we will focus on how this process worked in the life of Walter Wangerin, preacher and author. Wangerin tells of a painful crisis when he was boy:

> I cannot run. I am short, hampered by big buttocks, hunched with a miserable miscoordination, generally inferior in the contests of children— unable to run. But in the track meets of the fifth grade, they make me run the 100-yard dash. It causes me a vomitous anxiety. I have nightmares of running under water. My dreams are not untrue, for when the starting gun goes off, I stumble and am the last to leave the line; slowly, slowly I

> suffer my way to the end of the race, and when I
> arrive, people have departed to run in other races,
> I am humiliated. Ellery Yurchuck cries out, 'He
> walks like a girl!' I do. I burn with shame, I can-
> not do what other children do so thoughtlessly. I
> cannot run.[40]

How might a parent help a child with this kind of a problem? Some fathers might take a very insensitive approach: "Son, why don't you act like a man. If you really wanted to run, you could. Maybe you *are* a big sissy!" A more sensitive parent might say, "Son, I know what you are going through; I went through the same thing. Hang in there; as you get older, running will be less important to you." This second response, while more empathetic than the first, still doesn't provide much help in the present. Walter's father did not approach his son in either of these ways.

Instead, Walter's father buys a large picture less book containing the tales of Hans Christian Andersen, and begins reading them to his son. As the boy sits in his fathers arms, he hears about a duck uglier than all the others. Walter listens with unspeakable sympathy:

> I listen and laugh, and my father laughs, too. What
> is happening? Violence is being reduced to some-
> thing manageable; and because I am the one laugh-
> ing at it, scorning it, recognizing the blustering
> silliness of it, then I am larger than it, capable of
> triumphing over it. This story does not deny the
> monster in me or the cruelties of the general soci-
> ety. Rather, it empowers me.[41]

As an adult looking back on his experience, Wangerin writes,

> The tales of Hans Christian Andersen *were* my
> world for a while. They named and shaped the

universe in which I dwelt, and something of that
shape has remained forever; not the fantasy, but
the faith that created the fantasy continues even
now to explain existence . . . Those things that were
horrible and senseless in my external world were,
in Andersen's world horrible still; but his stories
gave them a sense (often a spiritual sense) that I
could grasp, by which the horror might be mas-
tered, if not by me then by someone, by goodness, by God. Andersen was my whispering, laugh-
ing, wise companion when I most needed com-
panionship.[42]

Young Walter appropriated the story of the ugly duckling and, in
the process, learned to *anticipate creatively.* Empowered by an appropriated story, Walter Wangerin would not be overwhelmed by
his inadequacies.

In my judgment, narrative preaching functions in a similar
manner. I particularly like the word *empowerment*; at the core of
his being Walter Wangerin appropriated hope and confidence that
no logical argument could provide. He relates, "As a child, I never
analyzed the tale I read; I felt it; I sank inside of it; I *lived* its
experience through to the happy conclusion."[43] That is precisely
what we want to happen in narrative preaching: God's Story connects with the revelatory experiences of both pastor and people so
that the gospel "names and shapes the universe in which we dwell."

Ordering Experience

For me, once "inner appropriation" has occurred, insight for a
possible sermon *explodes* into existence. I find myself highly motivated to develop a message evoked by my "priestly listening." Such
sermons are enjoyable to create and preach. When I try to preach
without this appropriation, sermon work is laborious; my efforts
almost seem counter-productive. I haven't tapped-in to the well-

spring of my spiritual and creative self. Consequently, the sermon never comes to *feel* right. Because the Living Word has not been released *in me*, I struggle to release it *through me*. Personally, preaching sermons where these appropriations have not been made is like a trip to the dentist; I keep my appointment but not with much enthusiasm. Without inner appropriation, narrative messages are much more difficult; with it, sermons almost write themselves. As Thomas Troeger comments:

> When we are attentive to what we see, feel, and hear, our imaginations are less capricious and more reliable. The vividness of the world feeds our creativity day by day. We are less anxious about finding homiletical resources because we have become sensitive to the richness of common experience. We use our imaginations to draw parables from life, from plain human stories that are marked by ambiguity, resolution, and renewed ambiguity.[44]

Sermons that grow out of fruitful encounters with God, his Word, his world, and his people are also refreshing to hear. Listeners *experience* the sermon; it resonates within their being. They sense that the preacher understands what it means to live, to suffer, to laugh—even to die. Preacher *and* congregation together are practicing the fine art of interpreting life through the lens of story.

Narrative communication then is not the "structuring of ideas" but the "shaping of experience." Eugene Lowry hits the nail on the head: " . . . the preacher who orders ideas into a structural form will focus on a theme, while the preacher who orders experience into a process will focus on events."[45] In other words, if the message is to evoke a response in listeners, it must be *an event;* only then, to use the language of the previous chapter, will the sermon remain "in the flow" where life-transforming communication happens. The perspective I have described views the text not as a "still-life picture" but like a "motion-picture film clip": "They are not static, still-life pictures full of things to look at objectively. No, they move like stories, episode by episode; or they travel along with the give and take of lively conversation . . ."[46] Henry Mitchell says it well: Preaching must move from " . . . argument to art—from syllogism to symbol—from awesome oratory to experiential encounter [with the Living God]."[47] Yes.

CHAPTER 4

THE NUANCES OF NARRATIVE

"Between teller and listener, there is a potent connection of the minds, a connection that stimulates the listener to create the story . . . from within, see characters and vivid landscapes, transparent, one upon another. It is then that the real tentacles of the story reach out and grab the listener and they become engaged at a very deep, personal level—a moment when he actually lives the story while he is imagining it, when he becomes so involved in the story that he ultimately forgets about me, the teller, and the story becomes his more than mine."[1]

Laura Simms as quoted by David Weber

Having stressed in the previous chapter the importance of living in the *receptive mode*, which leads to "inner appropriation," we now turn our attention toward understanding "story." We will focus on "plot" and how it functions in story (Chapter 4) and sermon (Chapter 5). Metaphorically, we are constructing a sermonic house—from the foundation up. The lengthy initial stages of building a house can be frustrating. An impatient family member may demand: "Why is so much time being spent 'underground'?" Yet, skilled carpenters caution us that a house is no better than its foundation; even an elegant home lacks structural integrity if constructed on a weak substructure. This chapter, then, will complete our foundational understanding of narrative; our sermonic house will begin to develop in the next chapter.

What is the shape of narrative? How does one plot a story? What elements are necessary for creating a story? I have referred several times in previous chapters to the "nuances of narrative." Only in understanding these subtleties will we be able to create effective narrative sermon designs.

Driving on the Other Side of the Road

A few years ago my family and I spent the summer in Northwestern England. We lived in the town of Wigan, which is sandwiched midway between Liverpool and Manchester. I preached in a small church on Sundays and during the week we traveled. The minister whose pulpit I was filling allowed us the use of his little car, a five-speed Fiat, Ono, in which we journeyed over five thousand miles. This was my first experience driving on the left side of the road. The steering wheel, of course, was on the right side of the car, and I had to shift the five-speed transmission with my left hand! What a transition to drive British-style; how intimidating to travel sixty or seventy miles per hour on the *wrong side* of the road. My American instincts had conditioned me to drive in a particular way, and I had to reverse those instinctive feelings. For the most part, the British drivers were patient with my learning process. By God's grace and a good bit of luck, we never put so much as a scratch on my friend's car. After my family and I adjusted to driving in the United Kingdom, we didn't give it much thought—we just did it. It was simply another way of moving from point A to point B.

To learn to drive in England, the first thing I did was saturate myself with the rules and regulations in the British auto manual. I memorized these rules of the road and the various signs that we would encounter. Then I sat down with pencil and paper, and I *imagined* myself into numerous situations we might experience on the motorway; I did this every day for a week or more. Then came our first tentative trips, short at first and expanding as confidence increased. Even after I had driven several miles, I made errors; driving just did not *feel* right. Becoming accustomed to British "roundabouts" was particularly difficult for me. With a roundabout, the driver must enter in the correct lane in order to exit properly; when in the wrong lane, one must drive around again and again till in the proper lane for exiting. Each evening I would review my mistakes and correct them mentally in preparation for the next day's travels. I could not have driven in that place had I not made extensive use of my imagination to reprogram my instincts. Soon, driving in the British style *felt* right. Of course, when we came back to America. . . !

Learning to compose and preach narrative sermons is a good bit like learning to drive on the opposite side of the road; we must retrain our instincts. Not only the way we preach, but also the way we think and feel must be altered; at first the process can be uncomfortable. This discomfort is especially intense if most of our preaching has been deductive. It is like replacing a favorite chair; the old thing might not be aesthetically attractive any more, but at least it is a known quantity. A man might say to his wife: "Honey, I don't want to get rid of this chair; it fits *my body!*" Constructing deductive sermons is an analytical process involving mostly the *left brain*;[2] the structure of these messages is rigid and predictable. Narrative sermons, however, are much more *right brain* oriented; they are intuitive, calling on our creative impulses. One might *think* a deductive sermon into existence, but story sermons must be *thought and felt* into existence. Deductive sermons march with the precision of soldiers at boot camp; narrative sermons *dance* their way into the world. Therefore, to preach in the manner we are describing, we must cultivate a "feel for story."

Often ministers have not developed the creative skills necessary for story preaching. Listening to lectures and writing academic papers in seminary can actually *diminish* our capacities for composing sermons—especially narrative sermons. Richard Jensen speaks for many seminary graduates, "When I was a student in seminary in the late '50s I was taught homiletics as a 'thinking in idea' discipline. I learned to study the text in order to find the ideas. . . ."[3] Ministers are often trained, argues Jensen, to preach for a "literate culture," i.e., a culture based primarily upon the written word.[4] But the domination of the printed word has been broken;[5] we live in a "post-literate world"; the electronic media have transformed ours into an "oral-aural" culture. Learning to preach narrative sermons demands, as Jensen maintains, that we develop a narrative mind-set, that we learn to "think in story."

But someone might ask, isn't this a shallow way of reasoning that excludes the use of the mind? Not at all. Western civilization, in the post-enlightenment world, taught us a truncated way of thinking which often excludes narrative thought-forms. Jensen declares,

> Our task is to learn a new way of thinking. Please note that storytelling is a way of thinking. It is not that we tell stories in order to do something other than think. . . . Literate culture taught us to think in ideas as the highest form of human thought. There is certainly nothing wrong with thinking in ideas. But there are other ways to think. One can also think in story.[6]

To preach narratively, we must learn the "logic of narrative."[7] This phrase comes from Harold Fickett who describes story as "a particular species of thinking."[8] Fickett argues that setting, character, plot, etc., are to the storyteller "what syllogisms are to the philosopher."[9] Narrative is not shallow or simplistic; it constitutes *a particular way of thinking* which must be understood and appreciated; we must cultivate a *feel* for story.

Shaping Stories

Stories come, of course, from a plethora of sources; like flowers, they might just grow anywhere. We read them in books and magazines, we watch them on TV or at the theater, we hear them in public places like restaurants or ball fields; in some cases they are born out of the context of living and then shared over a cup of coffee. Regardless of their origins, stories contain certain defining characteristics. They provoke *expectations* in the listener; disappointment and disinterest follow when those expectations are betrayed.

A "story" and the "plot" of the story are not the same.[10] The story begins earlier than the plot; further, the plot is the *action* of the story. Ryken defines plot as "the arrangement of the events."[11] This arrangement is not random, but is "a coherent sequence of interrelated events, with a beginning, middle, and an end. In other words, a whole completed action."[12] Tremper Longman quotes P. Brooks who indicates that plot provides an indispensable "principle of interconnectedness."[13] Plot ties the story together, gives it a sense of unity. Narratives demand *action*, forward movement which enlivens the story and sustains interest. *Something* at the end of the story pulls the listener along. That "something" may be suspense or tension; it might also be a danger, a test, a curiosity, or just the simple need for closure. In any case, plot will not succeed unless it causes the listener to creatively anticipate. Stories, like jokes, do not succeed if they take the listener on a path to nowhere. Recently, my wife and I walked out of a movie because it had no "plot" (or at least it was a very weak plot). There simply was nothing to hold our attention, to keep us to the end.

Given this general overview, precisely how is a story shaped? Let us examine Marsh Cassady's description as found in his book, *Creating Stories For Storytelling*.[14] Stories often begin with the introduction of the characters and their placement in a particular setting. As details are given and experiences revealed, readers develop an appreciation, even an identification with these characters. Often one person is the *protagonist* or hero of the story. At the inception of the narrative, the hero's life is in a state of balance or harmony, though there may be ominous clouds on the horizon. As the plot builds, opposition arises from an *antagonist*. Sometimes conflict emanates from self (a struggle with one's conscience, for example), or opposition may come from society, from disease, or many other sources. A specific situation involving the protagonist upsets the harmony. This precipitating event, the *inciting incident*, often places the hero in desperate circumstances. In the process, an important question is raised which must be answered if balance is to be restored and the main character survive. Then comes the *rising action* which heightens the tension; instead of resolution, the struggles of the hero are amplified into an intensifying crescendo. If resolution does not present itself soon, the protagonist may suffer or even die. For the story to work, the listener or reader must become convinced that the problem may never be solved; the main character is legitimately in crisis. Will the hero finally triumph or be defeated? A cul-de-sac has been created with no *apparent* outlet. At this point the story can go no further without some breakthrough—some unexpected means of escape; this is the *turning point*. Suddenly appears a thread of hope, a remotely possible route out of the dilemma—but it is extremely risky. To overcome the opposition and restore balance, the protagonist must risk total and irrevocable defeat. Failure will mean destruction, but success will bring triumph and the restoration of harmony. The point at which the central character wins or loses is the *climax;* the remainder of the story is the *falling action.*

As we have noted, for a story to have an adequate plot, it must embody a complete action with a beginning, middle, and end. The final outcome of the story, the "climax" and "falling action," is called the *denouement.* No matter how difficult or complicated the sequence of events, this final denouement or "coming together" must occur. R. V. Cassill maintains, "The principle that must be respected is that every story must have some resolution, some denouement. . . ."[15] Resolution is not simple or easy; many unusual twists and turns heighten the tension and put the protagonist in grave peril. The reader, of course, becomes a participant, experiencing every bump and bruise along the way. Effective stories will not allow the reader the luxury of passive or objective disinterest; the vicissitudes of the hero are keenly felt. (In the midst of a good story, I have found myself almost hyperventilating.) The storyteller creates escalating tension as the struggle develops; the reader feels uncomfortable, but also involved. In a sense, reading an effective story is like riding a roller-coaster; a kind of "miserable-enjoyment" is experienced. When we think the danger past, the hero safe, trouble strikes again! Deceptive endings are common; the storyteller lulls the reader into a false sense of complacency as the antagonist has been rendered powerless. Then occurs one final jolt; the tension is unexpectedly re-established. Finally, it is over; we can take a deep breath and relax, knowing that our hero is safe; with full resolution comes unspeakable relief. Once the resolution arrives, the story ends rather quickly.

Because plot develops around personalities, *characters* are important. Enough detail about characters is presented to help us form an opinion about them. We find ourselves identifying with a certain individual or individuals, usually the protagonist. We then experience anxiety as this person struggles against overwhelming odds. Often this main character searches for something, which may be a murderer, someone to love, or a life-enhancing quality like happiness. The antagonist attempts to stop the search, to block the protagonist from solving his or her problem. This resistance in the form of an evil or unlikable person is essential. A murderer, for example, may attempt to kill the sleuth before certain clues are uncovered. Skillful writers portray the antagonist in a variety of distasteful ways, causing feelings of animosity and anger toward this character. To think that a disgusting scoundrel could defeat or even kill the hero, with whom we have come to identify, is unacceptable.

A certain amount of description is essential to character development.[16] However, the storyteller cannot disclose everything about any one person, even about the main character. Instead, selective points are highlighted. In every story, the listener or reader is expected to infer the missing details. The teller gives just enough facts to incite the listener's imagination. Once that happens, the reader or listener fills in the gaps, often unconsciously. Specific descriptions of characters serve to pave the way for later events in the story. We might learn for example that the protagonist is gullible, accepting what he is told in a naive manner. This trait will serve as a future trap for the protagonist. The reader may even sense that the presence of a particular trait bodes evil for another given character. As noted, we come to care for the hero, sharing his or her dangers, anxieties, and concerns. Of course, we frequently know that the wit and resourcefulness of the protagonist will win the day; no harm could possibly overtake him. This would be the case, for example, in a TV show where the same person stars in each episode; the series could not continue if this individual were killed. Nevertheless, in our imaginations, we suspend disbelief: "Surely this will come out all right—but maybe it won't!" In some instances, the reader is aware of a danger of which the protagonist is unaware (under the table, a "ticking bomb"!). Escalating anxiety keeps us reading as we are pulled toward the denouement, like a tiny canoe swept toward a dangerous waterfall.

Identification between reader and story characters is vital; if there is no personality in the story in whom we see ourselves, we may have trouble staying with the story to its conclusion. Effective stories are shared experiences, involving us in the action. Ryken asserts: " . . . if we can see our own experience in the events and characters of the story, the story has captured something universal about life."[17] Amos Wilder defines this as "a prior sense for the real which pervades . . . all stories."[18] Earlier I quoted Wilder: "The world of a story is our own world in a higher register."[19] He explains,

> In all those features of storytelling, which exert their spell on hearer or reader, we can recognize the bridge between fiction and life itself. Stories

would not even exist or be heard if human nature
did not look to them avidly for illumination of its
own homelessness in time and circumstance. It is
just because life is labyrinth that we follow ea-
gerly the clues and traces, the impasses and de-
tours and open sesames of myth or tale.[20]

This "bridge between fiction and life" is imperative if any given
story is to become *our* story.

We have looked at *plot* and *character*; we now turn our attention to *setting*. Declares Ryken: "Storytellers put us on the scene in
the middle of an action. They pluck us out of our own time and
place and put us in another time and place."[21] The setting provides the background in which the characters live and act; it also
includes the physical location of the action, often in the process
adding atmosphere. Nancy Mellon refers to the various settings as
"storyscapes."[22] She demonstrates how different settings spark varying reactions in the reader or hearer.[23] Among the settings Mellon
examines are mountains, pools and lakes, dark woods, bogs and
swamps, and dark towers—each providing a unique mood. A story
set in downtown Washington, DC, for example, provides a completely different atmosphere than one cast in the deep recesses of
the Amazon forest. Good storytellers make the listener feel as though
he or she is on the scene, present at the place of the action.

My wife and I recently viewed the movie "Apollo 13" which is
directed by Ron Howard and stars Tom Hanks. This movie recounts the almost miraculous return to earth of three astronauts
after their space capsule developed problems. What a powerful
experience to feel one's self drifting in orbit around the moon with
the knowledge that returning to earth might never be possible. As
we watched, *we were there!* Being able to say that is a lofty compliment to any story.

What About Fantasy?

Even fantasy worlds come to life in the hands of a skilled storyteller. This actuality introduces an interesting question: "Must stories be realistic in order to seem real?" For example, what about narratives set on another planet in a far out galaxy? What is the value of fanciful stories like Tolkien's trilogy of the hobbits, or C. S. Lewis' space adventures? A man once said to me, "Don't expect me to get anything out of a fanciful story; if it can't possibly be true, I don't want to hear it!" I regard this individual as an exception; most people find it possible to identify with even highly imaginative characters and settings.[24] The popularity of the science fiction genre underscores this point. William Bausch declares that the ultimate question is not, "Is this story true?" but rather, "Is this story true for me?"[25] If a given narrative mediates reality *to* and *for* me, the setting makes little difference. Initially, I resisted reading Richard Adam's delightful book, *Watership Down*. Though I like fantasy, I did not think I could become engrossed in a story about rabbits. When I finally read the book, I enjoyed it thoroughly and had not the least problem seeing life through the eyes of a four-footed, fuzzy animal.[26] Marsh Cassady states that "reality" in stories has to do with establishing a "logical frame of reference."[27] The storyteller creates a world that, "although different from the one we inhabit, is consistent. It has certain natural laws, inhabitants, and physical characteristics that remain the same throughout the story."[28] It is only when elements of the story contradict the world *that has been created* that they become unbelievable.

In fact, *truth* is often best communicated through stories that are *not literally true*. Consider this Vietnamese folktale as an example of a story not real, but most *truthful*.[29]

> Mr. Kinh returned to his home village after many years of travel. There he met an old friend named Mr. Sanh, whom he had not seen since having left the village.

Said Mr. Sahn to his friend, 'You have been away from the village for a long time. What were your adventures? What have you seen?'

Replied Mr. Kinh, 'I sailed on a great ship. The ship was so long, I could not measure it. A young boy of seven years began to walk from the bow of the ship. He walked and he walked until he reached the giant mast. It took so many years to walk that great ship, his hair turned white and his beard grew long. Before he could reach the stern, he died of old age.'

Mr. Sahn listened with thoughtful patience.

Then Mr. Kinh asked Mr. Sahn, 'Old friend, while I was on that great ship, what did you see? What were your adventures?'

Mr. Sahn replied, 'While you were on that great ship, I walked through a vast forest. The trees were so tall that if you stood beneath them you would not see the sky. The birds that wished to nest in these tall trees flew higher and higher and higher. After they had flown for ten years, the birds reached the tops of the trees.'

Suddenly Mr. Kinh shouted: 'That's a terrible lie! Such trees are not possible!'

Mr. Sahn bowed reverently to his old friend and said, 'Please, my friend, if it is not the truth, where would one find a giant mast for the great ship that you sailed upon?'

Stories like this one need not be "real" in order to engage the listener or convey truth about human nature. Our world would be deprived of much great literature if stories were constrained by the boundaries of the "real world." I have discovered that it does not take long to become absorbed in any narrative in which I see myself, from which I gain insight into the nature of life. As Wilder writes,

Even in fables and fictions, these aspects may be strange, yet they involve us. These characters and their vicissitudes link up with our own predicaments and their options and constraints, their entanglements and fortunes are familiar. Even tales of the marvelous are not only exercises in spellbinding, in thrill and shudder; they speak to our own wrestling with necessity and fatality.[30]

William Bausch presents the ultimate test of any story in his paraphrase of Pogo: "We have met the story and it is us."[31]

The Narrator

Stories are told by someone; they come from a particular "point of view" or perspective—they are narrated. In some instances, the word "tone" is used instead of point of view. Explains Eugene Lowry, "tone refers to the work's *created subjective presence*—the world view that stands silently articulate behind the writing."[32] Being aware of the narrator's perspective is imperative for he or she "is the one who mediates perspective on the characters and events. . . ."[33] As I have indicated, stories are related in a selective manner— not every detail is given but only those which serve the author's purpose. Longman uses an analogy of the camera:

> In a film, the eye of the camera grants perspective as it moves from place to place, coming in for a close-up here and then panning to another shot. The camera guides and limits the audience's insight.[34]

The writer or storyteller utilizes the narrator's point of view to select and emphasize certain crucial details.

In some instances, for example, the story is told from a *first-*

person perspective which means that one of the characters in the story does the reporting. Other stories are recounted from a *third-person* perspective, i.e., someone outside the narrative recounts the story.[35] If the narrator does not figure into the events of the story, then the perspective is most often third-person.[36] In this instance, the narrator usually displays a certain amount of omniscience and omnipresence; the reader is made aware of the thoughts, feelings, or sensory experiences of the characters.[37] Longman reminds us that readers tend to respond to third-person narrative with what he calls an "unconscious submissiveness."[38] This compliance means, among other things, that the reader may miss the narrator's bias in telling the story.

A Simple Story

Having examined the nuances of narrative, let us consider a simple story from Elaine Ward's book, *The Art Of Storytelling*.[39] Each year a rich apple grower would send a basket of his finest apples to the king. On one occasion the grower's oldest son was walking toward the palace with a basket of apples when he was stopped by an old woman. She asked him: "Where are you going and what are you carrying?" The young man was annoyed: "Old woman, if you must know, I am taking a basket of dried grass to the king. Now leave me alone!" When the young man arrived at the palace, the king removed the covering from the basket. To the astonishment of both the boy and the king, they discovered a basket filled with dried grass! The king ordered the boy be thrown into prison. The apple grower then sent a second basket of his finest apples to the king; this time his second son was the courier. Again the old woman imposed herself, "What, my young friend, do you bear in your basket?" Answered the boy, "What do *you* think, old hag? I carry a basket of garbage!" When this boy reached the king, he confidently removed the cover. A stench permeated the room as a basket of garbage was revealed. "To the dungeon with him," said the king. "I will not be so insulted again!" With trepidation, the anxious father sent his youngest son to the king bearing apples. This time the boy was also interrupted, "What do you carry in your basket?" begged the old lady. "I take my father's finest apples to the king," responded the boy. "Would you like one?" Thankfully the woman accepted the gift; a bright smile flooded her face. Upon discovering the third son at the palace, the king was furious: "If this is another of your tricks, I will hang the lot of you!" But when the king removed the covering, the basket was filled with *golden* apples. The king was so pleased that he set all the brothers free.

This brief story has setting, characters, and plot; it is told from a third-person perspective, and it contains the tension or conflict necessary in any plot. Donald Davis refers to this tension as a kind of *crisis*.[40] He defines "crisis" as "any event or happening that takes a part of the world we have grown comfortable living with and turns it upside down."[41] Davis calls "crisis" the "plot center" of all stories: "Without a crisis to be experienced and endured by the main character, we may have a portrait but we do not really have a story."[42] In the above narrative, the crisis is precipitated by the disrespectful responses of the older brothers. The youngest brother becomes the hero of the story by simply treating the old lady with a measure of kindness. Who is the old woman and by what power does she transform the contents of the baskets? We do not know, nor does it matter. Only the strictest literalists demand that all the mystical details be explained—or eliminated. Stories like the one above communicate *experienced* truth; they reflect what I called earlier the "logic of narrative." There is no need for the storyteller to conclude by saying, "We must be sure we treat elderly people with the respect they deserve." Such a propositional directive would actually diminish the force of the story. Granted, there are times when our sermons must go beyond the story to expand and expound upon the central lesson of the narrative. Most often, however, if we will just leave it alone and trust it to work, the story itself will communicate with our listeners.

The Sermon Event

Narrative sermons, like good stories, are built around a crucial question, conflict, or crisis; they take the listener on a quest which leads to self-discovery. These sermons are plotted so that "the question, the quest, and the discovery" occur in the context of actual human experiences. Like stories, our sermons will be *events:* "ordered form[s] of moving time."[43] Our listeners will do more than hear the sermon; they will *experience* it. Our goal in narrative preaching is not simply to illustrate or explain by using story or stories. We want our listeners *to participate* in the story; therefore, we make careful use of "metaphors of participation."[44] As we have observed, stories give birth to stories; our sermons *evoke* theirs. Further, their stories connect with The Story, so that the gospel "names and shapes the universe in which they dwell."[45]

We must remember that narrative sermons *pull* the listener along by the power of *creative anticipation,* as opposed to pushing the listener by logical argumentation. Effective narrative sermons function like effective stories. They move toward a creative denouement which often sneaks-up on the listener, causing him or her to question long-held assumptions. Jerome Brunner, while speaking primarily of art and literature, claims that the hallmark of creativity is what he calls "effective surprise."[46] He asserts, "Effective surprise is . . . the unexpected that strikes one with wonder and astonishment."[47] This is not to say that all narrative sermons leave the audience spellbound and breathless; no preacher could guarantee such sermonic endings—even if they were desirable. Salmon quotes Paul Ricoeur: " . . . instead of being predictable, a conclusion must be acceptable."[48] Our goal in narrative sermons is to leave the listener with *unexpected insight* into his or her life—a *fresh hearing* of the gospel. Sermons of this nature may indeed sneak up on the hearers, forcing self-examination, sometimes even self-incrimination. Because listeners have appropriated the story, they are less defensive, more open to self-reformation. And, of course, that reformation does not take place apart from the inner working of God's Spirit.

This brief analysis of story completes our foundation. Grab your hammer and saw, because in the next chapter our sermonic house begins to take shape.

CHAPTER 5

THE QUESTION, THE QUEST, AND THE DISCOVERY

"But our parson's no gift at all in that way; he can preach as good a sermon as need be heard when he writes it down. But when he tries to preach wi'out book he rambles about, and doesn't stick to his text; and every now and then he flounders like a sheep as has cast itself, and can't get on its legs again."[1]

George Eliot in Amos Barton

Having examined the shape of narrative in the previous chapter, we are now ready to apply our understanding to the sermon. Previous chapters have established the groundwork for the more practical applications. Our sermonic foundation is complete; the time has come to build our narrative house.

I am assuming in this chapter that the text has been carefully studied and its message appropriated by the preacher; therefore, the minister is prepared to formulate the sermon. When I arrive at this point, I find it easy to feel intimidated. Research is my cup of tea; I could go on indefinitely reading commentaries and doing word studies. But Sunday approaches like a runaway train; God's people will gather expecting a Word—I must not disappointment them. The sermon drafting must begin. If our goal were a deductive sermon, we might start by reviewing our research and writing a thesis or proposition; points would be developed to break the thesis into component parts. Exegetical work would then be transported to the appropriate locations and additional illustrative material added in order to apply scriptural truth to our listeners. The difference between deductive and inductive sermon preparation might be described in this manner: "Sermons completely controlled by rational logic focus on a logical exposition of propositional Truth. Sermons controlled by narrative strategies are plotted as story qua story—'truth' emerging out of shared experience."[2] Because we are creating a narrative sermon, our concern is *movement*; the sermon must be *plotted*. As Shea says it, the time has come for us to "join the chain of flawed and halting storytellers."[3]

In this chapter we will view, in a general sense, the process of plotting a narrative sermon; our goal will be to see the operation in overview, in broad terms. In future chapters, more detail will be given as we study specific biblical texts. Likewise, later we will address important textual issues like the following: What role do exegesis and hermeneutics play in story preaching? How does the form of the text shape the form of the sermon? Is it ever acceptable for the sermon's form to be different from the form of the text? How does a biblical narrative itself influence the way we plot the sermon? How does the sermon create "narrative interest" in a manner similar to the biblical story? How do we choose contemporary stories which sit comfortably alongside the biblical narrative? These questions and others will receive attention as we examine the various narrative designs for telling the Story. For now, however, we shall apply our amassed understanding of story to the sermon.

Connecting Bible and Life

We begin by returning to a basic assumption mentioned earlier: *Narrative sermons come into existence at the point where the message of the text, the preacher's experience of the text, and the congregation's need overlap.* Let me stress again that a narrative sermon cannot be developed unless the preacher has personally appropriated the message of the text. Milton Crum cautions, "The preacher functions as a listener to God through the Bible before he or she serves as a messenger of God through the sermon."[4] If, for example, our study has focused on one of Jesus' parables, we must ask ourselves, "what redeeming power have I found in the story?" Declares Shea, "There is no escaping this personal foundation for retelling. Without it, all telling lacks persuasion and passion."[5] If God has indeed spoken to me, I am now ready to plot the sermon, so that God speaks through me. Our work in this chapter assumes that the preacher's spirit has absorbed the biblical text, as a sponge soaks up water; the text has been *remembered* or *imagined* into the preacher's life. Now the communicator confronts the question, "How can I retell the story so that listeners will assimilate and appropriate God's truth?"

Gardner Taylor advises that regardless of its structure, a sermon must deal with the "revelant" and the "relevant."[6] The revelant is God's message as revealed in his Son and as reflected in the sacred text of Scripture. The relevant, of course, refers to the contemporary world and the pressing needs of people. Taylor states, "The sermon's task is to swing the light of proclamation, not mechanically, from what is 'revelant' to what is 'relevant,' to show how one touches the other and the demands made in the name of the sovereign Lord of them both."[7] The *form* and the *content* of the text will be taken into consideration as we plot the sermon. Grady

Davis is correct in stating that "form does its work immediately and at deeper levels than logic, persuades directly and silently as it were. . . ."[8] We must avoid imposing rigid or mechanical structure on the sermon, lest we block the release of the Word. Our goal is not to produce a lifeless lecture but a living organism, *a dynamic vehicle of participation* and communication. Grady Davis asserts that in such a sermon, "the right thing is said rightly."[9] When this has occurred, the preacher will sense a rare satisfaction: "Once the right thing is said rightly, there is a feeling of finality about it, as if it could never be said so well in any way but this."[10]

Connecting Text and Story

In my childhood I watched many westerns on television in which wagon trains made the long, dangerous overland journey to the far west. These wagon trains were supervised by a captain who depended on the guidance of a man called a "scout." The scout's job was to determine the best route for conducting the people from "here to there"—from their old home to their new one, with minimal discomfort and loss of life. Along the way he would ride ahead to look for obstacles like rivers, mountains, or hostile Indian tribes. The scout would then devise a strategy for overcoming these difficulties. The journey west was never easy; unexpected dangers and hardships could arise at any point. The scout anticipated these hazards and contrived means for overcoming them. I see the preacher as a kind of "scout;" he goes ahead of his listeners to scout-out a particular text of Scripture. After careful study, reflection, meditation, and appropriation of a specific passage, a sermon is constructed that will take listeners from "here to There." The preacher-scout helps the congregation overcome the distance and surmount the obstacles that stand between them and their appropriation of a particular portion of God's Word.

Sometimes a human experience, what I have spoken of in a previous chapter as a "revelatory experience," has come to the preacher's awareness. These revelatory insights make a good starting point for narrative sermons, but, in my judgment, they must be connected with Scripture before a sermon can emerge. As much as I believe in the power of stories, I am uncomfortable with sermons that ignore the texts of Scripture. What preacher, however, has not heard, discovered, or experienced a particular story and exclaimed, "That will preach!" F. Dean Lueking labels these potent stories "grace-filled-moments;"[11] or "people stories."[12] He writes, "The genius of artful people stories lies in their simplicity, their capacity to capture moments that are so transparently meaningful that everyone who hears can find involvement."[13] Such stories are not necessarily extraordinary events; sometimes they are simply a discernment of the mysteries of God in ordinary life circumstances. Revelatory moments happen to all of us, but only a few have eyes trained to see them and ears, to hear them.

Lueking gives this example of a "people story."[14] A man and his wife were separated, a result of years of insensitivity on his part. He had moved out and was staying in a second-floor room in the home of an older couple who were acquaintances of his. On a February morning, Valentine's Day, the troubled guest looked out his second-floor window to see that a light snow had fallen during the night. The man of the house, a retired physician, was cleaning snow from the walkways. Suddenly the elderly gentleman laid aside his snow shovel and began to tramp carefully in the snow. The guest was curious: what was the old man doing? It soon became obvious that the elderly doctor was forming a large heart in the snow. He then stamped out a love note to his wife, to whom he had been married for more than sixty years. Lueking finishes the story:

> The second floor guest, who was observing it all unseen, was overcome by the simple, whimsical, beautiful expression of an old man telling his wife that he loved her. It was a moment of such power that the guest had to lie down on his bed and weep in the realization that in all his own years of

marriage, amidst all his own striving and accomplishing, he had never done anything close to that. It was the turning point in his interior process of repentance and looking in new directions for the power of love to heal him and his marriage.[15]

Such stories provide excellent starting places for narrative sermons. Do not forget the *two pistons* which keep the sermon moving: *Bible and life*. When stories like the one above are connected with biblical truth, powerful occasions are created for the working of grace.

The Living Question

How does one compose a narrative sermon? As we delve into my proposed strategy for developing narrative sermons, the reader should be aware that other strategies are available. Milton Crum, for example, thinks of the sermon in terms of *situation, complication, and resolution*.[16] Eugene Lowry speaks of *aim, turn, and focus*.[17] In discussing the "web and flow" of an inductive sermon, Lewis and Lewis picture inductive movement as a whirlpool which begins with "common ground" and moves from "specifics-to-the-general" or from "evidence-leading-to conclusion."[18] Though my approach to narrative sermons is somewhat different, I have benefited from each of these authors and others; I recommend them for further study.

In the previous chapter we stressed the importance of "thinking in story." Plot, we said, is built around some form of conflict which moves toward resolution; this conflict is often portrayed in opposing persons, called "the protagonist" and "the antagonist." As we indicated, plot involves a "whole action" with a beginning, a middle, and an end; our goal in the narrative sermon is to get our listeners involved in the action of the story so that he or she anticipates the ending—the denouement. We noted that the end of the story is characterized by some "turn" which ultimately leads to resolution. Narrative sermons progress in a similar manner. I describe the movement of narrative sermons as a *question, a quest and a discovery.* The question I call a "living question" or a "central question." In the sermon itself, this question is often presented through the telling of a story. Once the congregation understands this question, both preacher and listeners proceed on a difficult journey toward discovery. This discovery provides the "answer" for the living question. As I shall discuss later, narrative sermons do not necessarily provide perfect answers, but they always lead us to The Answer. In sermon preparation *the preacher must isolate this living question and its Biblical resolution before the sermon can be plotted.* This *diagnostic* process is essential; it precedes the plotting of the sermon.

Before we focus more attention on the "living question," let us think about *questions* in a general sense. Karl Albrecht states that if asked to choose only one of humankind's symbols as the most important, he would choose a question mark.[19] Albrecht proposes that choice because "the investigative attitude lies at the foundation of all advances in the human condition, from the progression of science to the ordinary business of living a happy life."[20] I *almost* agree with Albrecht. I say "almost" because, for me, the most influential symbol is the *cross*. I am stimulated by intriguing questions, but my life is determinedly patterned after God's ultimate symbol, the cross. However, I agree with Albrecht that the question mark is a dynamic symbol, necessary for expanding knowledge and understanding. Questions constitute an indispensable tool in the preacher's workshop. The composition of sermons, especially narrative sermons, requires a refined skill in asking, not just questions, but the *right* questions. After all, if we do not ask the right questions, we will get wrong answers every time. A tourist who got lost on the back roads of Vermont stopped his car to ask directions from an elderly gentleman leisurely rocking on his front porch. "Say, old-timer, am I on the road to Montpelier?" "Ee-yup," responded the old man. The stranger hastily drove off, but suddenly had a peculiar hunch. He backed his car to the old man's house, leaned out the window, and asked, "Am I going in the right direction?" "Nope," replied the old fellow, as he continued to rock. Wrong questions send us in wrong directions.

Sermon preparation involves bombarding the text with questions; or, more correctly, the text bombards the preacher with questions. In any case, questions of varying significance surface. Eventually, the preacher will isolate a single "living question," around which the sermon will be plotted. Discovering this fundamental question is a *diagnostic enterprise* which requires the utmost precision. This "living question" *arises at the point where the message of the text, the preacher's experience of the text, and the congregation's need overlap.* Discerning this "overlap" is essential; otherwise, the sermon will most likely fail. Eugene Lowry writes, "the greatest single weakness of the average sermon is the weakness of diagnosis. What is lacking is concrete perceptive insight into the multifaceted ambiguities of the human situation. . . ."[21] When parishioners complain that they get little out of their minister's sermons, the problem often lies in this very area. One man said to me, "I heard the preacher's sermon this morning; I even understood part of it. But I said to myself as he was preaching, who cares about this stuff?" Faulty diagnosis is intolerable; it leads to sermons that are irrelevant. Life's serious spiritual and emotional wounds require the restorative ointment of God's Word; the living question must *hit the mark.* If not, a superficial question will surface which leads down the long, tedious road to No-wheres-ville. Sermons built around an inaccurate or irrelevant question are a waste of the listener's time; they lead to absurd, superficial answers. They are not much fun to preach either.

The "living question" must meet two criteria: First, it must be a vital question that *connects at a story-level* with both the one who preaches and those who will listen. Recall my definition of preaching given in an earlier chapter: "Preaching is the integrating of God's Story, their story, and the preacher's story, so that souls are saved, wounds are healed, and Christ is exalted." Like a correctly sized glove, the living question fits the people who will hear the sermon. Second, a question is not a "living question" *unless the gospel provides an "answer" to it.* In some instances the gospel provides a direct answer to our living question; in other instances the gospel offers us the faith and courage to live with an incomplete answer. In the latter case, the preacher will assist the listeners by "softening the irresolution"; I will discuss momentarily what I mean by that phrase.

Our living question leads us to some "piece of the gospel" which provides resolution. As Francis Rossow affirms, we must "develop a gospel awareness, sniffing . . . for its traces of gospel."[22] In some instances, this "piece of the gospel" surfaces first, and we must work back from it to fashion our living question. There are also occasions when a Scripture passage raises a significant living question, but does not provide a gospel answer. In these instances, we may need, as Rossow states, to "import the gospel from elsewhere in the Bible."[23] In any case, the narrative sermon emerges when it is carefully plotted so that the "living question" connects with the "Living Word." In future chapters I will illustrate the process with Scripture passages.

At this juncture I want to discuss the origins of my concept of a living question. Jensen argues that narrative sermons are built around a "living center" which "takes the form of proclamation."[24] Writes Jensen, "The living center ought most often to be first or second person, present tense language that enables Jesus to speak words of proclamation through us."[25] While accepting his idea of a "living center," I alter his use a bit. I think the center of a narrative sermon, at least initially, is a question, not an answer. Of course, and I stress this point, a question is not a "living question" unless the gospel provides an "answer" to it. However, I advocate the living question due to the influence of Lowry; he emphasizes the difference between exploring the text to find its *answer* and exploring to find a *problem*. The first, asserts Lowry, "puts us in command. The second, while prompting similar exegetical work, positions us as investigator rather than explainer."[26] Lowry's assumption, and mine as well, is that narrative preaching works best when the preacher accesses the text as an *investigator* rather than an *ex-*

plainer.[27] Our initial concern in preparing story sermons is finding a problem or conflict, rather than simply serving as an "answer-person." As stated earlier, this central question may emerge from a text or from a contemporary story; but whatever its origin, it forms the core around which we plot the sermon.

Before I discuss "the quest," I wish to explain my use of the word "answer." When I state that the living question leads to an "answer" I am not implying that every living question can be easily or completely resolved. Sometimes in preaching we can only acknowledge the ambiguity and "soften the irresolution." What John Collins says about stories is also true for narrative sermons:

> [Stories] provide images and ways of thinking about the imponderables of life. . . . They are not rational arguments. They are illustrations of experience, offered with the invitation: 'he who hath ears to hear, let him hear.'[28]

In the throes of human suffering, all answers seem superficial; yet, the preacher must not hesitate to provide God's Answer. Narrative sermons demonstrate sensitivity to suffering and loss, but they do not always furnish completely satisfying resolutions. While voicing this quandary, I am in no way diminishing the power of the gospel. I believe that Christ is our strength and comfort in life's most difficult struggles. However, sometimes we must say to hurting people, "I do not fully understand this suffering, but I know that *God's work in Christ* proves that he loves us more than you and I are able to comprehend. Through Christ, we know that God is with us even in pain and sorrow."

Story sermons function well in addressing ambiguous situations for which we have only partial answers. When I pastored a church in Indianapolis, a little eight-year old boy was killed in front of the church building as he crossed the street to attend Vacation Bible School. His death was an agonizing experience, not only for the boy's family, but also for the church family. When I preached the funeral, I could not give the parents a "perfect answer" for their son's death. Had I tried, they would have walked out of the funeral home. I could, however, give The Answer. With a gentle narrative, I attempted to "soften the irresolution" and assure the family of God's steadfast love. I knew there was no way to remove the pain of this tragedy; yet I encouraged my listeners not to sorrow, "even as others who have no hope."[29] Echoing the words of Paul: "Now we see but a poor reflection as in a mirror; then we shall see face to face. Now I know in part; then I shall know fully, even as I am fully known,"[30] I prayed that these grieving people would have the faith and courage to hold on, to keep believing until, at last, we see "face to face." If our preaching is to be authentic, it must be realistic; for me that means not pretending to have all the answers. As Lueking expresses it, "Jesus came to *this* fallen world and not some other, unburdened by sin."[31] I am thankful that when we do not have all the answers, we still possess The Answer.

The Quest

Once we have isolated the living question, we are ready to plot our journey—our quest. If we have arrived at an appropriate inquiry, a great distance and many obstacles will stand between this question and its answer. Our narrative sermon will grow out of the *tension or torque* that we create between this living question and its resolution. The plotted sermon will lead the congregation on a quest to discover (or *rediscover*) God's answer (or Answer). The various turns and twists on this journey from question to answer form the *plot*. As in stories, narrative sermons *pull* listeners along by the power of *creative anticipation*. Just like narratives, these sermons trigger expectations; something (or *Something*) ahead sustains interest. And, just as I stated in describing the nuances of narrative, that "something" emerges as some sort of an *incompleteness* which is resolved; resolution may take the form of a danger to overcome, a test to pass, a curiosity to satisfy, or a simple need for closure.

The sermonic process I am describing is not unlike the genre of stories called "murder mysteries." Over the years I have devoured hundreds of these mysteries by writers such as Arthur Conan Doyle, Agatha Christie, Charlotte MacLeod, Ellis Peters and Rex Stout. Most murder mysteries follow the same basic pattern. The narrative opens by describing the setting, i.e., the location where the events will take place. Characters are introduced even as we are plugged into the setting. Then, a murder is committed and the question is established: "Who murdered Edward Jones?" As the characters are portrayed (often with descriptive scenes), we like some, and we dislike others ("That despicable character must be the murderer!"). The mystery provides a limited number of possible suspects. Character sketches are intertwined with action to give the reader insight into the individual personalities. As the storyline progresses, a master sleuth questions one person after another, gathering clues that will eventually reveal the murderer. The clues point first in one direction and then another; the reader matches wits with the detective in a frantic effort to discover the culprit before she strikes again. As the detective closes in on the guilty party, the tension builds; another murder or attempted murder may surface. The local police (if the detective is not one of them) do their best, but overlook or misinterpret vital clues—which, of course, the master sleuth perceives. Finally, the detective names the man (or woman), and lays out the evidence that proves the case. Very often the identity of the murderer startles the reader, who has missed minor details along the way. The culprit may even turn out to be someone the reader had come to respect.

Narrative sermons contain the same basic elements as murder mysteries: a question, a quest, and a discovery. In mysteries, the living question is: "Who did it?" Not only does the reader of these stories identify with the sleuth, she *becomes the sleuth*. The frantic quest to detect the culprit before he strikes again is also *the reader's quest*. This participatory dimension is essential to good stories and effective sermons. Jensen helps us understand this dimension; he reviews the work of John Dominic Crossan on the parables of

Jesus.[32] In this context, Jensen discusses the importance of "metaphors of participation" in stories and sermons. Stories and parables, as it happens, are extended metaphors. To paraphrase Crossan, anyone hearing a parable enters into it "and experiences it from the inside out."[33] That is precisely what we want to happen in our sermons; our listeners are "in the story" and "on the quest."

An elementary school teacher recently told me of her initial effort to use storytelling in her classroom. She was quite anxious about how the children would respond. She was telling the story from memory when the unthinkable happened; she forgot the next episode of the story and had to return to a book to refresh her memory. Usually, she said, her children would become restless and talkative when she had to pause in the middle of a lesson. What amazed her on this occasion was that her children sat perfectly still, eyes fixed on her, while she reviewed the details of the story. "Well, what happened?" someone finally whispered. The children were *caught-up* in the story; they were suspended in a story-world—a "metaphor of participation." Remember Wilder's assertion as quoted in an earlier chapter: "the first axiom of good storytelling is that it should capture and hold our attention."[34]

Narrative sermons, like effective stories, often have tension and conflict; they transport the listeners into troublesome situations; they travel over rough terrain. The sermonic quest does not cruise down an interstate highway in an air-conditioned Cadillac. Instead, both preacher and listeners, with machetes in hand, chop their way through a dense and foreboding jungle. Giant snakes hang from the trees, and, a short distance off the path, hungry lions roar. Why do I use such metaphors to describe the narrative sermon? Sermons must reflect reality; the quest ought not deny the deep complexities and ambiguities of life. In life the snakes have real fangs, and the lions, real teeth and claws. One of us could, on this day or any other, lose a mate or child in an automobile accident; anyone reading these pages could learn today that he or she has a life-threatening illness. Narrative sermons are not preached in a Pollyanna world. The human race is alienated from

God; Satan is the "prince of this world." Our struggle "is not against flesh and blood, but against the rulers, against the authorities, against the powers of this dark world and against the spiritual forces of evil in the heavenly realms."[35] Life's journey is not simple or easy; sermons must reflect reality, if they are to be taken seriously. This does not mean that our cosmic struggle against evil and the evil one will defeat us. No matter how difficult the quest, *God will have the last Word.*

The Discovery

The *living question* sends us on a difficult journey with bumps and barriers, twists and turns. As with any plot, the listeners feel somewhat anxious, wondering where this quest will take them and if there is any possible release from the ambiguity which the sermon has established. The plot of the sermon vaults the listeners into a cul-de-sac, from which there appears no way out. Then comes the denouement, a significant *turning point* which reverses the direction of the sermon and convinces the listeners that they were on a *High Quest.* In homiletical parlance, this is sometimes called the "aha"; for the listeners, it "signals a decisive and sometimes peculiar form of knowing which illumines the entire plot."[36] I cannot stress enough the importance of the denouement in a narrative sermon. Long declares, "Everything in a plot strains forward, anticipating the end, working toward its consummation."[37] This break-through comes as a *Discovery*, an unexpected offering of grace in which the gospel provides a way out. When we are trapped in our dilemma, overwhelmed by sin and guilt, a gentle Voice breaks through the ambiguity: "Do not weep! See, the Lion of the tribe of Judah, the Root of David, has triumphed."[38] Through the use of "creative anticipation" listeners have been brought anew to the old, old, story. Stephen R. Lawhead characterizes the purpose of art and literature as a High Quest which searches for, captures, "and offer[s] to view the three verities: Goodness, Beauty, and Truth."[39] Narrative sermons function in a similar manner;[40] they point the listener to Truth and to the God of Truth. These sermons may focus on any of hundreds of Biblical characters and stories, but *God and his Son will always be the heroes* of the story.

The process I have just detailed is illustrated in a simple story which appears in Jon Hassler's novel, *A Green Journey*.[41] Hassler tells of an Irishman who travels to the United States and visits New York City. During his stay in New York, he becomes preoccupied with the thought that he might be mugged. The Irishman describes his feelings as he walks down Broadway: "[I was] afraid every step I'd be beaten and robbed of what little money I was carrying back to Ireland."[42] Sure enough, his fears were realized; someone bumped him roughly; he reached quickly, only to discover his billfold missing. Seeing the young man who had jolted him, the Irishman set off to apprehend the suspect. He caught him within a block or so: "I came up behind him, I did, and I turned him around rough as you please and I took the lapel of his checkered coat. . . . The wallet now, hand it over and be snappy about it!"[43] The young man reluctantly reached in his pocket, "swearing like a sailor as he did so," and handed over the billfold. The Irishman felt very proud of himself: "If only more people took it upon themselves to stand up to muggers, then they would soon change their ways!"[44] When the Irishman returned to his hotel room, he found, laying on his bed, *his own billfold*— where *he* had left it that morning. The billfold which he had demanded from the young man was just like his—but it wasn't his. The Irishman was stunned as the realization settled upon him that *he* was not the "muggee" but the "mugger"!

In Hassler's story, the conflict centers around the question: "Is it possible to walk the streets of New York without being mugged?" Notice that the conflict is revealed through an actual person and experience. The problem is not just theoretical or factual, as it might be if one were writing an essay on "Crime in the City of New York." The conflict is incarnated; it takes flesh in an Irishman walking down Broadway in New York City. Once we are introduced to the Irishman and made aware of his fear, we know that some action is going to ensue; we begin to anticipate. The story carries us on a journey, which turns out to be a quest for self-understanding. The tale reveals a kind of reverse logic; what seemed patently obvious was not true; the outcome differs radically from what we expect. This reversal, a common technique in well written stories, is an important element in narrative sermons. Lowry calls this element the "principle of reversal."[45] He states, "It is not quite what one expected, and 'arrives' from where you were not looking. And *it turns things upside down.*"[46] In this story, the Irishman turns out to be both the protagonist *and* the antagonist. Of course, many thieves do their dirty work in New York, as in most large cities, but the enemy encountered by the Irishman was *himself.*

Effective narrative sermons function like Hassler's story; they cause us to rethink our assumptions about the nature of both ourselves and others. We are shocked into self-examination; maybe the enemy really isn't *out there.* We often discover that evil is not simply someone else's problem; it lurks in our own hearts. We are not victims but perpetrators; we are not the "muggees" but the "muggers." Like Paul on the road to Damascus, we suddenly view ourselves from a new and often uncomfortable perspective. We have thought ourselves the "good guys" (and "gals") until stunned into *a new reality* by the words of Jesus: "Why do you persecute me?"[47] Sermons of this kind sneak up on the hearers forcing self-examination, sometimes even self-incrimination. As we have said, because listeners are co-creators of the sermon, they are less defensive, more open to self-reformation.

The profound importance of *the ending* or denouement is not a characteristic unique only to stories and narrative sermons. In humor, for example, it is not simply how you tell the joke, but how well you deliver the punch line. A trip with the family to the beach means, if the excursion is to be successful, you eventually must arrive at the ocean. Even a simple journey with the children to McDonald's leads *somewhere,* even if it is only to a hamburger. Long argues, "[Narrative] sermons are not propelled by powerful beginnings; they are evoked by significant endings."[48] The end of a sermon sits in judgment on its beginning; if the denouement falls flat, the sermon will die a thousand deaths, no matter how effectively the question and the quest have been established. Sermons *go somewhere* or people go *elsewhere*. As one fellow informed me, "If it gets too bad, I just reach up and turn off my hearing aid." All of us have heard sermons (and probably preached some) that made us *wish* we wore hearing aids. People approach the church with expectations— requiring spiritual food; the sermon must not give them stones when they come for bread. It does not take very many disappointments for auditors to ask, "Why am I wasting my time?" Of course, both preacher *and* congregation have responsibility in the communication process. If listeners are not prepared to hear, it matters little how the preacher finishes the sermon. But most often people will listen to the end—if they have learned through experience that the pay-off is coming; the sermon leads to a Destination.

Sometimes the sermonic denouement will strike like lightning; resolution will arrive with shocking suddenness and unexpected clarity ("effective surprise"). Yet, I am not suggesting that the sermonic quest will *always* lead to a spectacular conclusion. Sermons are not murder mysteries or adventure novels. I have preached long enough to know that we preachers do not hit a home run every time we go to bat; often we are thankful even to get on base. However, the denouement, if not spectacular, *must at least be insightful*. Otherwise, people will not waste their time listening—and we cannot blame them. Our goal is not to leave our listeners spellbound, but to leave them Spirit-filled. The skill and knowledge of the preacher are not unimportant, but neither are they *the* decisive factor; God works in the process. We want the message to be spoken "with a demonstration of the Spirit's power," so that our congregation's "faith might not rest on men's wisdom, but on God's power."[49] Sometimes the Spirit comes, as it did on Pentecost, with a mighty rushing wind and tongues of fire. Often, though, the Spirit convicts like a gentle summer breeze after a hot, humid day—the breath of God himself.

In the next few chapters, we will turn our attention to specific narrative sermon designs. This general description of the narrative sermon will become concrete as we work with particular biblical texts and sermon examples. Through preaching we want "to make the gospel happen in human lives."[50] Narrative sermons can sometimes serve as effective tools for delivering a prophetic word, as with David and the prophet Nathan;[51] stories can cause listeners to pronounce judgment *on themselves*. But self-incrimination is but one purpose of these sermons. They also bring about personal transformation *by making available to listeners a Word of grace and hope.* When the gospel happens *in them*, they are made aware of God's judgment on sin. Beyond that, they come alive to the reality of *God's grace* made known in the person of Jesus Christ. That, I believe, is the ultimate goal of preaching. I agree with E. Stanley Jones who declares, "I would not be God's able lawyer, but I would be a witness to grace."[52] In a troubled world, preaching provides a God-shaped haven of courage, hope, and possibility.

CHAPTER 6

TEXT AND SERMON

"Jesus loved to tell us about the Father, about his will and purpose and about his love and compassion for us. He tried to tell us what the Father and the kingdom were really like. So again and again he tells us they are: Like a man who . . . , like a mustard seed, like yeast, like ten virgins, like a king. When we listen to him, we can always find a peg on which to hang the truth he comes to share."[1]

Bob Benson in "See you at the house"

I have described preaching as a *diagnostic enterprise* that involves learning to listen to the message of the text, to one's personal experience of the text, and to the congregation's needs. This statement implies that the biblical text has a God-given message and a "determinate meaning"[2] which the preacher attempts to understand, and, subsequently, to communicate. Learning to listen *thoroughly* to the text presents an unrelenting, lifetime challenge; it requires skill not attained through some arcane technique or a few numbered suggestions. In the concluding chapters of this book, we will examine several narrative sermon designs; at the same time, we will hone our skills for engaging the text.

How do we move from text to sermon? How does a narrative sermon *evolve* out of a biblical narrative such as a parable without simply reiterating the parable itself? How do we *listen* to the text and preach it so that parishioners receive a *fresh hearing* of the Gospel? Such questions are the focus of this chapter. Dan McCartney and Charles Clayton declare that both "study and sane imagination" are necessary in engaging any text.[3] *Study* makes the interpreter aware of differences between the biblical and the modern worlds. A *sane imagination* allows the interpreter to determine "how those cultural differences would affect the meaning of a text."[4] I have indicated that "Bible and life" are the two pistons that keep the sermon moving. The narrative sermon designs we will examine venture to reflect fidelity both to the biblical text *and* to the contemporary context. Though not easily learned, there is perhaps no greater prerequisite to narrative sermon development than the preacher's capacity to listen to the Word, to self, and to congregation. Also indispensable is the capacity to interpret Scripture against the backdrop of contemporary culture. As Thomas Troeger asserts,

> . . . not only the text will shape the sermon but also the modern consciousness of the listeners. The sermon will not come 'straight from the Bible.' It will come crooked from the Bible, bent into a new shape by the Spirit who is at work in my listeners' lives, though they have difficulty seeing that.[5]

In this chapter we will address the question: *How might a sermon be shaped allowing the form of a biblical narrative* (a parable in this instance), *to become the form of the sermon?* I call this design "simulating the biblical text." Our sermon example will be plotted around *a question, a quest, and a discovery.* The sermon model for this chapter comes from the parable of "The Pharisee and the Tax Collector" (Luke 18:9-14); the sermon bears the title "The Comfortable Cat." Have you ever heard or read a sermon preached to a cat? Your fortunes (misfortunes?) are about to change. But before you return this book for a refund or file heresy charges against the author, exercise a little restraint (some feline curiosity might be helpful as well!). Prior to the "The Comfortable Cat," we will briefly review the process for engaging Scripture. Just how does one engage a text (such as a parable), and *translate* it into a contemporary sermon? My purpose is not to give a detailed or extended description of exegesis; many biblical study resources provide that service. Rather, we will focus on the artistic and stylistic dimensions of exegesis; we will then apply these observations to the "Pharisee and the Tax Collector."

In preparing a sermon, we must encounter the text afresh; rediscovered or newly discovered import must erupt like a long dormant volcano. Our preparation will often lead us to surprise, to discovery, to a rekindled openness to God's Word and Spirit. Keck explains: "Developing this opening for the possibility of discovery and surprise is the most important dimension of learning to listen, because without it one merely hears confirmations."[6] In other words, both preacher and listeners become stuck in ruts; we just do not have "ears that hear." Walter Brueggemann contends that often in sermons, "There is no danger, no energy, no possibility, no opening for newness!"[7] We ask the wrong questions and get the wrong answers; we know it so well that *we don't know it at all.* In describing the communication process, Craddock writes:

> But how much more pressing, albeit more difficult, is the challenge to help them hear what they hear every day, to learn what they already know. . . . Many who say, 'Here we go again' have not in fact ever gone before.[8]

What we face, then, according to Craddock, is the "illusion of knowing."[9] Be certain of this: the *illusion of knowing* can only lead to the *illusion of proclamation.*

"Ears That Hear"

Learning to *listen to the text* in the manner I have just described might best be understood alongside a simple metaphor. A little boy of seven leaves New York City to spend a month with his grandparents on a farm in Iowa. Nothing about the visit thrills him more than being allowed to play in a shallow creek that meanders through the homestead. This small body of water and its surrounding area enthrall the boy beyond words. He observes moss, minnows, tadpoles, frogs, dragonflies, and a zillion other things never viewed before. In order to comprehend this new world, the boy splashes the water with rocks, pushes sticks down unusual holes, examines stones and leaves, and dangles his feet in the water; unbounded curiosity drives his exploration. The best part of his adventure comes in the evening as his grandfather, after a busy day on the farm, joins him at the creek; what fun they have. The boy discovers that his grandpa is an expert in "creek things." Such wonderful knowledge he imparts: tadpoles turn into frogs, caterpillars become butterflies, some insects actually walk on water. The three underground springs that feed the stream have not gone dry in some two hundred years. But beyond all of this, the boy learns that his father, his grandfather, and his great grandfather all played in this creek when they were boys. The channel has shifted positions over the years, but the same stream flows through the farm. For the boy, this small body of water becomes sacred ground, his adventures, a kind of baptism into the family. He *belongs* in this place and *with these people;* he feels it in his bones.

The preacher must come to the text with the eyes of a small boy investigating a newly discovered creek. At least initially, seminary-trained perspectives on the text should be laid aside as the text is explored with "right-brained" curiosity. This approach is sometimes called having a "beginners mind."[10] Observes Shunryu Suzuki, "In the beginner's mind there are many possibilities; in the expert's mind there are few."[11] With this beginner's mind, the preacher pushes and pokes at the text, turns it this way and that *tasting* its cool water; in so doing the "basic issue is understood and its living thrust is felt."[12] It is during this time that the preacher confronts the text *experientially*, processing it through personal memory, experience, and imagination. The result of this encounter with the text is that the biblical narrative becomes what James Earl Massey calls "a word-event for the preacher."[13] If that does not occur, the text will not be fully appropriated, nor will listeners be influenced at a *story level*. Their stories can only be *evoked* when the sermon connects with them at this heartfelt level.

The preacher's experiential encounter with the text is only the beginning. We must then take the next step: *we turn to grandfather* for wisdom and knowledge. That is, the preacher goes to biblical scholars to discern their perspectives on the text. This objective involves researching various translations, commentaries, word-study resources, hermeneutical aids, and other helpful materials. After all, the text has been "in the family" for hundreds of years; the insights of these more experienced members of the family should be heard. Advises Timothy George, "We must learn to 'read alongside' the church fathers, reformers, and theologians of ages past. . . . we will do well to heed what [God] has been saying to the people of God throughout the history of the church."[14] Our own exegetical skills can now be pressed into service as we compare our observations with theirs. These scholarly insights, combined with our more creative and experiential appropriation of the text, often open unanticipated discernments. Of course, the Holy Spirit also performs a substantial role in helping us to comprehend and assimilate this portion of God's Word. McCartney and Clayton say it well:

> Generations of Christians have gone before, building a framework of understanding which we have

inherited. The framework is far from perfect, but is much better than starting from scratch. And most importantly, the Holy Spirit has guided the development of his people's understanding through history and continues to work in us now, opening our eyes to see and our hearts to obey the wondrous things that are in his Word.[15]

If we have so engaged the text, listening "to it, with it, and through it,"[16] our reward is fresh, creative insight into its message. Our goal is not so much novelty as a rediscovery or reappropriation of what has already been encountered but forgotten. The investigation of this portion of the Living Word confers a *new identity* on us. We become aware of a kinship with multitudes of faithful believers who have gone before us in exploring this piece of Holy Ground, this well-spring of Living Water.

"Priestly Listener" and "Prophetic Listener"

I appreciate Leander Keck's analysis of what happens in exegesis. He refers to the minister as a "priestly listener."[17] According to Keck,

> The preacher listens for a word not only as a private citizen but as a representative of the church. The preacher's listening and hearing is a priestly act. . . . [It is done] in solidarity with the people . . . on behalf of the congregation.[18]

Keck compares the task of biblical exegesis to playing and replaying a cassette tape until the message is finally understood.[19] Another metaphor he uses is that of a skilled counselor who, through thousands of hours of trained listening, has become a "perceptive listener." The preacher who does not become a skilled, artistic listener will never, in my judgment, become an effective communicator. This perceptive style of hearing begins by *listening-in* on the conversation between the biblical writer and the original readers. Before the task is finished, the preacher must "hear the original meaning as clearly as possible in order to be able to respond, in order that genuine conversation can occur with the writer about the subject matter."[20] This conversation often *evokes* within the preacher questions, doubts, bafflement, resistance, perhaps at times even feelings of hostility.[21] Keck observes that the preacher must not be guilt-ridden about these responses. Rather, we "should recognize them as signs that an issue has been located that needs to be worked through, as symptoms that a word is being heard."[22] Since the congregation will often respond to the text with similar thoughts and feelings,[23] these reactions are inherently valuable in isolating the "congregation's need." Listening to the text demands time; it cannot be rushed. Cycles of engagement and disengagement, throughout the preacher's week, will give this textual encounter space to happen.

As we work with the text in the manner I am advocating, a subtle shift occurs, moving us ever closer to the narrative sermon itself. Keck depicts this shift as the "priestly listener" metamorphosing into a "prophetic listener." States Keck: "A word that is heard is compelling; it grasps us in our imagination; it causes us to reassess other worlds, values, and the web of assumptions and trusts that make up our lives."[24] God is voicing a Word for his church; we must not fail to hear. Walter Brueggeman, among others, has stressed the significance of cultivating a "prophetic consciousness."[25] Exegesis goes beyond a simple historical encounter with the text to discover "what it meant." Again I quote Keck: "Exegesis becomes fruitful for preaching when the text confronts the exegete, in solidarity with the congregation, with a word that intersects prevailing understandings and loyalties."[26] The fact is, we do have "prevailing understandings and loyalties"; these often obstruct our hearing of God's Word. Fee and Stuart express it well: " . . . we are convinced that the most serious problem people have with the Bible is not a lack of understanding, but the fact that they understand most things too well."[27] Familiarity often breeds misunderstanding, if not outright indifference to the message of Scripture; the Word of God no longer penetrates the shell that has progressively encased us over the years. It takes a prophetic word to shatter that encasement and *let the Gospel happen to us again.*

In the process of listening to the text, the preacher actually changes roles "in order to become a prophetic spokesman on behalf of the text."[28] Why must the "priestly listener" become a "prophetic listener" before the sermon can develop? The nature of Christianity itself demands it; *verbs* express the meaning of our faith: serve; grow; repent; love; forgive; go; etc. Where the Gospel is preached and heard, people change; little by little they become more like Christ. Counterfeit preaching only confirms us in our present state, reinforces our "prevailing understandings and loyalties."[29] Genuine proclamation does not stroke egos, but creates a climate for the growing of souls;[30] such expression requires both a *priestly and a prophetic* Word. Paul wrote to Timothy, "Preach the Word; be prepared in season and out of season; correct, rebuke and encourage—with great patience and careful instruction."[31] *Encouraging* believers and reminding them of the ever-present reality of grace is important; but preaching also *corrects and rebukes*— though with gentleness and compassion. Prophetic communication calls the church to be what God has already declared us—his people who daily live-out the claims of Jesus Christ. Brueggemann describes preaching as a "dangerous, indispensable habit of speech."[32] He declares, "The poet/prophet is a voice that shatters settled reality and evokes new possibility in the listening assembly."[33] If we have truly engaged the Word, the text *possesses us*; we feel a compulsion to proclaim that Word in the contemporary setting. As Jeremiah illustrated it, "his word is in my heart like a fire, a fire shut up in my bones. I am weary of holding it in; indeed, I cannot."[34] Without the preacher's prophetic voice, the church cannot be the Kingdom of God on earth.

Both Form and Content

Before we look at Luke 18:9-14 and the subsequent sermon which developed from it, let us establish one more point regarding scriptural study. To determine the meaning of any passage of Scripture, both *content and form* (genre) demand examination. "Genre" may be defined as "a group of texts that bear one or more traits in common with each other."[35] Sidney Greidanus identifies seven "genre": Narrative; Prophesy; Wisdom; Psalm; Gospel; Epistle; and Apocalypse.[36] He then divides these seven into subgroups, which he calls "forms," such as parables, dreams, laments, etc.[37] In my present description, I am using the words "form" and "genre" interchangeably, though I acknowledge the distinction between larger and smaller units as indicated by Greidanus. Longman, drawing from the thoughts of E.D. Hirsh, compares genre to a game: "Just as a sentence is a game, so too is genre. In games there are rules which shape the play of the game."[38] In other words, just like games, genres have specific rules that must be followed. We would not use basketball rules when playing football; doing so would destroy the game. Longman contends that, consciously and unconsciously, various genre trigger expectations on behalf of the reader.[39] The interpreter (preacher) must respect these expectations (rules) if his preaching is to be biblical. When interpreting apocalyptic texts, for example, we must not use the same literary rules that govern parables. To do so would dishonor the text, not just in its form but also in its content, because *the two are inseparable*.

In composing sermons we want not only the content but also the form of the text to shape the form and content of the sermon. Ron Allen asserts, "Each text has its own design, and we live in it according to the type of space it is."[40] Craddock reflects the same sentiment: "Let doxologies be shared doxologically, narratives narratively, polemics polemically, poems poetically, and parables parabolically. In other words, biblical preaching ought to be biblical."[41] The question then is determining how the form and content of the text can *participate* in the form and content of the sermon. It is worthwhile, therefore, for the exegete to be sensitive to the biblical genre of the text, so that the interpretive nuances of that literary form can participate in shaping the sermon. Deductive preaching is legitimately criticized because it sometimes ignores scriptural form and imposes an inflexible structure on the text. For example, a parable might be preached deductively by stating a proposition and announcing points.[42] Previously, I stressed the importance of asking *the right questions* when interpreting a particular text. If we do not respect the genre of a passage, we will not raise the right questions, i.e., "questions that are appropriate to the form of the text."[43]

If the form of the sermon must, in some manner, reflect the form of the text, does this imply that narrative sermons can only come from "story passages"? While we are primarily focusing in this volume on the narrative genre, I am not suggesting that narrative sermons *always* require biblical narrative. Our preaching goal is not "to copy slavishly the biblical form,"[44] though we do want to respect the form and learn from it, even if the resulting sermon does not duplicate the biblical genre. I quoted Long in an earlier chapter: "The preacher's task . . . is not to replicate the text but to regenerate the impact of some portion of that text."[45] The preacher is attempting to "regenerate the impact" that the text had *upon first century hearers*, to re-create their experience. Sometimes this is best accomplished by using a form *different* from the text itself. But whatever the form of the sermon, it must not ignore or detract from the message of the text as it appears *in both form and content*. This means, for example, that a parable or biblical narrative preaches best when presented in a similar manner; after all, the first century believers were responding to a story.

"The Pharisee and the Tax Collector": Luke 18:9-14

The sermon example in this chapter ("The Comfortable Cat") takes its form from the parable; it "simulates the biblical narrative." Lowry refers to this approach as "running the story," In this instance, he writes, "the shape of the text will be the shape of the narrative sermon."[46] This is not to say that the preacher simply tells the biblical story. Rather, the "preacher will highlight, elaborate, amplify, and creatively enflesh certain portions while moving through the text."[47] As will be true of most of the narrative sermons we examine, these messages do not consist entirely of story or stories; each contains a good bit of dialogue and even instruction. Again I quote Lowry: "In a typical narrative sermon—moving, for example from opening conflict into complication—it is often the case that rational discourse is the means being employed in order to 'thicken the plot.'"[48]

Let us talk briefly of the biblical genre of "parables." William Barclay calls Jesus' parables " . . . lovely improvisations in the dust and heat of conflict."[49] Ryken reminds us that parables "obey the literary principle of verisimilitude (lifelikeness)."[50] These colorful stories of Jesus are rooted in real life. In one sense, the parables are simple; in another sense, they are quite profound. In one of his novels, Robert Parker describes an unusual scene in a play:

> The houselights dimmed. The play began. On stage there were men dressed as women and women dressed as men, and white people in blackface and black people in whiteface, and a Rabbi named O'Leary and a priest named Cohen. . . . There was someone in a dog suit who kept saying meow.[51]

To an extent, the parables of Christ follow a similar pattern. In them the world is turned upside down, and in the process, hearers are forced to reexamine some assumption about themselves and life. Parables often sting like a bumblebee, and *the stinger remains in the listener.* As Lowry explains, the story has "some seed or germinal quality that does not quit with the teller's last word."[52]

Barclay reminds us of the importance of knowing the specific social context in which any parable was spoken: "the parable must always be interpreted in light of its background."[53] Luke introduces the parable by explaining: "To some who were confident of their own righteousness and who looked down on everybody else, Jesus told this parable."[54] In this particular parable, the typically perceived good man (a Pharisee[55]) is a *bad man,* and the typically perceived bad man (a tax collector) is a *good man* (or at least a justified man). One can imagine the anger among the religious establishment upon hearing Jesus' words. The listeners would have been shocked by a *justified* tax collector; such persons were universally despised by the Jews for their unjust collection of revenues and their collusion with Rome. Fee and Stuart tell us that the parables have certain "points of reference," the understanding of which are necessary if the parable is to have an impact upon hearers. For example, the audience who heard this parable had an immediate response to both "Pharisee" and "tax collector"; those words are the "points of reference." One problem we face in preaching parables is that a contemporary audience does not connect with these first-century points of reference. Therefore, in order to preach parables, the preacher must have a sense of how first century listeners responded to these referrals. Then, the sermon must create "contemporary points of reference" that *evoke* a similar response. In the sermon you are about to read, note the manner in which I have tried to accomplish this task; I will reflect on my approach after the sermon.

In appropriating Luke 18:9-14, I attempted to *remember* or *imagine* the text into my own life, to connect with it at a *narrative level.* During my reading of the text, and listening to Jesus' message to the Jewish religious leaders, I became aware of a certain amount of personal discomfort. I asked myself, "What if Jesus were not simply characterizing the Pharisees? What if *religious leaders* in a more generalized sense were the objects of his characterization? What if this text is not simply addressed *to them* but also to *me?*" In asking these questions, I began to feel some sympathy for the Pharisee: a life of good deeds and good behavior goes unrewarded while the tax collector's open-hearted confession allows him to leave the temple "justified." That does not seem fair. In contemporary society, ministers are often portrayed falsely and unfairly; I can almost hear the critics: "Preachers are nothing but self-righteous bigots, out to glorify themselves!" Is Jesus making the same accusation regarding the "preachers" (Pharisees) of his day?

As I roamed the corridors of memory, bits and pieces of an experience began to collect in my consciousness. Once, when calling on behalf of the church, a man said to me, "You preachers are pompous windbags; you have no constructive purpose in life but to convince society of your indispensability. You don't need to come back to our home; my family and I will do fine without your God and your church!" I felt hurt and humiliated; I had neither done or said anything that deserved this outburst. Might the Pharisees have had a similar response to Jesus' parable? Of course, I recognize that Jesus was not simply trying to humiliate the religious leaders; his words *hurt* so that he could *heal*; he turned the world *upside down* so that his listeners could understand the world *right side up*. Nevertheless, seeing this parable through the eyes of the Pharisees allows me to capture the *sting* of Jesus' story. This must happen before I can communicate that sting to my listeners.

The next step in the sermon preparation was to decide how to convince my congregation that this parable is Jesus' prophetic word *to us*. I wanted my listeners to experience thoughts and feelings like those triggered in the religious establishment of first-century Palestine (like I experienced when preachers were labeled "pompous windbags"). As I made the move from "priestly listener" to "prophetic listener," I noted that the primary opposition Jesus faced during his ministry was from *religious* people. The prophetic message of this text speaks not just to the Pharisees, but to religious people who read and hear the parable. When I finally arrived at a *living question*, it retained this prophetic edge: *"Is there something about the nature of being religious which causes Jesus to become our adversary?"* I might say it like this: "What is there about the nature of being *religious* that so often closes hearts and minds to God's Truth—even when that Truth is revealed in his Son?" This question refuses to allow the text to remain distant, either from myself or from the *religious people* who hear it. As I plotted the sermon, I took my listeners on a quest; the result, I hope, was a new awareness of the *poverty of religion*, and a new sense of *our need for God's grace*, revealed in Christ Jesus. I will allow the reader to decide whether my approach "regenerated the impact" of Jesus' parable, and subsequently opened my listeners to a *new hearing* of the Gospel.

I should also note that the sermon you are about to read uses a literary technique called "gapping" or "narrative reticence." A gap is "an unstated piece of information that is essential to the understanding of the story, for instance, an unstated motive."[56] This unstated information is crucial to a proper understanding of the story. Narrative reticence also involves the listener by arousing curiosity, suspense, or surprise. In my sermon, the metaphor of the "comfortable cat," along with my use of narrative reticence, serves as a *reinforcing metaphor* to drive home the resolution of my living question. I will not tell you what information I withheld, but will allow you to discover it as you read the sermon.

Before we examine the sermon entitled "The Comfortable Cat," I give one last word. Throughout the remainder of this book, I will give several sermon examples, all of which have been preached to congregations. These sermons have been heard and critiqued by students, ministers, and professors. I have gained some degree of confidence in them or I would not offer them as examples. Yet, I know that my readers will encounter them in a different form; you will not *hear* but *read* them. All printed sermons have peculiar obstacles to overcome. They were initially oral-aural events; to read them rather than hear them, in some ways, diminishes their power. Furthermore, they were spoken for specific congregations and preached for particular occasions; when printed they become, to an extent, decontextualized. Let me use this analogy: Suppose a noted French chef prepares a dish that, at its serving, is acclaimed as a culinary delight. Americans, hearing of this wonderful dish, want to taste it. So a sample is frozen and shipped by jet to New York City, where it is thawed and served. Will Americans who taste this food be able to appreciate fully this culinary achievement? Of course not; time and distance will inevitably have their impact. My sermons will serve their purpose in helping us understand various narrative sermon designs; they may not retain all the flavor that was present when first preached. Having expressed this qualifier, we move on to a sermon which *simulates* the biblical narrative.

The church bulletin announces that the setting for the sermon is *a large midwestern city.* A minister *sits on his patio reflecting aloud* on sermon possibilities for the parable of "The Pharisee and the Tax Collector." The minister's audience is a cat named Fluffy.

****

The Comfortable Cat
Luke 18:9-14

"Well, here I am again, sitting on my patio, working on my Sunday sermon. This is my favorite place to prepare sermons; my ideas flow here on the patio. Fluffy likes it when I sit out here; don't you Fluffy? He and I are buddies; he is the first listener for all my sermons. He hasn't complained even once; I wish I could say that for *all* my listeners.

"'FLUFFY, YOU SURE LOOK *COMFORTABLE* LYING ON THAT NARROW FENCE AROUND THE PATIO; YOU DON'T SEEM IN THE LEAST BOTHERED BY HIGH PLACES.'

"I've been preaching through the parables; this coming Sunday my text is Luke 18:9-14, 'The Pharisee and the Tax Collector.' This parable follows another of Jesus' parables, that of the unjust judge; in my Study Bible those two parables together are labeled, 'Concerning Prayer.'

"Let's see. Jesus says that two men went up to the temple to pray, one a 'Pharisee' and the other a 'tax collector.' In first-century Judaism, the Pharisee was the very model of what it meant to be religious. The tax collector was the exact opposite, the essence of a *religionless* man, hated for his collusion with Rome. Called a 'publican' in the KJV, the tax collector was considered "a traitor to the nation and religion of his people."[57] In his temple prayer, the Pharisee told God: "I thank you that I am not like other men—robbers, evildoers, adulterers—or even like this tax collector. I fast twice a week and give a tenth of all I get" (Luke 18:11).

"The tax collector stood in the temple at a distance from other worshippers; he beat on his breast, as if to drive his confession of unworthiness from his body. Without raising his eyes to heaven, he cried out saying, 'God, have mercy on me, a sinner.' 'This man', said Jesus, 'rather than the other, went home justified before God' (Luke 18:13,14).

"Fluffy, what in the world is Jesus trying to say? Is Jesus the enemy of religious people? Does a life of religious devotion mean nothing? Does God not credit us for the evil from which we abstain (thievery, adultery, etc.)? Does he not bless us for the good we do (fasting, tithing, etc.)? Having spent a lifetime in the pursuit of goodness, are we to find ourselves barred from heaven, while wicked, unjust, and unethical people are welcomed with open arms at heaven's gate? That doesn't seem fair. Fluffy, I wonder how Jesus might tell this parable today?

Perhaps in this manner?

> Two people went into a church building to pray. They were shocked when the Lord verbally responded to their prayers.
>
> **Elder Edwards:** "Lord, I had some free time and wanted to drop by and let you know how my Christian life is going. Actually, I am fairly

pleased. The Christian life takes a lot of dedication but I'm willing to pay the price. I know you hear me when I pray."

The Lord: "I not only hear; sometimes I *talk* to people who pray."

Elder Edwards: "LORD! IS THAT YOU? What a shock! I did not expect to hear your voice. Why are you speaking *to me?*"

The Lord: "I would like to ask you some questions."

Elder Edwards: "Of course, Lord. Anything at all."

The Lord: "Elder Edwards, you have been a church member all your life?"

Elder Edwards: "Yes, Lord! I have been an elder for forty-two years at First Church in Graysville. I have never received less than 82% of the congregational vote. I don't think any of the other elders have even come close to that percentage."

The Lord: "You're faithful in Church and Sunday School attendance?"

Elder Edwards: "You can say that again! I have so many perfect attendance pins, I quit wearing them; I didn't want anybody to think I was being prideful. I had them framed and hung in my living room."

The Lord: "You are a man of prayer?"

Elder Edwards: "Absolutely! My piety is beyond question. When people have prayer needs, they bring them to me. When I lead the congregation in prayer, I spend hours crafting my prayers. When people compliment me, I pass the compliment on to you. I tell them, 'Just like I do, give your best to The Lord; that's the only way!'"

The Lord: "You read your Bible on a regular basis?"

Elder Edwards: "I have participated in our church's

'Read-Your-Bible-In-A-Year-Program' eighteen
times. No one else has even come close!"
The Lord: "You share your faith with non-Chris-
tians and let them know about my Son?"
Elder Edwards: "You bett'ya! I tell it straight:
'Change your ways or chance the fire!' You'd better repent because my God don't brook no sin-
ners!'"
The Lord: "I think that will do it; I have heard
enough."
Elder Edwards: "But Lord, I haven't told you half
of it! I work every year in church camp. I made a
mission trip to Haiti. I led an effort to shut-down
an X-rated bookstore in Graysville. There's so
much to tell. I could fill a book with all the good
deeds I've done."
The Lord: "Elder Edwards, your life is a sham and a
disgrace. You have only *one god*, and it's not me.
I grant you no justification!"
Elder Edwards: "Lord, You misunderstand! I collected clothes for an orphanage. I contributed to
feed-the-hungry programs. . . . I . . . I . . . I . . ."

Jesus were telling the parable today, we might listen-in on
the prayers of Mary the prostitute as she too visits the church
building.

Mary: "Lord, I don't feel very comfortable inside
this church building, but I wanted to talk to you.
I'm not even sure you listen to the prayers of a
person like me."
The Lord: "Mary, I am listening to your prayers."
Mary: 'WOW! THIS ISN'T POSSIBLE! You are
actually talking *to me!*"
The Lord: "Yes, Mary, I am talking to you. I have

some questions to ask you. You have spent most
of your life as a prostitute?"

Mary: "Yes, Lord. I am ashamed to admit it, but
that's how I have made my living."

The Lord: "You seldom have attended church?"

Mary: "Yes, Sir, that is correct. I keep think'in I
should, but I just don't feel worthy because of
my lifestyle. I could never take the holy com-
munion."

The Lord: "You have lived with at least two men
without being married to them?"

Mary: "Lord, I can't deny this charge either. I
shouldn't of done it. The men didn't love me,
even though I wanted them to. I have been
search'in for someone who really loves me, but I
know that that don't make sin right."

The Lord: "Mary, you have lived an evil life. You
have violated the holiness that I desire for my
children. What do you have to say for yourself?"

Mary: "Lord, I really can't defend myself. I have had
some bad breaks in life, but that ain't no excuse
cause I know what's right and wrong. I am an
awful person, and I deserve whatever punishment
you give. God . . . , it scares me to say it, but *I
desire above all else your mercy and forgiveness.*

The Lord: "Mary, I have heard your prayer; *you are
justified in my sight.*"

"What do you think, Fluffy? Does the road to hell run down
the middle aisle of the church? Does the road to heaven run through
the middle of a house of Prostitution?

"'LOOK OUT, FLUFFY! CHASING AN ANT ON THAT
NARROW LEDGE! I CAN'T IMAGINE HOW YOU CAN BE
COMFORTABLE UP THERE."

"Fluffy, do you understand Jesus' parable of the Pharisee and the tax collector? Does it make any sense to you? The 'good man' was a *bad man* and the 'bad man' was a *good man*. I can't say that I am all together pleased with the way Jesus told it. It almost makes me feel like living a good life doesn't count, as though Jesus viewed religious people as enemies of his cause. It's true, I guess, that Jesus spent much of his life in conflict with *religious* people. The Pharisees were so blind to spiritual reality, so closed to the work of God in the world. It makes me think that it's downright *dangerous* to be religious. 'Fluffy, *Is there something about the nature of being religious which causes Jesus to become our adversary?*'

"I wonder why Jesus had so many confrontations with religious people? Would the same thing happen today if he were on earth? Once, the Pharisees were severely critical of Jesus because his disciples picked and ate some heads of grain on the Sabbath Day. Jesus reminded them that David and his men violated ceremonial law by the very act of eating consecrated bread (1 Samuel 21:1-6). But Jesus seems to say they were not guilty because *human need supersedes law*. Even the priests, said Jesus, desecrate the Sabbath by working on it, and yet, 'they are innocent' (Matt. 12:5). Somehow, the Pharisees' religion had separated them, not only from God, but also from the people God loves. 'Fluffy, my friend, do I ever allow that to happen to me?'

'FLUFFY, WHAT IN THE WORLD ARE YOU DOING— HANGING OVER THE EDGE LIKE THAT? YOU ARE NOT A BIT AFRAID ARE YOU? YOU REALLY ARE *COMFORT-ABLE* IN HIGH PLACES.'

"On another occasion the Pharisees attempted to trap Jesus by asking him this question: 'Is it lawful to heal on the Sabbath?' Jesus responded, 'If any of you has a sheep and it falls into a pit on the Sabbath, will you not take hold and lift it out? How much more valuable is a man than a sheep! Therefore it is lawful to do good on the Sabbath' (Matt. 12:11). Jesus then proceeded to heal a man with a shriveled hand, again raising the ire of the religious leaders. Though the Pharisees were religious, they refused to acknowledge Jesus as God's Son. Indeed, 'the Pharisees went out and plotted how they might kill Jesus' (Matt. 12:14). I do not understand how healing sick people, even on the Sabbath, could engender such hostility. *Is there something about the nature of being religious which causes Jesus to become the adversary of religious people?*

"Religious people are supposed to love the truth, to be always open to it; after all, 'grace and truth came through Jesus Christ' (John 1:17). Yet, the Pharisees set themselves against God's purpose in the world as revealed in his Son. They would not accept Jesus' authority or even consider the possibility that he *might be* the Messiah. Jesus said to them, 'You diligently study the Scriptures because you think that by them you possess eternal life. These are the Scriptures that testify about me, yet you refuse to come to me to have life' (John 5:40). The Pharisees spent their whole lives waiting for the Messiah and were unprepared to receive him when he came. It seems that Jesus threatened their *comfortable* religion and their easy answers. 'Fluffy, is that what religion does to humans?' Does religion close person's sensitivity to God's Truth—even when that Truth is revealed in his Son?'

"'FLUFFY, LOOK AT YOU: STRETCHING AND TWISTING UP THERE ON TOP OF THAT FENCE! YOU'RE NOT A BIT CONCERNED ABOUT A FALL.

"Fluffy, have religious people changed since Jesus' day? Do we still value ceremonial laws over people? Do we still tend to think that we have all the answers? Is our religion, like that of the Pharisee in Jesus' parable, just a personal ego trip? Are we more concerned with *self-righteousness* than *God's righteousness?*

"You know what troubles me most about Jesus' parable of the Pharisee and the tax collector? *I too am a religious person and leader.* If I am honest, I must admit that sometimes I feel *comfortable* with *my answers.* Just like the Pharisee in Jesus' story, I often feel proud of my spiritual achievements. I have been tempted to 'hang my Sunday school pins in the living room.' At times I even catch myself thinking, 'Boy, am I glad I am not like that guy.' 'Fluffy, does Jesus view me the way he did the Pharisee? *Is there something about the nature of being* religious *which causes Jesus to become our adversary?*'

"'You know, Fluffy, maybe Jesus wasn't against religious people; perhaps He was simply against *religion*. Maybe Jesus doesn't want us to be religious at all, but *Christian*. That is, he wants us to be Christlike—'little Christs.' Someone once wrote, '[Religious people] are trying to reach God, find God, please God through their own efforts. Religions reach up toward God. Christianity is God reaching down to man. Christianity claims that men have not found God, but *that God has found them.*'[58]

"Maybe the Pharisee's problem in the parable was his religion; he no longer needed God; he was a self-made man who didn't need God's grace. Perhaps the Pharisee was his own 'god' worshipping his own 'creator.' Rather than genuine communication with God, his prayer was a 'monologue of self praise.'[59] Jesus said, 'Blessed are those who hunger and thirst after righteousness, for they will be filled' (Matt. 5:6). The Pharisee was not hungry for God's righteousness; he fed his soul on the empty husks of self-glorification. Consequently, he did not need the Lord in *his* system of justification. He saw himself as superior to other persons, and his superiority was a product of his *own achievement* .

"The tax collector, on the other hand, was starving spiritually; he needed God and recognized that need. In one sense his heart was pure, for he made an honest confession and admitted his need for God's mercy. Jesus was not praising or approving the tax collector's lifestyle, any more than he was the prostitute's in my story. Nor was Jesus condemning the good deeds of the Pharisee—or those of Elder Edwards. It was the Pharisee's *attitude*, his exaggerated self-confidence and comfortableness that brought God's judgment. Likewise, it was the tax collector's confession, humility, and need for God's grace that led Jesus to say, 'this man, rather than the other, went home justified before God. For everyone who exalts himself will be humbled, and he who humbles himself will be exalted' (Luke 18:14).

"When we are religious rather than Christian, God's righteousness becomes *my-rightness.*

"When we are religious rather than Christian, God's truth becomes *my understanding* of God's truth.

"When we are religious rather than Christian, dogma makes us *dogmatic.*

"When we are religious rather than Christian, being a good person means being *a better person than someone else.*

"When we are religious rather than Christian, believing becomes less important than that *others believe what I believe.*

"Fluffy, I don't want to be religious, it's just *too dangerous*; I want to be *Christian.* I want to be like Jesus who said, 'Take my yoke upon you and learn from me, for I am gentle and humble in heart . . .' (Matt. 11:29).

"'Well, Fluffy, I guess you and I will have to do some more work on this sermon tomorrow. I just don't have it all figured out, but I will keep plugging away; yes sir, my feline friend, I'll have something to say when Sunday arrives.

"'FLUFFY, THERE YOU GO AGAIN! LEANING WAY OUT OVER THAT EDGE TO SWAT AT A BUG! MY, YOU ARE *COMFORTABLE* UP THERE.'

"'You just don't realize do you? You lie on the edge of that fence as though it were twenty feet wide! You twist and turn on that narrow ledge as though you had a safety net under you. Like most cats, you really are *comfortable* in high places. I just wish you were smart enough to understand that I live in a high-rise apartment complex; my patio is twenty-four floors off the ground! Fluffy, if you ever fall, you will be little more than a spot of grease on the road below.'

"I guess, sometimes it's dangerous to be comfortable."

****

Simulating the Biblical Narrative

Ryken refers to what he calls the "cracks" in the realism of the parables: "there is often an element of exaggeration or improbability in them."[60] In the parable of the Pharisee and the tax collector this exaggeration is obvious. The culturally despised tax collector leaves the temple justified rather than the Pharisee who has lived a good life, but fails to recognize his need for God's mercy. This reversal of roles triggers an emotional response in Jesus' listeners. These cracks or exaggerations cause the import of the parable to burst forth. This parable came alive for me as a *religious* person and leader, when I viewed it through the eyes of the Pharisee. I connected my experience of this text with a narrative experience from my own life ("You preachers are pompous windbags . . ."). Though I chose not to tell this story, still it was beneficial in helping me plot the sermon, because it allowed me to identify with the emotional response of the Pharisees to Jesus' parable. Such identification was necessary, I believe, for the meaning of the parable to erupt.

Parables, Ryken reminds us, mean what they say, "and something besides, and in the parables of Jesus that something besides is the more important of the two."[61] As I have attempted to demonstrate, the preacher's goal in preaching parables is to recreate, as much as is possible, the impact that the parable had on the first century audience. In so doing, this "something besides" can happen again in a contemporary setting. In the above sermon, I attempted to accomplish that goal by substituting new "points of reference." The Pharisee and the tax collector became Elder Edwards and Mary, the prostitute. Hopefully, these *points of reference* evoke feelings in my listeners like those triggered in the first century audience when they heard "Pharisee" and "tax collector."

In this sermon my living question is this: "Is there something about the nature of being religious which causes Jesus to be our adversary?" The answer, of course, is that religious people often become comfortable with themselves, and subsequently, blinded to their need for God's mercy. I attempted to create tension and ambiguity in the sermon by portraying Jesus' conflict with religious people—*which means us*. The denouement in this sermon is not dramatic. The *turning point* in the sermon arrived when I stated: "You know, Fluffy, perhaps Jesus wasn't against religious people; maybe He was simply against *religion*." "Religious people," as I am using the word *religious*, do not need God's Son or his mercy; they are comfortable with themselves, apart from anything God might supply.

As I plotted my sermon, I used the metaphor of the cat for several reasons. It allowed me to create a situation of *overhearing*, where my congregation *listened-in* as the sermon was prepared. The metaphor was also designed to foster anticipation. Furthermore, I used it as a "reinforcing metaphor" to drive home the prophetic word: Religious people are often comfortable, and *comfortable is dangerous*. As indicated earlier, I made use of the literary technique of "gapping" or "narrative reticence." Earlier, I defined a "gap" as an unstated piece of information that is essential to the understanding of the story. In the above sermon, that omission is the fact that the cat lies *comfortably* on a narrow ledge—which is *twenty-four stories off the ground*. Once this fact is stated, the word "comfortable" takes on an even more ominous meaning. Narrative reticence was also employed to arouse curiosity, suspense, and even surprise: "Why does he keep talking about that cat lying comfortably on the patio fence?"

I plotted "The Comfortable Cat" so that it *flows* like Jesus' story. In imitating the genre of the text, I am attempting to regenerate the parable's impact on first century listeners by substituting contemporary "points of reference." In our next chapter we will examine a narrative design where the sermonic form *does not* follow the form of the text. I call this next design, "sustaining the narrative"; it consists of a simple story which connects with Scripture, but makes no effort to *apply* the message of the story; indeed, *the story is the sermon*.

CHAPTER 7

SUSTAINING THE NARRATIVE

"We want our preacher-boys to say it fast and tell it plain! 'Tain't no scuse fer no preacher to preach more'n one hour. Remember three points and a poem and no souls are saved past noon."
Quoted by John S. Workman in Fireflies In A Fruit Jar[1]

In the previous chapter we viewed a narrative sermon model which takes its form from the text—it *simulates* the biblical narrative. In the next five chapters we will examine five additional designs, each accompanied by a sermonic example. As we look at these possible designs, we will see similarities between them, as we should, for they belong to the same literary family. All, for example, are inductive in the sense that they move toward resolution rather than working from a prestated thesis or proposition. These designs all make use of story, plot, and movement—but not in precisely the same manner. I classify these five narrative designs as:

Creative Anticipation

1) *sustaining* the narrative; 2) *supplementing* the narrative; 3) *segmenting* the narrative; 4) *sequencing* the narratives; and, 5) *suspending* the narrative. As these names suggest, the distinctiveness of each design is determined by the manner in which each uses story. My goal in naming these designs is not primarily to *classify* but to *clarify*. I am saying to the reader: "Here are possible approaches for shaping narrative sermons." In identifying these five, I am not declaring, "These are the only ways to design narrative sermons." Indeed, the sermon models that I offer are meant to be suggestive, to encourage the preacher's experimentation with story and plot. As I expressed earlier, I am attempting to prime your pump, not to fill your bucket; my desire is to both liberate and stimulate. Having escaped the prison of "three-points-and-a-poem," I am not trying to impose a new set of constraints which stifle creativity and promote sermonic monotony.

Bear in mind that all of the narrative sermon designs we will explore utilize "creative anticipation" to lead listeners toward a *new hearing* of the gospel. As with stories, they move inductively toward a conclusion. Sermonic form *and* content march forward toward a plotted denouement "in which the table of life gets set for us in a new way by the gospel."[2] With the exception of "sustaining the narrative," these sermon designs do not consist entirely of story or stories; each contains a good bit of dialogue and even instruction. To quote Lowry: "In a typical narrative sermon—moving, for example from opening conflict into complication—it is often the case that rational discourse is the means being employed in order to 'thicken the plot.'"[3] How might story be used to shape the sermon? That question is preeminent in the next five chapters.

The Shape of the Sermon

In the previous chapter, we began our examination of sermon designs that are plotted like story with "a question, a quest, and a discovery." We said that plot is established by the torque or tension that exists between a living question and its ultimate resolu-

127

5418-ENYA

tion. We also indicated that a biblical parable or narrative preaches best when the sermon adopts *the form of the text*. In such a sermon, the contemporary audience encounters the sermon in the same fashion as first century listeners encountered the parable or story. When successful, the contemporary listeners will *experience* the text with the power and feeling as when the words were first spoken. We looked at a narrative sermon design that derives its form from the text itself (as in "The Comfortable Cat"). When the form of the text becomes the form of the sermon, the central thrust or focus of the biblical story becomes the thrust of the sermon. Bruce Salmon informs us, "The aim of preaching is not to rob the biblical narratives of their force, but rather to focus that force."[4] This narrative sermon design, as described in the last chapter, is perhaps the most *biblical* way to preach the genre of biblical narrative because it *simulates* the passage, i.e., the text itself shapes the sermon. But sermonic form does not *always* need to duplicate the form of the text; our goal in preaching is not "to copy slavishly the biblical form."[5] Indeed, textual genre is but one of many factors that influence the shape of the sermon. Others include: the nature of the audience, the personality of the preacher, the purpose of the discourse—all have a bearing on the final shape of the sermon. In my opinion, the narrative format comes as close as any to providing a kind of universal format for pulpit communication. But, as we have already acknowledged, in preaching we must use a variety of sermonic shapes, both inductive and deductive.

Thomas Long offers a metaphor that illustrates the move from text to sermon.[6] He says the text is like a stone tossed in a pond.

> Its immediate impact is felt where it falls—the historical situation into which it originally landed—but this impact creates ripples which flow in time across the surface. As the ripples move away from the center in ever-expanding circles, their motion is impelled by the original event of the text, but their shape is altered as they strike

objects in the water and blend with other waves. The task of preaching is not merely to recover the text's original breaking of the surface but to express what happens when one of the ripples sent forth by that text crosses our spot in the pond.[7]

Let us think of each congregation as a unique "spot in the pond." The preacher then must understand the text in its first-century setting, while at the same time remaining sensitive to the contemporary audience that will hear the sermon. As expressed in the homiletical thought of David Buttrick: "Of more importance than a compulsive replication of the pericope's structure is faithfulness to its hermeneutical intention. . . ."[8] Therefore, the preacher must ask, "How can I best release the meaning of this text into the lives of my listeners?" Or, as Buttrick expresses it, "The object for the congregation is not so much to hear the sermon as to have it form in their consciousness."[9] When this happens, listeners do more than listen to a sermon, they internalize it (appropriate it). Such appropriation is indispensable if the sermonic story is to evoke the listener's story or stories.

Sustaining the Narrative

Our focus in this chapter is on "sustaining the narrative." In this design, *the story is the sermon*. The story may develop either from the text (a narrative passage) or from a source outside the Scripture text. As I shall demonstrate in the sermon that follows ("One of the Least of These"), even though the story itself may not come from the Bible, Scripture finds its way into the sermon. In "sustaining the narrative," the preacher never moves outside the story; everything the audience hears, they *overhear*. Contrast this approach, for example, to our emphasis in the next chapter called "supplementing the narrative." In supplementing, the listeners also hear a story, *but it does not stand alone*. The preacher *supplements* the story with comments that clarify, explain, amplify, and support the thrust or focus of the story.

Previously, I indicated that the text must be *remembered* or *imagined* into the preacher's life before the narrative sermon can unfold. Most frequently this happens at a narrative level, i.e., the preacher connects the text with some personal story or stories. The resulting sermon is more likely to *evoke* the stories of congregants if the preacher has allowed the text to evoke personal experience. But what if the preacher has no such experience? What if no story provides a connection between preacher and text? In that case the preacher's imagination must supply that connection. The sermon example for this chapter illustrates this point. As I read Matthew 25:31-46 ("The Separation of the Sheep and the Goats"), I could not associate this text with a personal narrative. I had, however, read a fictional story of a medieval monk that connected well. Using my imagination, I altered the fictional story to fit my sermonic purpose (See Appendix A for the brief original version[10]). In one sense I actually *became* this monk so that his story might live through me. I appropriated text and story by thinking *and feeling* my way into the monk's experience.

In creating or adapting any story, we should pay attention to carefully laying out the place, the time, and the people. Donald Davis stresses that any given story, with its setting, time, and character development, is a kind of "container" for the story's plot.[11] My story of the humble, thirteenth-century monk, Reeam, became the *container* that would carry Jesus' ethical teachings. In this sermon text (Matthew 25:31-46), Jesus pictures the judgment with the separating of the sheep from the goats. Jesus portrays the King as saying, "I tell you the truth, whatever you did [or did *not* do] for one of the least of these brothers of mine, you did for me."[12] I wanted my listeners to identify with Reeam; to that end I painted my word-portrait of this character. The sermonic goal for my story was to cultivate an increased sensitivity for *disenfranchised persons*—those who may not normally be reached or ministered to by any given church. I settled on the following as my living question: "*Who* do we *actually serve* when we give aid to the less fortunate?" In this particular sermon, the question, quest, and discovery are never directly stated. As is often the case with a sermon that sustains the narrative, these are only implied through the story itself. Let us look then at a sermon where *the story is the sermon.*

****

"One of the Least of These"
(Matthew 25:31-46)

There once lived a simple and humble monk named Reeam. He served in an insignificant rural monastery called Wingsferr, located in northern Greece. Reeam was small in stature and was not a particularly gifted individual. He was not a scholar nor was he deeply educated in the writings of the church fathers. Though he loved the Word of God, Reeam was not an effective teacher or preacher. He had absolutely no musical talent of voice or instrument. It took many job changes before Reeam discovered his gift and was assigned a position within the monastery. At first, the Abbot tried to make a builder of him; unfortunately, Reeam did more damage than good. Then they placed him in the kitchen, helping prepare meals for the brothers. That assignment came to a quick end when he almost turned supper into a deadly poison. Finally Reeam found his place—working with mop and dust rag to clean the monastery chapel. This job he performed with loving care, feeling honored that he could look after the House of God. He spent hours on hands and knees polishing the ancient stones of the chapel.

Reeam did not want or ask for much out of life; he was a simple person with simple needs. However, he had one great dream that he shared with anyone who would listen. Before his death Reeam wanted to make a pilgrimage to the Holy City and walk where Jesus walked. All his life he had saved from his meager earnings so that he could fulfill this dream. "Before I die," said Reeam, "I shall make the long journey to Jerusalem. I shall walk where

Jesus walked and pray where Jesus prayed. I will visit the Garden of Gethsemane where the Lord prayed, 'Not my will but thine be done.' I shall stand before Mt. Calvary and ask God's forgiveness for my sins. Then I shall come to the Holy Sepulcher where once Jesus' body lay entombed before God raised him from the dead. When I arrive at the Holy Sepulcher, I will walk three times around it, then kneel to thank God for Jesus the Messiah. I will then make the long journey home and return to my duties in the chapel. I know that when I return from my pilgrimage, I will be a new person; when I pass through the gates of Wingsferr, my heart will be light, my soul will be full of joy, and I will be ready for my eternal rest."

Sometimes visitors to the monastery would hear of Reeam's dream and give him small coins. Other monks also shared of their meager earnings so that Reeam could keep his dream alive. But in truth no one really thought that he would ever set out on such a long and perilous pilgrimage.

As Reeam grew older his dream continued to burn within his heart. If anyone happened through the chapel while he was cleaning, he would stop them and tell his story again. "Before I die I shall make the long journey to Jerusalem. I shall walk where Jesus walked and pray where Jesus prayed. I will visit the Garden of Gethsemane where he prayed, 'Not my will but thine be done.' I shall stand before Mt. Calvary and ask God's forgiveness for my sins. Then I will visit the Holy Sepulcher where once Jesus' body lay entombed before God's miracle raised Him from the dead. When I arrive at the Holy Sepulcher, I will walk three times around it and then kneel to thank God for Jesus the Messiah. I will then make the long journey home and return to my duties in the chapel. I know that when I return from my pilgrimage I will be a new person; my heart will be light, my soul will be full of joy, and I will be ready for my eternal rest."

How shocked was everyone when, one evening in vespers, Reeam stood and announced that he had accumulated the necessary funds and in two weeks he would begin his pilgrimage. After his trip, he told the brothers, he would return to the monastery and resume his duties in cleaning the chapel. "Just think," said Reeam, "when I return from my pilgrimage, my heart will be light, my soul will be full of joy, and I will be ready for my eternal rest."

The night before Reeam set forth on his journey, the brothers said prayers on his behalf in vespers; they prayed for his safety and protection on the road. The Prior read the lesson for the evening from Matthew's Gospel (25:31-45). Reeam listened carefully to the reading of Scripture; he thought that God might communicate to him some special message for his journey. The text spoke of judgment and the separation of the sheep and the goats:

> "When the Son of Man comes in his glory, and all the angels with him, he will sit on his throne in heavenly glory. All the nations will be gathered before him, and he will separate the people one from another as a shepherd separates the sheep from the goats. He will put the sheep on his right and the goats on his left.

> "Then the King will say to those on his right, 'Come, you who are blessed by my Father; take your inheritance, the kingdom prepared for you since the creation of the world. For I was hungry and you gave me something to eat, I was thirsty and you gave me something to drink, I was a stranger and you invited me in, I needed clothes and you clothed me, I was sick and you looked after me, I was in prison and you came to visit me.' "Then the righteous will answer him, 'Lord when did we see you hungry and feed you, or thirsty and give you something to drink? When did we see you a stranger and invite you in, or needing clothes and clothe you? When did we see you sick or in prison and go to visit you?'

"Then the King will reply, 'I tell you the truth, whatever you did for one of the least of these brothers of mine, you did for me.'

Reeam listened intently. Was God saying something to him? The Prior continued to read:

"Then he will say to those on his left, 'Depart from me, you who are cursed, into the eternal fire prepared for the devil and his angels. For I was hungry and you gave me nothing to eat, I was thirsty and you gave me nothing to drink, I was a stranger and you did not invite me in, I needed clothes and you did not clothe me, I was sick and in prison and you did not look after me.'
They will answer, 'Lord, when did we see you hungry or thirsty or a stranger or needing clothes or sick and in prison, and not help you?'
He will reply, 'I tell you the truth, whatever you did not do for one of the least of these, you did not do for me.'
Then they will go away to eternal punishment, but the righteous to eternal life."

Moved by the Scripture lesson, Reeam reminded himself not to forget those in need, even as he made his pilgrimage to the Holy City.

The Abbot closed the service with prayer. He prayed for the safety of Reeam in his travels, that he might return to his home in the monastery. Said the Abbot, "When Reeam returns to us, he will be a new person; his heart be light, his soul be full of joy, and he will be ready for his eternal rest."

The next morning, Reeam arose with the first light; he had already packed his meager belongings, along with his small bag of coins. As he departed, a steady rain fell, but Reeam was not in the least concerned. His heart was full of sunshine and excitement, anticipating his visit to the Holy Land. The brothers all waved farewell as he walked through the gates of the monastery; they wondered if they would ever see their friend again.

Reeam had traveled only a short distance when he encountered a strange sight. A small family stood huddled together in the rain. The father used a crutch because he had only one leg; the mother held a baby, and two other small children clung to her dress. Their clothes were tattered and dirty; the whole family looked gaunt and sickly. Inquired Reeam, "Why do you stand in the rain? Why are you not in your home seated before the fire?" "We have no home," said the father. "When I lost my leg in an accident, I could no longer work. My wife has ill health, and does all she can to care for the children. We are left to beg for our food. We sleep in caves or wherever we can find shelter. We stand here to ask alms of those who come and go from the monastery." Their story touched Reeam's heart.

Said the one-legged man to him, "Where are you off to this cold, rainy morning?"

"I am going to Jerusalem," responded Reeam. "I have saved for this pilgrimage all my lifetime. When I get to Jerusalem, I shall walk where Jesus walked and pray where Jesus prayed. I will visit the Garden of Gethsemane where he prayed, 'Not my will but thine be done.' I shall stand before Mt. Calvary and ask God's forgiveness for my sins. Then I will visit the Holy Sepulcher where once Jesus' body lay entombed before God's miracle raised Him from the dead. When I arrive at the Holy Sepulcher, I will walk three times around it, then kneel and thank God for Jesus the Messiah. I will then make the long journey home and return to my duties in the chapel. I know that when I return from my pilgrimage, I will be a new person; my heart will be light, my soul will be full of joy, and I will be ready for my eternal rest."

"Well," voiced the one-legged man, "good fortune to you as you travel. We will detain you no longer; be on your way with God's blessing."

Reeam gave them a small coin and quickly moved away. He was sorry for the family's sad state, but he could give nothing more; he would need all his meager possessions for his pilgrimage. Reeam had not gone far when he suddenly stopped; he turned and looked back at this pitiful family huddled together in the rain. Though the thought shocked him, he knew he could not continue his journey. The Scripture lesson from vespers the night before danced on his mind: "For I was hungry and you gave me something to eat, I was thirsty and you gave me something to drink, I was a stranger and you invited me in, I needed clothes and you clothed me, I was sick and you looked after me, I was in prison and you came to visit me. . . . whatever you did for one of the least of these brothers of mine, you did for me" (Matt. 25:35,36).

Slowly, and with little joy, Reeam returned to the unfortunate family: "I have decided that I cannot spend this bag of money on a pilgrimage, while you have no home or food or clothes." "No!" said the father. "We cannot take your money and keep you from your pilgrimage to the Holy Land!" "You must," said Reeam. "I could never enjoy my journey with the thought of you and your little family in such a state of deprivation." When the father and mother realized that Reeam actually wanted them to have his bag of money, they were overjoyed: "To us this will mean a place to live and food to eat and even some decent clothes to wear! But it is costing you everything!" Without much enthusiasm Reeam responded, "I know it is the right thing to do; God be with you."

With heavy heart, Reeam slowly turned back toward the monastery. He had acted rightly, but his lifetime dream was shattered. He knew the brothers would understand and support his decision. Suddenly, as he trudged toward Wingsferr, an impulse overtook Reeam. He turned back to the little family; they were still celebrating their good fortune. At first, they thought he had changed his mind and returned to retrieve his gift. To their surprise, Reeam walked three times around them; then he knelt and asked Jesus to forgive his sins. He then thanked God for Jesus the Messiah. With that, he stood and turned again toward Wingsferr.

To Reeam's surprise, he discovered that his sadness had departed; a deep satisfaction filled his heart.

When Reeam reached Wingsferr, he felt himself accompanied by a Divine Presence. Indeed, when he entered the gates of the monastery, Reeam "felt like a new person; his heart was light, his soul was full of joy, and he was ready for his eternal rest."

The brothers expressed surprise at seeing him so soon. But after Reeam explained, they congratulated him on making the right choice. One of the brothers comforted Reeam: "I am so sorry that you will not get to visit the Holy Land. I know this has always been your dream." "Thanks for your kind words," said Reeam. "But you need not feel sad for me. I have truly walked on Holy Ground."

With that, Reeam went to gather his bucket, mop, and rags. He softly whistled as he made his way to the chapel. The words of Jesus continued to echo through his mind: 'I tell you the truth, whatever you did for one of the least of these brothers of mine, you did for me.' AMEN

****

The Risks of Indirection

In the sense the word is often used, this sermon is not "expository." It makes no attempt to set the biblical context of Jesus' words. Nor does the sermon *explain propositionally* what Jesus meant, or *teach lessons* on viewing the less fortunate as though they were Christ himself. I simply wanted to set the text in the context of a real human dilemma. I wanted my listeners to *experience vicariously* what it is like to surrender one's own desires for the sake of another. In this message, I assume that *Truth experienced* will serve as a greater motivator than Truth *defined or explained*. If the simple story of Reeam influences my listeners deeply, they will be more likely to *imitate his example*. Especially for regular church attenders; the problem is not a lack of *knowledge*; it's a lack of motivation—of *action*. If my sermon only tells them what they already know, the chances are they will continue to do what they have always done (or have not done). Instead, I planted narrative seeds in my listener's hearts; only God knows what acts of Christian benevolence will sprout from my "spiritual gardening."

"Sustaining the narrative" means creating a sermon that is entirely indirect—*the story is the sermon*. Trusting listeners to respond to the sermon's indirect message is essential. The risk, of course, is that some may fail to make personal application. We do not know *how* or *if* listeners will complete the story and appropriate the message. Declares John Shea,

> The wager has been ventured. The story has been told. What people will find in it, they will find in it. Some will laugh and be forced to consider. Others will dismiss it and go on to better things. There is no control on what people will find or where the discussion will go once the story is heard.[13]

Most listeners, however, are much more able and willing to apply the story than we sometimes credit. Jesus occasionally explained his parables to his disciples but not, for the most part, to the crowds; he let the people ponder the meaning of his parabolic word. And, of course, we must not forget that the Holy Spirit continues to move in human hearts, even after the sermon itself is over. Sustaining the narrative means, among other things, trusting God and his Spirit to convict men and women—leading them to an appropriate response. As stated in an earlier chapter, we want to "release the Word" and "get out of the way" so God can do his work.

Richard Jensen tells of preaching a narrative sermon to a seminary community. Two days later, a student came to his office to inform him that "this form of preaching didn't work."[14] The student said that he and another student had discussed the text and sermon for two hours and could not reach a consensus on the

sermon's meaning. Jensen responded, "Let me get this straight. . . .
I preached a sermon on this text which led you and your friend to
have a two-hour discussion of the text and I failed?"[15] If listeners
"think it through" or "talk it out," the sermon has not failed. Indeed, getting parishioners to ponder and discuss is often more
valuable than simply giving them some prepackaged answer to a
problem. At best, "the listener makes the connection between the
story, the text and his or her own life story."[16] Writes Shea: "When
a story has religious impact, it always leads to a larger conversation
and further reflection."[17] Out of the chemistry of personal interaction with story and text, the Word of the Lord may break through
in marvelous and mysterious ways. Like the wind itself, the Spirit
"blows wherever it pleases."[18]

An Action Response

I indicated earlier that my living question for the above sermon, though not specifically stated, is: "*Who* do we *actually serve*
when we render service to the less fortunate?" The answer, of course,
is Christ himself. The church is only the church when she gives
herself in faithful ministry to the cultural and social outcasts—the
lonely, the lost, the suffering, the imprisoned. When we love and
serve these, we are loving and serving Christ. I offer a suggestion:
after a sermon like "One of the Least of These," why not invite
listeners to volunteer for a ministry of service to the poor, the sick,
the imprisoned? The community in which I live has a program
called COMPEER, where individuals can volunteer to spend time
with a patient from an area mental hospital. Our local newspaper
recently carried an article on COMPEER entitled, "Someone to
talk to. . . ."[19] Volunteers in this program are not therapists but
friends: "Once every 10 days or so, [the volunteer and patient] go
to the mall, have lunch and hang out together."[20] After a sermon
like the one above, a chaplain from the mental hospital might
explain a program like COMPEER, and invite church members to
participate. Obviously, not everyone would feel called or qualified

for such a ministry, but just a handful of volunteers could provide care and needed friendship. Not only would the church reach into the community, but Christ would be served through fidelity to "the least of these."

This ends our emphasis on "sustaining the narrative." We march forward toward a narrative design which "supplements the narrative."

CHAPTER 8

SUPPLEMENTING THE NARRATIVE

"As he delved into Elisha's career, it became terribly evident that [he], now freed from his text and moving away from the pulpit and into the aisle and bracing himself with one hand against pew after pew and speaking thunderously, considered himself to be Elisha and was searching the chapel for those children who had mocked him in their hearts, to whom God had sent the bear as punishment. He couldn't stop himself. He recited his many efforts in their behalf, his dedication, his hard work, and their offenses, their indolence, their unworthiness. 'Why?' he shouted. 'Why? Why has thou forsaken me?' Nobody made any attempt to stop him. Everyone in the room was making his own plan for escape."[1]

Garrison Keillor in Lake Wobegon Days

In the previous chapter we examined a narrative sermon design which "sustains the narrative." In that particular model, *the story is the sermon.* At no point does the preacher move outside the story to explain, clarify, or drive home the central thrust of the text. Story and text, with the able assistance of the Holy Spirit, do their work in listeners' hearts. Now we move to another narrative design: "supplementing the narrative." Story is also important in this design, but *not just story.* Sermonic narrative is supplemented with material that amplifies, interprets, and helps the listeners appropriate the truth conveyed by the story. A sermon that *supplements* the narrative, as with all the designs we will examine, is *plotted* with some conflict or tension which moves toward resolution. Again, in this design, the sermon is shaped around "a question, a quest, and discovery." We noted in the previous chapter that the "living question" often goes unstated in sermons that *sustain the narrative*; the story implicitly raises the question but does not necessarily state it. In contrast, sermons that *supplement the narrative* are more likely to state the living question and its resolution, as will be the case in our sermon model for this chapter. Our sermon text in this chapter focuses on God's command for Abraham to offer his son, Isaac (Genesis 22:1-19). In this instance, the living question becomes the sermon's title: "Does Faith Make Sense?"

We have established the fact that the genre of the text must be respected; *both* form and content convey the message of a text. The text *says* something and it *does* something; both dimensions must have a voice in shaping the sermon. Often, the form of the text itself will become the form of the sermon. In Chapter 6, for example, we looked at a narrative sermon design ("The Comfortable Cat") that *simulated the biblical text*; it took its shape from the parable of "the Pharisee and the tax collector." Our sermon model from chapter seven ("One of the Least of These") was also based on a parable—"the separation of the sheep and the goats." However, the form of this text had little influence on the final shape of the sermon—even though the sermon follows a narrative format. There is not, therefore, *always* a *rigid* correspondence between the form of the text and the form of the sermon. A *non-narrative* text, for example, might sometimes be communicated using a *narrative* sermon design. On a rare occasion, a narrative text might best be heard when preached in a more deductive or discursive manner. As previously noted, some listeners respond to narrative sermon designs and some do not. Richard Lischer remarks,

> Those who spend many of their waking moments on the assembly line or at the computer terminal may not respond to story because it has been drummed out of them. That is not to say that they do not need story, only that it has ceased to be a reputable currency.[2]

For nearly all individuals, however, story does function as a "reputable currency." Most often, the preacher will not go wrong in shaping the sermon like a story.

Before we turn our attention to a sermon which "supplements the narrative," we will briefly review some important points from earlier chapters. This review will help us maintain continuity as we progress through these various narrative sermon designs.

Evoking Their Stories

We established early on that "story" can be a powerful means of releasing the gospel into the lives of listeners. We defined preaching as "integrating God's story, your story, and their story so that souls are saved, wounds are healed, and Christ is exalted." "God's Story," we noted, grants the sermon authority; "the preacher's story" contributes personal passion and conviction; "the stories of the people" provide immediacy and relevance. We have referred to the narrative sermon as a "metaphor of participation" because the listeners become engaged by the story. In the prologue we listened in as one minister (Douglas Chadwick) wrote his "Monday Memoirs." Over the years, this minister discovered that the real test of a sermon's effectiveness is what happens *in the listeners*. Douglas Chadwick testified that effective sermons have the power to *evoke* the personal stories of listeners. As this occurs, men and women *preach their own sermons*; this "second sermon" is self-created and self-directed. A sermon preached to one's self is a powerful instrument for personal transformation.

In discussing sermonic "words and phrases," Craddock maintains, "the goal is not to utter but to evoke, not to express anything about one's education, values, life, or views of a text, but to effect a hearing of a text."[3] "How can I 'effect a hearing' of this text?" This question remains paramount as we move toward a sermon based on any given text. Preacher and homiletician Henry Mitchell describes the goal of preaching as "to [so] involve the audience that they are moved to sense identity with the biblical character [or story] . . . , affirming the message with their total being."[4] Facilitating this process, instructs Mitchell, involves the use of the "literary folk genres" or "vehicles of encounter." [5] Among these he enumerates: narrative; character sketch; group study; dialogue; monologue; personal testimony; metaphors, similes, analogs; and finally— "the stream of consciousness."[6] The latter he defines as "getting inside the flow of thought of a person and identifying with her or his struggle."[7] To these "vehicles of encounter" I would add: a question; questions; repetition; and parable. These function as "evoking devices"; they effectively *draw* listeners into the story/sermon. Note that these devices are the building blocks of everyday conversation; they reflect the way people think and interact. Over the next few chapters, we will examine some of these devices in more detail.

"The Father of the Faithful"

Genesis 22:1-18 is the culmination of a "hero story" that focuses on Abraham as the "father of the faithful." Abraham, the protagonist of the story, faces an incredulous spiritual test by God: "Take your son, your only son, Isaac, whom you love, and go to the region of Moriah. Sacrifice him there as a burnt offering on one of the mountains I will tell you about."[8] This command directly contradicts God's covenant promise to Abraham.[9] How could his descendants become "a great nation" if Isaac is sacrificed on the altar? To analyze any biblical story, Ryken asserts that we must ask, "Exactly what accounts for the narrative interest that this story elicits from me?" and "How does it make me a participant in the action?"[10] How then does Genesis 22 generate interest? What is its central conflict and how is it ultimately resolved? How can we connect the *Old Testament context* of Genesis 22 with our *contemporary context*? Do we have situations that in any way parallel Abraham's experience? Claims G. Walter Hansen, "What the text means to me now must be rooted in what the text meant then. What the text meant then must be related to what it means to me now."[11] Assuming that this text has two "horizons" (the "then" and the "now"), how do we "fuse these two horizons" so that the message of the text is released into the lives of our listeners?[12] We will answer these questions as we work toward a sermon which "supplements the narrative."

In commanding Abraham to offer his son, "God tested Abraham."[13] Why was it necessary for Yahweh to prove Abraham? A brief review of the circumstances leading up to this testing might be helpful. God had promised Abraham that from his descendants would come "a great nation."[14] Because it appeared that Sarai could bear no children for Abraham, she had given him her Egyptian maidservant, Hagar: "The Lord has kept me from having children. Go, sleep with my maidservant; perhaps I can build a family through her."[15] But when Hagar became pregnant, Sarai could not contain her jealousy; the pregnant concubine became "a festering thorn in Sarah's side."[16] With Abraham's permission, Sarai mistreated Hagar, causing her eventually to flee the camp.[17] When the Lord questioned Hagar on her reason for running away, she responded, "I am running from my mistress Sarai."[18] The Lord then commanded Hagar to return: "Go back to your mistress and submit to her."[19] The son born to Hagar was named Ishmael.[20]

Some fourteen years later, Sarai's name was changed to Sarah. God promised Abraham another son, to be born of Sarah—even though she was ninety years old.[21] Abraham, finding this promise incredible, laughed at God.[22] God proved true to his word and Sarah conceived; the child she bore was named Isaac. He, not Ishmael, was to be the "son of promise" through whom God's eternal covenant with Abraham would be fulfilled.[23] Of Isaac, God affirmed, "I will establish my covenant with him as an everlasting covenant for his descendants after him."[24] After Isaac's birth, Sarah continued to display jealous anger toward Hagar and Ishmael. Sarah demanded of Abraham: "Get rid of that slave woman and her son, for that slave woman's son will never share in the inheritance with my son Isaac."[25] Although Abraham was greatly distressed by this treatment of Hagar and Ishmael,[26] he acceded to Sarah's wishes.[27] The boy and his mother were driven into the desert with little food or water, ostensibly to die.[28] Only God's miraculous intervention spared their lives.[29]

So Abraham, prior to the offering of Isaac in Genesis 22, is not the most admirable of characters. He often chose the path of least resistance, vacillating "between faith and expediency."[30] Twice Abraham lied, saying that Sarah was his sister rather than his wife.[31] He had allowed Hagar and Ishmael to be severely mistreated; he had laughed at the possibility that God could give a son through Sarah in her old age. Additionally, when God informed him of the impending destruction of Sodom, Abraham challenged God: "Will you sweep away the righteous with the wicked? What if there are fifty righteous people in the city?"[32] It became necessary, therefore, for Abraham to prove himself—to demonstrate his fidelity to God. As Herman E. Schaalman proposes, "If Abraham was to become the ancestor of a people who, because of its covenant with God, would be tested over and over again in excruciating ways, then God needed to be sure that Abraham was in fact capable of passing ultimate questions of faithfulness and obedience."[33] Abraham's willingness to sacrifice Isaac demonstrates his choice of *faith* over expediency; this event solidifies him as the father of the Jewish nation.

"Take your son, your only son, Isaac, whom you love. . . ." For

Abraham this was the ultimate test of faith. The Scriptures reflect no questioning or hesitancy in the actions of the Patriarch. In literary terms, Abraham is generally a *round* character, but in this particular story he is a *flat* character. According to Longman, "A round character appears complex, less predictable, and therefore more real. A flat character has only one trait and seems one-dimensional."[34] Because the Scriptures record nothing of his anxiety, some interpreters would have us believe that Abraham's faith delivered him from inner turmoil; surely this was not the case. While I do not question Abraham's confidence in God, I also know that he was human. The contradiction between God's covenant promise and God's unbelievable command to sacrifice Isaac must have confused Abraham; surely he felt the staggering absurdity of God's command. Schaalman raises the question: "Is this the reward for submitting oneself to [God]. . . ? Did the father of the covenantal people, himself a covenant partner of the covenantal Lord, deserve this fate?"[35] Could Abraham be blamed if he did think: "Why, God? This doesn't make sense!"

Abraham passed the test. I doubt that any "student" ever felt more relief over a "test-grade": "Now I know that you fear God, because you have not withheld from me your son, your only son."[36] Ultimately, Abraham's faith transcended human reasoning; God meant what he said, and his commands demanded unquestioning obedience. The writer of Hebrews informs us that Abraham possessed the full assurance that God was able even to "raise the dead."[37] He was willing to live with the confusion and ambiguity of Isaac's death because he trusted that God's plan was right. The Apostle Paul records, "Abraham believed God, and it was credited to him as righteousness."[38] From this faithful Patriarch, whom Paul designates "the father of us all,"[39] we learn to trust God—even when his way does not *appear* to make sense.

"Why God?"

In studying this Old Testament narrative, we are struck by the absurdity of God's directive to Abraham. Do we have similar experiences, our own personal Mt. Moriahs? David Buttrick suggests that the "problem for Christians is in deciding what kinds of human experience are to be lined up with biblical texts."[40] As I appropriated this Old Testament narrative, I recalled a time some twenty-five years ago when I cried, "Why God?" My father and I had planned a major fishing trip together; we had discussed such a vacation for years, but lacked opportunity. The day before our trip, I drove home from seminary with a tingle of excitement. More than the trip itself, I was looking forward to spending time with my father. When I arrived home, my wife broke the news: "Your father died early this morning of a massive heart attack." He was forty-six and had had no previous heart attacks. Others, I know, have suffered great losses (like the death of a mate or the loss of small child). But that fact did not lessen the pain I felt. I knew that God did not *cause* my father's death, but did he not *allow* it? It is so easy to have all the answers when *someone else* has suffered the loss. I could not deny the questions that came: "Why did I lose my father at such a young age? Why didn't the doctors discover this potential problem and correct it through open-heart surgery? My father was a good man; why not take someone evil?" In a broader philosophical sense, "Why must we sometimes accept the unacceptable?" My sad experience may not perfectly parallel Abraham's. Yet, it raised in me the same fundamental question that he faced: "When life does not make sense, does *faith* in God make sense?"

When I reflected on the death of my father, I felt again the pain of losing a family member. In so doing, I was able to identify with Abraham as he faced the loss of his son. This identification was essential because I wanted to tell the story from a first person point of view, i.e., from Abraham's perspective. We learn through life's experiences that faith often travels over bumpy roads; how difficult it is to do it God's way when that path appears overtly irrational. Yet, God's way is *right* because *he is God.* In Abraham's example, many a suffering soul discovers, as did I, that "The Lord Will Provide."[41] With this brief background, we turn our attention to a sermon which "supplements the narrative."

****

"Does Faith Make Sense?"
(Genesis 22:1-19 and Isaiah 40:31)

" . . . but those who hope in the Lord will renew their strength. They will soar on wings like eagles; they will run and not grow weary, they will walk and not be faint" (Isaiah 40:31).

"Abraham."
"Yes, Lord, I hear you."
"Take your son, your only son, Isaac—you know, the one you love, and offer him as a sacrifice on the mountain that I will instruct you."

"COME TO THE EDGE!"
"No, we will fall!"
"COME TO THE EDGE. "
"NO, WE WILL FALL!"

Why does God take us to the very edge—and sometimes even push us over the edge? Why does he ask us to do what seems foolish, even absurd? *Does faith in God make sense?*

Has God ever taken you to the edge? Have you ever faced an experience like Abraham's? Have you ever cried out to God, "This just doesn't make sense!"

I recall such a time in my own life; it occurred some twenty-five years ago. I was a seminary student working hard to complete my education for ministry. For several years my father and I had spent little time together. We had discussed the possibility of a major fishing trip; finally we had fixed the date and made the plans. The day before our trip, I drove home from seminary tingling with excitement. More than the trip, I was looking forward to spending time with my dad. When I arrived home, my wife broke the news: "Your father died early this morning of a massive heart attack." I felt emotionally crushed. He was forty-six and had been, we thought, in good health. His death was such a shock; it seemed unfair. So many words were left unsaid; so many good times together would never be experienced. In the small church where I preached, I had ministered to others in times of grief; now it was my turn. Initially, I found it very difficult to accept the reality of God's love in the face of this crushing loss. I could not prevent myself from asking, "Why?" "Why did I lose my father at such a young age? Why didn't the doctors discover this potential problem and correct it through open-heart surgery? Why take such a good man when the world is filled with so many evil men?" I struggled to accept the unacceptable. Like Abraham, I could but ask, "Does faith in God make sense?"

Perhaps you too have been forced by life's circumstances to journey to the edge. If so, you too understand how Abraham must have felt.

"COME TO THE EDGE!"

"No, we will fall!"

"COME TO THE EDGE."

"NO, WE WILL FALL!"

A bit of background and then we will let Abraham tell his story. Abraham had journeyed to Beersheba; there he entered into a treaty over water rights with Abimelech, the Philistine King of Gerar (Gen. 21:22-34). In the latter part of Genesis 21, we are told that Abraham planted a tamarisk tree and called "upon the name of the Lord the Eternal God" (Gen. 21:33).

Then came that fearful Voice in the night which must have fallen upon Abraham like a "peal of thunder from a cloudless sky".[42]

"Take your son, your only son, Isaac, whom you love, and go to the region of Moriah. Sacrifice him there as a burnt offering. . . ."

Genesis 22 indicates no doubt or hesitancy on Abraham's part; he simply "set out for the place God had told him about" (Gen. 22:3). Do you think Abraham was calm on the inside? What were his deepest thoughts and feelings? Perhaps this: "Well, God, if that's what you want, I will do it. I don't really have any plans for today anyway! I'll just march up the mountain and sacrifice Isaac, whom I love more than life itself!" This I doubt! Though we cannot be certain precisely how Abraham responded on the inside, let us bring him on the scene and imagine how he might tell his story.

> I still remember *that* day, the day when Yahweh called my name. "Abraham, Abraham." Startled, I answered, "Here I am, my Lord, here I am."
>
> "Take your son, your only son, Isaac, whom you love, and go to the region of Moriah. There, sacrifice him as a burnt offering on the mountain I shall show you."
>
> When God spoke those words to me, they chilled my heart. How could he ask such a thing of me?
>
> The night after God's command, I slept not one bit; I tossed and turned, worried and wept. I prayed to God, desperately attempting to figure out what he was asking. I simply could not believe God would ask me to sacrifice Isaac. His command did not make sense!
>
> Quietly I slipped into the tent of my sleeping son; his face was so beautiful, so innocent. I thought, "Oh, my son, my son! I would gladly die in your place. I am old and withered; my days on this earth are few. Oh, that God would take

me and leave you! You are the sole joy of my heart and the hope of generations to come. Why? Oh, why? Oh, why?"[43]

God had promised me that a great nation would come from my descendants; all the peoples of the earth would be blessed through my seed (Gen. 12:2,3). Isaac was the "son of promise" given to Sarah and me in our old age. How could God possibly ask me to offer him as a sacrifice?

Don't ever say that it was easy! Never have I done anything more difficult! The morning after God gave his command, I got up, saddled the donkey, took Isaac and two servants, and set our path for the region of Moriah.

That was the longest trip I have ever taken. Every step my mind was perplexed, my heart in excruciating agony. The seeming contradiction between God's command and His promises over-whelmed me.

As we made the long lonely journey to Moriah, I looked northward and eastward, and I saw the altar fires blazing upon the hilltops. These were the high places where children were sacri-ficed to the heathen gods of Moloch, Baal, and Chemosh. But my God is not like that! Does some evil power send me on this journey? With each tormenting step toward Moriah I asked myself, "Does faith make sense?"

Once I had doubted God. When he told me that my aged wife, Sarah, would give birth to a son, I was so astounded that I actually laughed at the absurdity of God's promise. But Yahweh kept his word! Sarah gave birth to Isaac. I pledged after that birth that I would at no time ever again ques-tion my God. That pledge was never more difficult to keep than on this solemn journey to Moriah.

One voice within me said, "God has power even to raise the dead!" But another voice questioned, "Why would God require the death of my beloved Isaac? It did not make sense!"

My nights were awful on that dark, troublesome journey to Moriah; every sound in the night seemed to whisper: "Take your son, your only son, whom you love. . . ."

When we reached the great mountain, I commanded my servants to wait. Isaac and I began our trek up the side of the mountain. I laid the wood for the sacrifice on the back of Isaac, while I carried the knife and the fire.

On the way up the mountain, Isaac asked a question that cut to my heart: "Father, I see the fire and the wood, but where is the lamb for the burnt offering?" With trembling voice, I answered, "God himself, my son, will provide the lamb for the burnt offering."

I asked myself, "Should I turn back and tell not a soul of this dark and mysterious journey?" My son is the "staff and joy"[44] of my old age; how will I live without him? Suppose my vision at Beersheba "was all a mistake, a false and feverish dream?"[45]

"No! God has spoken and I will obey!"

Finally we reached the appointed place. I built the altar and arranged the wood. I feel certain that Isaac understood what was to happen; yet, he would follow my lead, even if it cost him his life. He could easily have resisted and overwhelmed me in my feebleness, but Isaac trusted me even as I struggled to trust my Father.

I bound Isaac with cords and laid him on the wood on top of the altar. Tears flowed from my eyes, and my hand trembled as I raised the knife to penetrate the heart of my son. I turned my head away so that I would not see his blood. That knife was so heavy, so very heavy; no power on earth but the power of my faith in the Living God could have lifted that knife!

Why would God make such an irrational request of Abraham? The false gods were often appeased with human sacrifices. Is the Living God no different from gods made of stone and wood? *Does faith in God make sense?*

You and I have chosen to live our lives by faith; we trust him and believe that the future is in his hands—even when He takes us to the edge.

Why did God take Abraham to the edge?

Why does he take us to the edge?

"COME TO THE EDGE!"
"No, we will fall!"
"COME TO THE EDGE."
"NO, WE WILL FALL!"

We go with Him not just to the edge of sorrow, of suffering, of sanity, but to the edge of life itself.

He takes us *to the edge of the water:* "Yet as soon as the priests who carried the ark reached the Jordan and their feet touched the water's edge, the water from upstream stopped flowing. It piled up in a heap a great distance away . . ." (Josh. 3:15,16).

He takes us *to the edge of rationality:* "The virgin will be with child and will give birth to a son, and they will call him Immanuel . . ." (Matt. 1:23).

He takes us *to the edge of absurdity:* "Why do you look for the living among the dead? He is not here; he has risen!" (Lk. 24:5,6).

Can we not be forgiven if sometimes we cry out with Thomas? "Unless I see the nail marks in his hands and put my finger where the nails were, and put my hand in his side, I will not believe!" (Jn. 20:25).

In spite of the apparent failure of human reasoning, we too trust him—both in this life and in the world to come. In choosing this life of trust, have we chosen the sensible way, the reasonable way, the right way? the rational way?

Have we, as our culture so often claims, committed our lives to absurdity? Are we religious Looney-Tunes marching to the beat of a demonic drummer?

Does faith in God make sense?

"COME TO THE EDGE!"

"No, we will fall!"

"COME TO THE EDGE."

"NO, WE WILL FALL!"

The humanist or rationalist might answer: "No! How foolish to live your life by faith. After all, "a bird in the hand is worth two in the bush!" You Christians have nothing but a handful of promises; how ridiculous to live by faith!"

Yet, pain or no pain, fear or no fear, questions or no questions—Abraham climbed the mountain. Listen again as Abraham finishes his story:

> I raised the knife to penetrate the heart of my beloved son. I turned my head away, so that I would not see his blood. A fraction of a second before the knife came down, I heard the voice of the angel of the Lord: "Abraham, Abraham." "Here am I." "Do not lay a hand on the boy. Do not do anything to him. Now I know that you fear God because you have not withheld from me your son, your only son." I cannot describe the unspeakable relief that

flooded my soul when I heard those words. To me, my son *was dead*, and Yahweh gave him new life! Then I saw a ram caught in the thicket; it became my sacrifice. On that mountain I learned that Yahweh can be trusted; I called that place "The Lord Will Provide."

Can we hear the words of Abraham without thinking of another Faithful Father who freely sacrificed his Son on a cross-shaped altar? "For God so loved the world. . . ." IT IS TRUE! "The Lord *Does* Provide."

Abraham had a grand faith, believing God able even to raise the dead (Heb. 11:19). At God's command, Abraham walked to the very edge of rationality. But his faith did not make his actions simple or painless.

My wife, a third grade teacher, recently asked her children for a definition of "brave." Several children said that brave meant "not being afraid." "No!" responded my wife. "Brave is marching on *in spite of one's fear*. Brave means declaring, 'My fear shall not stop me!'"

Abraham's faith did not take away his anxiety. After all, Jesus himself agonized as he faced the cross: "My Father, if it is possible, may this cup be taken away from me. Yet not as I will, but as you will" (Matt. 26:39).

Faith is not whistling on the way to surgery, or humming our way to the funeral home. Nor is faith dancing one's way up Mt. Moriah to sacrifice one's beloved son. Faith takes us to the very edge!

"COME TO THE EDGE!"
"No, we will fall!"
"COME TO THE EDGE."
"NO, WE WILL FALL!"

Does faith in God make sense? Of course not! Faith is not faith if it makes sense *to us*! "Now faith is being sure of what we *hope* for and certain of what we *do not see*" (Hebrews 11:1). Faith means that we trust our Father to make a way, even when we do not understand his workings. Just like Abraham we will struggle at times with faith's apparent absurdity. Yet, God sees the big picture; he is concerned for our *eternal* welfare. He can be trusted—even when his requirements appear irrational. We serve a God who "is able to do immeasurably more than all we ask or imagine" (Eph. 3:20).

The people of God *live* and *act* by faith. The Hebrew writer affirms this truth in a litany of examples: "By faith Able . . . By faith Enoch . . . By faith Noah . . . By faith Abraham . . ." (Hebrews 11:4-39). All who trust and obey have their names added to this "honor roll of the faithful."

Not many people in the modern world are prepared to walk in the footsteps of Abraham; few are willing to go with God *even to the edge*. Often faith is redefined into something far less than that the Patriarch demonstrated. Writes Virginia Stem Owens, faith "has been bowdlerized, tamed, and packaged by the culture of which the church is a part, and when one in need of spiritual relief reaches for the faith-remedy, one often finds instead a cherry-flavored placebo."[46] She continues:

> No one, I'm convinced, should be allowed to claim faith who knows where his next meal is coming from or where he will sleep tonight. Faith is a word we should fear to have on our lips, lest it be defined for us in ways we cannot imagine. . . . You should not talk about faith unless you are prepared to stand . . . with the knife raised over your child's body.[47]

Does faith in God make sense? No, faith does not always make *sense*, but it surely makes *saints*! The Apostle Paul expressed it correctly when he echoed the words of Habakkuk: "The righteous shall live by faith" (Hab. 2:4; Rom. 1:17).

"COME TO THE EDGE!"
"No, we will fall!"
"COME TO THE EDGE."
"NO, WE WILL FALL!"
THEY CAME TO THE EDGE!
And he PUSHED them,
AND THEY FLEW!

Closing prayer: "Our heavenly Father, sometimes life does not make sense. Teach us to trust you, to believe that your way is right, even when we do not understand it. God of Abraham, *test us* that we might to learn to know you and trust you. Give strength to the weary and power to the weak. Teach us, oh Lord, to fly; we would soar on wings like eagles. . . . Amen."

****

First Person Portrayal

With each text and sermon the preacher must decide how best to *effect a hearing;* that is part of the *challenge* and the *fun* of preaching. In the above sermon, I could simply have allowed Abraham to tell his story without adding any "preacherly" perspectives; that would be "sustaining the narrative." However, in this instance, I opted for a different narrative design; I *supplemented* the story with exposition and theological reflection.

The plot of this Old Testament narrative is tied closely to characterization—to the person of Abraham. The "thread" that holds the sermon together is the question: "*Does faith in God make sense?*" Through the voice of the preacher, Abraham told *his own story.* As I imagined myself into Abraham's life, I could *feel* what he experienced. First person portrayal does not come naturally to me, but slowly I am growing to value this rhetorical technique. Eugene Lowry is of the opinion that, within any given sermon, such first person portrayal should be limited: "most of us can believably sustain only brief moments of characterization."[48] There may be danger in routinely crossing the line from *preacher to actor*. Some congregations, for example, might have trouble accepting the metamorphosis from preacher to biblical character. I have been pleased, however, at the positive response from listeners to first-person-portrayal; it provides a fresh way to hear biblical narratives. Should the preacher ever dress like a biblical character and preach a first person monologue? I advocate occasional sermons of this kind. With practice and a little coaching (like assistance from a high school drama teacher), most preachers will surprise themselves in their ability to do characterization. The objective, of course, is not to transform the preacher into entertainer, but to allow the biblical characters to speak with authority in contemporary settings.

Even though feelings are not mentioned in the text, my sermon reports on Abraham's inner anguish. Do I violate the Scripture when I have Abraham describe his discomfort? I think not. After all, Isaac was more than Abraham's bridge to the future descendants; he was a son, greatly loved. I have a friend who was criticized because he described the emotions Joseph must have felt when he discovered that Mary, to whom he was betrothed, was pregnant. Said the critic to my friend, "You have no warrant to say what the text of Scripture does not say. You take away from the biblical story by suggesting the feelings of Joseph." My friend disagreed; he argued that by reflecting Joseph's emotions, the biblical story became *more real* to the listeners. If Abraham was human, he must have felt fear and confusion that God would make such a request. When I portray this inner turmoil, I believe that I am enlivening the biblical story—not contradicting it. I want my listeners to say to themselves, "If Abraham, who was a human being just as I am, could walk by faith when faced with such ambiguity, perhaps I can do the same."

Grounded in Human Experience

According to Ralph and Gregg Lewis, "Inductive preaching begins with the particulars—facts, illustrations, experience, examples; deduction starts with assertions, conclusions, propositions, generalizations or principles."[49] Lewis and Lewis repeatedly stress the importance of beginning the sermon on "common ground."[50] All forms of inductive communication, including narrative sermon designs, are grounded in *human experience*. In the initial stages of my sermon, I identify with my listeners: "Has God ever taken you to the edge? Have you ever cried out to God, 'This just doesn't make sense!'" My own story (the death of my father) also had the intent of moving me *along-side* my listeners, preparing them for Abraham's story. I want listeners to admit to themselves, "I have asked that question!" or, "I had an experience like that!" In one sense, the sermon does not begin until we establish this "common ground." To paraphrase Craddock, "We can't pull out of the station till all our riders are aboard the train!"

Interestingly, this Old Testament narrative reflects a mutual process of discovery; even as God examined Abraham, *Abraham was examining God*. Abraham "was overwhelmed by the ultimacy of that catastrophe that loomed before him. What did God have in mind? How could he possibly understand God's workings? He was thoroughly confused. He needed to probe God's will and intent. He, Abraham, had to test God, as it were."[51] What distinguishes Abraham's God from the deities worshipped by the Canaanites? Will Yahweh routinely ask his followers to offer their children on altars of appeasement? Abraham revealed himself as a person whose obedience had no limits. He learned that God's commands could appear most irrational. At the same time, God vindicated himself to Abraham; he proved himself the Living God who, unlike gods made of wood and stone, both *acts* and *speaks*. On the surface it may seem that Abraham is the hero of this biblical narrative. In reality though, God is the true hero of this story, as with most Old Testament narratives. State Fee and Stuart: "Old Testament narratives are not just stories about people who lived in Old Testament times. They are first and foremost stories about what God did to and through those people." [52]

In the above sermon, the resolution (or "discovery") comes with the completion of Abraham's sacrifice. In another sense, however, the concluding paragraphs provide the resolution as a fuller answer *evolves*. Henry Mitchell stresses the importance of a sermon's final words or climax. He believes the message should build toward a kind of "grand finale" or "crescendo" "when the theme is finally restated and lifted to its highest expression." [53] This is not to suggest a loud or flamboyant conclusion; indeed, a quiet but passionate ending, like prayer, can be the most influential closure. Often, narrative sermons end abruptly; listeners are somewhat shocked that it is over. However the preacher chooses to conclude the sermon, it should not be allowed, warns Mitchell, "simply to dribble to the end or peter out." [54]

As biblical readers and interpreters, it is important for us to pay close attention to the use of repetition in biblical narrative. Writes Longman, "Instead of weeding out redundancies, scholars thus pay close attention to the way redundancies function in the text." [55] Such repetition is similar to our use of italics or underlining. It signals, "This is especially important in the story." Sermonic repetition will often pattern itself after the repetition found in the biblical narrative itself. Repeated questions, phrases, verses of poetry, or Scripture help tie the sermon together and pull listeners into the story. The living question is repeated in the above sermon: "Does faith make sense?" A recurring verse of poetry is also present:

"COME TO THE EDGE!"
"No, we will fall!"
"COME TO THE EDGE."
"NO, WE WILL FALL!"

Hopefully, the echoing of these poetic lines causes listeners to say to themselves, "What does this mean? What edge? Who is coming to the edge and why?" This measure of *ambiguity* stimu-lates anticipation, pulling listeners toward the "grand finale." Clearly, God took Abraham to the edge; he sometimes does the same to us. Why? The answer comes at the conclusion of the ser-mon:

THEY CAME TO THE EDGE!
And he PUSHED them,
AND THEY FLEW!

The metaphor of a bird being pushed from the nest becomes what I called in the last chapter a "reinforcing metaphor." God has a purpose in our most painful testing; he wants us *to fly on wings of faith*. I wanted the congregation to get this message, without say-ing it directly. I read Isaiah 40:31 at the beginning of the sermon but made no other mention of it until the concluding prayer. This final prayer ties it all together; God pushes us over the edge be-cause he wants us to " . . . soar on wings like eagles."

Our "sermonic house" continues to rise as we explore creative ways to *effect a hearing* of the gospel. We have examined a narrative sermon design that simulates the movement of the text itself. We have also viewed designs that "sustain the narrative" and "supple-ment the narrative." In the next chapter we will "segment the nar-rative."

CHAPTER 9

SEGMENTING THE NARRATIVE

"Dr. Watt spoke at morning chapel a marathon sermon that left his congregation as weak as if they had spent the time struggling through snowdrifts. His opening prayer consumed twenty-six minutes . . . and touched on many points of Old Testament history."[1]

Garrison Keillor in Lake Wobegon Days

We come now to one of my favorite narrative sermon designs; I call it "segmenting the narrative." This approach parallels a literary technique employed by some writers: the telling of a story "within a story." "Segments" of a completely different story interrupt the primary narrative; this intrusive second story *seems* totally unrelated. I say "seems" because the second story is very much related to the primary story, but the reader does not yet realize this connection; at some point, the two narratives converge. A character in both stories, for example, may turn out to be the same person, though operating under an alias. Perhaps, the events transpiring in this segmented story alter the plot outcome of the primary narrative. Often, the reader becomes intensely curious as to the impact of one story upon the other. When the two come together, the reader may think, "Why didn't I see that connection?"

I define a "segmented narrative sermon" as any sermon which tells a story in *pieces* or *segments*. A contemporary story, for example, may be woven into a biblical narrative. The outcome of the biblical story provides the clue to the resolution of the segmented narrative, while it in turn sheds light on the biblical story. In some instances, as in our sermon example for this chapter, the segmented story is woven into *biblical exposition and reflection*, rather than into a biblical narrative. In this model, the sermon has two tracks; one track is a story "told in pieces," while the other track consists of scriptural exposition and instruction. The main *idea* or biblical truth *collides* with the *climax* of the story, thus providing for the listener what we called earlier an "aha experience." Lowry describes such an occurrence as being "the lighted light bulb in the old comic strip";[2] "its coming signals a decisive and sometimes peculiar form of knowing which illumines the entire plot."[3] Consistent with the other narrative designs examined, we plot the segmented sermon around a *question, a quest, and a discovery*. In this case, both tracks lead to the same resolution—one presented *logically*, the other *narratively*. As we shall discuss later in more detail, proper *timing* is essential for all narrative sermon designs. That is particularly true when "segmenting the narrative"; the two tracks must converge at *just the right moment*.

"Segmenting the narrative" overcomes at least two obstacles faced in preaching: 1) How do we create interest in a biblical story that has been heard hundreds of times? 2) How do we sustain audience attention throughout ponderous or didactic material? A "segmented narrative" provides possible answers to both questions; it stimulates curiosity and keeps listeners attuned as they *creatively anticipate*. Lucretius, a Roman philosopher from the first century

BC, wrote a lengthy philosophical statement in a poem.[4] Why put such heady material in poetic form? Lucretius explained:

> A doctor who wants to get children to drink a bitter medicine first rubs a little honey on the rim of the cup. The children, unable to imagine what lies ahead, drink the medicine, lured on by the sweet taste of honey. . . . My purpose is to lure the mind so that, once engaged with these ideas, it might be led into the nature of the universe.[5]

In this narrative sermon design, the segmented story supplies the "honey on the cup"; it induces people to stay tuned-in. Author Captain Marryat uses a similar metaphor for novels; they entice "the reader to take a medicine."[6] I might add that, in a segmented narrative sermon, the story is *both honey and medicine*. With all my efforts to convince the reader of the value of stories, I would not want to leave the impression that the biblical exposition constitutes the *real medicine*, while the story simply supplies the "sweet taste" that induces them to take it. In a segmented narrative sermon, *both* tracks contribute to the overall effect of the message.

But we must be honest; some biblical material is tedious to present (though not unimportant). Furthermore, many believers have heard the biblical stories all their lives. How do we keep these folk interested? Why not weave in a relevant contemporary story? Again I quote Marryat who indicates that one purpose of a novel is to "convey wholesome advice in palatable shape."[7] The same applies to a sermon. Like it or not, a part of the preacher's job is to present material in *palatable form*; the best spiritual medicine will have little benefit if the patient refuses to take it. *Creating and sustaining interest* are worth the effort, though I am not suggesting that these constitute our primary goal. Reasons Thomas Troeger, "Our goal is not simply to become more relevant or eloquent or engaging. We want to redeem language so that our words may more genuinely invite belief in the Word who redeems the world."[8]

Narrative preaching helps people listen—not just to the story, but also to some exposition and theological reflection. This form of communication *does not* preclude the use of instruction, or even argumentation; sermons that *teach* biblical truth can be *plotted.* Let the reader recall our observation made earlier: *preaching involves the productive interplay between "creative anticipation" and "logical argumentation."* A segmented narrative sermon adeptly illustrates this interplay; it consists of a contemporary story woven *into* and *around* either a biblical narrative, or around didactic/expositional material.

The Sermon on the Mount

In the next few paragraphs we will review the *diagnostic process* whereby I arrived at a living question and its gospel resolution. As previously indicated, *I must search for the overlap between the message of the text, my own experience of the text, and the congregation's need.* Having identified this material, I will then plot the sermon around a question, a quest, and a discovery.

The segmented sermon for this chapter comes from Matthew's recording of the Sermon on the Mount (chapters 5, 6, and 7). Our text (Matthew 6:1-4) develops into a sermon entitled "What are Your Secrets?" We note again that this narrative design originates from a nonnarrative text. Matthew 6:1-4 reads as follows:

> Be careful not to do your acts of righteousness before men to be seen by them. If you do, you will have no reward from your Father in Heaven. So when you give to the needy, do not announce it with trumpets as the hypocrites do in the synagogues and on the streets to be honored by men. I tell you the truth, they have received their reward in full. But when you give to the needy do not let your left hand know what your right hand is doing so that your giving may be in secret, then

your Father who sees what is done in secret will
reward you.

Before discussing the sermon, a few comments about Matthew's
Gospel and the Sermon on the Mount are in order. Most interpreters believe that Matthew wrote both to *convince* and *instruct.*
Matthew wanted to persuade Jews that Jesus was the long awaited
Messiah, whose coming was predicted in the Old Testament. At
the same time, this gospel probably served as an instructional instrument for new Christians (some who were Gentile). As Gundry
indicates, "The Gospel of Matthew is the gospel of the Messiah
and of the new people of God, the Church. . . ."[9] The Kingdom of
God which Jesus ushered in was quite different from the prevailing Jewish understandings of the coming kingdom. Many Israelites were anticipating a political and military Messiah who would
deliver Israel from the yoke of Roman domination. Matthew wrote
to clarify this confusion; God's Messiah would surely rule over a
Kingdom—but not an earthly kingdom. Rather, Jesus ushered in
the *Kingdom of God—the church.* This Gospel is structured around
five divisions (like the Pentateuch), which alternate the teachings
of Christ with narratives announcing both the *presence* and the
coming of the Kingdom of God. Matthew assumed that his readers
reverenced Jewish law, and that Jesus came to fulfill that law.[10]
Like Moses, Jesus conveyed a new revelation from God, but this
new word emerges as *both* a continuation and fulfillment of the
old: "You have heard that it was said to people long ago . . . But I
tell you."[11] Matthew also intended Gentile Christians to appreciate the connection between Judaism and the new covenant built
on King Jesus. Therefore, Matthew's Gospel "is the link between
the Old Testament and the New, the old Israel and the new world-
wide church of God's people."[12]

Matthew repeatedly portrayed Jesus as a *new* and *greater* Moses.
Like Moses, Jesus ascended a mountain to communicate God's
Word to humankind. Jesus is not against the Old Testament Law:
"until heaven and earth disappear, not the smallest letter, not the

least stroke of a pen, will by any means disappear from the Law until everything is accomplished."[13] Jesus came not "to abolish the Law or the prophets . . . but to fulfill them."[14] In the Sermon on the Mount, Jesus called for a *new* righteousness. Explains Ralph Martin, Jesus described "the disciples' goal as set at no less a standard than 'perfection,' meaning 'the wholeness of consecration to God.'"[15] In many respects, the Old Testament religious system had failed. The "scribes and Pharisees" exemplified this failure; they observed the outward forms of religion without allowing it to alter them within. Later in Matthew's Gospel, while describing the religious leaders, Jesus quoted Isaiah: "These people honor me with their lips, but their hearts are far from me."[16] The Jewish religious leaders *looked* good; they were not much interested in *being* good (except as they defined goodness). The ethic of the Kingdom of God, Jesus taught, must go beyond the artificial ritualism of the Pharisees.[17]

In our sermon text, Jesus excoriated the Jewish religious leaders as "hypocrites" who did their "acts of righteousness before men."[18] Jesus taught that when deeds of kindness (like giving to the needy) are done primarily to display one's *piety*, no reward is received from God.[19] God perceives not only *what* we do but *why* we do it. The Lord's concern extends to the hearts of his disciples; *thoughts* and *motivations* do matter. Cautioned Jesus, our Heavenly Father sees us from within—and rewards us accordingly.[20] Jesus attacked the self-righteous showmanship of the hypocrites: "For I tell you that unless your righteousness surpasses that of the Pharisees and teachers of the law, you will certainly not enter the kingdom of heaven."[21] According to Jesus, murder often originates with anger,[22] and adultery with lust.[23] He appealed for a new kind of obedience in the Kingdom; one based on an *inner transformation*. Explains Joachim Jeremias,

> Jesus says, in effect: 'I intend to show you by means of some examples, what the new life is like, and what I show you through these examples, this

you must apply to every aspect of life. You your-
selves should be signs of the coming of the Kingdom of God, signs that something already has
happened.'[24]

Under the ethic of the Kingdom, pleasing and serving God becomes the supreme goal of the religious experience; loving and
serving human kind becomes the practical result.

Appropriating the Text

To appropriate the text, I reflected on God's nature. He looks
within us; our thoughts, motives, and attitudes are forever visible
to the All-Seeing Eye. I asked myself: "How much of my Christian
life is lived out so that others will be impressed with my spirituality? Am I a man of prayer, or do I simply want others to *think* so?
Am I *righteous* or *self-righteous?*" This text stipulates that, in one
sense, *we are according to our secrets*. I remembered reading something similar written by O. Hobart Mower.[25] Also connecting his
thoughts to the Sermon on the Mount, Mower comments,

> Most of us live *depleted* existences: weak, zestless,
> apprehensive, pessimistic, 'neurotic.' And the rea-
> son is that when we perform a good deed, we ad-
> vertise it, display it—and thus collect and enjoy
> the credit then and there. But when we do some-
> thing cheap and mean, we carefully hide and deny
> it (if we can), with the result that the 'credit' for
> acts of *this* kind remains with us and 'accumu-
> lates.'[26]

This perceptive observation drives us to self-examination.
"*What Are Your Secrets?*" Behind this question stands a powerful biblical truth: *God requires the children of the Kingdom to conceal
their good deeds and confess their misdeeds.* This truth, somewhat

broader than Matthew 6:1-4, expresses New Testament teaching as a whole: "Therefore confess your sins to each other and pray for each other so that you may be healed" (James 5:16). With most of us, *flaunting* our goodness and *hiding* the evil that lurks within seems the more *natural* thing to do. It requires *supernatural* power to overcome fallen instincts and comport ourselves in God's way. I am not suggesting that we can somehow save ourselves by attaining this noble ideal. Even as we struggle for the ethical perfection demanded by Jesus, we acknowledge that salvation comes only by *God's grace*. Ultimately, only God's righteousness as revealed in Christ can make us *truly* righteous and work in us an inner transformation.[27] Yet, in both our actions *and* attitudes, we continue to reach for the high standard prescribed by Jesus. I will not necessarily state all these details in the sermon, but they provide the essential foundation as the message develops.

My study and reflection lead to this living question: "Has the gospel of Christ worked in us an inner transformation?" This question will be phrased a bit differently, but the primary thrust of the message will raise this introspective issue. Behind this question is my *thesis* or central biblical truth: *Christians demonstrate inner transformation by concealing their good deeds and confessing their misdeeds.* In the sermon, I want to create *torque* between my living question and its resolution. My segmented sermon will have two tracks, both of which assist in creating this torque or tension. One track consists of logical argumentation (didactic and expositional material), and the other, a contemporary story woven *into* and *around* this cognitive material. If handled correctly, both of these tracks will assert the central biblical truth. In fact, this truth will be distinctly asserted twice: as the conclusion to my didactic material, *and* as the *denouement* of my segmented story.

"Pieces" of Story

David Buttrick reminds us: "In preaching every idea must be imagined and, if possible, connected to actualities in human experience."[28] Because the text awakened in me no personal narrative, I turned to my *imagination* to connect the biblical truth with human experience. My story, which I tell in "pieces," revolves around a hypothetical minister (Pastor Williams), who has some *deep secret*. This minister's congregation is anxious; if only they knew his secret. After each segment of the story, I ask my listeners, *"What are your secrets?"* Other powerful questions stand just below the surface: "What secrets do we hold within ourselves?" "What do they reveal about our character?" "Do we *conceal our good deeds and confess our misdeeds?*" Hopefully, searching for Pastor William's secret will help us grasp something of the nature and demands of the Kingdom of God. My use of the repeated question ("What are your secrets?"), as in our previous sermon example, serves to hold the sermon together; it also calls my listeners to personal introspection. What does God see in us that others do not?

When a segmented story is first introduced, it often appears to have no connection to the sermon; it "hangs in mid-air." The listener might think, "Why is this story being told?" "Isn't the preacher going to finish that story?" These "loose ends" occur frequently in books and movies; they serve to foster anticipation. Steven Spielburg's powerful film on the holocaust ("Schindler's List") illustrates this technique. The movie begins with several seemingly disjointed scenes that eventually come together as the larger story emerges. In a sermon, listeners may feel a bit irritated that this incomplete story keeps peeking its head out from under the covers. That is acceptable; our concern is the impact of the *entire sermon*. As the denouement evolves, listeners encounter a "complete, unified experience . . . a point of fulfillment."[29] However, we do not want this to happen prematurely; the goal of a plotted sermon is to hold the tension as long as possible. When the segmented narrative reaches its climax, it may have an unusual twist or unexpected reversal. As we have noted, such a twist or reversal serves to reinforce the resolution of the central conflict. With these words of introduction aside, let us look at a sermon that "segments the narrative."

****

"What Are Your Secrets?"
(Matthew 6:1-4)

Members of his congregation called him Pastor Williams. He had been at First Community Church for a little over six months and had been well received. The church was growing and morale was generally favorable. The only potential source of trouble was Wednesday afternoon. On Wednesday afternoon, for about two hours, Pastor Williams disappeared; no one knew where he went or what he did. Other times when he left the church office he would say, "I'll be back at such and such a time"; or, "If you need me, you can reach me at this number." But on Wednesday afternoon he just disappeared. When asked about this, the pastor seemed reluctant to give information, which was enough to fuel the rumor mill.

We all have secrets, do we not? *"What are your secrets?"*

In the first century, three chief acts of Jewish piety were considered the pillars of the Jewish faith: almsgiving, prayer, and fasting. The Pharisees invented ways to turn these religious expressions into acts of self-glorification, by which they flaunted their goodness and their right-standing before God. We might translate the actions of the Jewish religious leaders into a contemporary setting with a simple example. Imagine a man in the worship service; as the offering plate is passed, he stands, trumpet in hand, and plays an ostentatious tune. Then, with great ceremony, he drops his check into the plate. Though they did not do it quite that way, the Pharisees were truly the *religious peacocks* of their day. To them *and us*, Jesus said, "When you give your alms, do not announce it with trumpets (Matt. 6:2)."

What did Jesus mean by the phrase "sounding trumpets before men"? In the synagogues, the offering utensils were often shaped like trumpets in order to discourage pilfering. With these narrow-topped trumpets, the hand could not be inserted to steal the gifts. Maybe Jesus was making a play on words and referencing these utensils. Also, the public fasts were announced by the *sounding of trumpets*. These fasts became occasions of great ostentation for the religious leaders. Perhaps Jesus was referring to these occasions when he spoke of "sounding trumpets before men." Or maybe his words simply meant, in modern vernacular: "Don't toot your own horn!"

In principle, the Pharisees knew that the best way to give a gift was anonymously. There was a room in the temple called "The Chamber of the Silent."[30] Here gifts could be given quietly, without anyone's awareness. Yet, as is often true, a great gap existed between *precept* and *practice*, as we might note in a first century example.[31] In Israel, water was an especially valued commodity because of its scarceness. Certain "water carriers" would stand in the marketplace to distribute drinks to the needy. After receiving a drink, the thirsty person had to say loudly: "O thirsty ones, . . . come to drink the offering."[32] The water carrier would respond in a loud voice, "Bless me, who gave you this drink."[33] Jesus condemned this kind of ostentatious behavior.

Jesus also denounced the public prayers of the hypocrites because they "love to pray standing in the synagogues and on the street corners so that they may be seen of men" (Matt. 6:5). Even when fasting, the religious leaders "disfigure their faces to show men they are fasting (Matt. 6:2)." The attitude seemed to be: "Let me show you how spiritual I am!" In this polluted religious environment, Jesus proclaimed: "Be careful not to do your acts of righteousness before men to be seen of them" (Matt. 6:1).

Yes, the rumors were flying. What was Pastor Williams doing on Wednesday afternoon? Could he be carrying on an affair?

"What are your secrets?"

Before we look at our text more carefully, we must address a possible textual contradiction. In the Sermon on the Mount, Jesus also said:

> You are the light of the world. A city on a hill cannot be hidden. Neither do people light a lamp and put it under a bowl. Instead they put it on a

> stand and it gives light to everyone in the house.
> In the same way let your light shine before men
> that they may see your good deeds and praise your
> Father in Heaven (Matthew 5:14-16).

Just a chapter later the Lord instructs that when giving to the needy, do not "let your left hand know what your right hand is doing, so that your giving may be in secret" (Matt. 6:3,4)." How do we reconcile this statement with the previous command to "let your light shine before men?" We must note the qualifier that Jesus assigns: "that they may see your good deeds *and praise your Father in Heaven."* Jesus seems to be saying, "When you do your good deeds publicly, as sometimes you must, *be certain that the praise and the glory goes to God.* Do not be like the Pharisees who simply gave alms to be honored of men, who offered prayers to be seen of men, and who fasted in a way that would bring praise and glory to themselves."

Refusing then to let "your left hand know what your right hand is doing"[34] addresses *motive.* Jesus is asking, "What motivates you to perform good deeds?" This verse, explains James Montgomery Boice, "points to an absence of ostentation, not only before men, but also before the giver himself. It is indicative of a charity inspired by the presence of Christ in the heart."[35]

A couple of deacons from First Community Church expressed concern: "We must find out what's happening! Where does Pastor Williams go on Wednesday afternoon? People are talking; some even suggesting involvement in a romantic tryst. Let's follow him and settle this matter once and for all. "

"What are your secrets?"

Notice in our text that Jesus grounds his discussion in the very nature of God. He establishes ours as a God who *sees*: "Then your Father who sees what is done in secret . . ." (Matt. 6:4). But not only does he see, he is also a God who *rewards*: "Then your Father . . . will reward you" (Matt. 6:4). The author of Hebrews describes God's nature: "Nothing in all creation is hidden from

God's sight. Everything is uncovered and laid bare before the eyes of him to whom we must give account" (Heb. 4:13). Through Jeremiah, God says, "Can anyone hide in secret places so that I cannot see him?" (Jer. 23:24). No secret sin can we hide from God: "Nor is there sin concealed from My eyes" (Jer. 16:17).

Recall the Old Testament story of Joseph and Potiphar's wife. Time after time she pleaded with him to commit sexual sin with her: "Come to bed with me!" (Gen. 39:12). Joseph steadfastly refused her seduction, declaring, "How then could I do such a wicked thing and sin against God?" (Gen. 39:9). Against God! Joseph knew that with God there are no secrets! Joseph would not betray the God he worshipped. In our day many people act as if sin is only sin *if discovered!* A small number of television preachers, for example, have adopted this attitude with respect to their sexual indiscretions. Surely their behavior has caused God to weep!

Achan in the Old Testament also forgot that God *sees* and *rewards* (Joshua 7). The Children of Israel were fighting the Amorites at Ai. God had given them overwhelming victories until they came to Ai where the Israelites were severely routed. Joshua said, "Ah, Sovereign Lord, why did you ever bring this people across the Jordan to deliver us into the hands of the Amorites to destroy us?" (Josh. 7:7). What happened to cause this great defeat? Against God's specific instructions, Achan had seized those goods from Ai which God had forbidden ("devoted things"). He took a beautiful robe, two hundred shekels of silver, and a wedge of gold. When his sin was discovered, Achan confessed to Joshua, "They are hidden in the ground inside my tent with the silver underneath" (Josh. 7:21). Achan, Achan, what you thinkin'? Do you really believe that the God of Heaven cannot see through a flimsy tent and a few inches of dirt? Achan's deception cost him his life (Josh. 7:25).

Those two deacons felt uncomfortable as they sat in their car that Wednesday waiting for their minister to leave the church building; they were not used to playing private detective. But something had to be done; the rumors had to stop.

"What are your secrets?"

Ananias and Sapphira in the New Testament thought they could get away with deception (Acts 5:1-11). They sold a piece of property, giving a *part* of the proceeds to the church. They told Peter that they had contributed *the entire amount*; their sin was the deception, not the amount they gave. Peter asked, "How is it that Satan has so filled your heart that you have lied to the Holy Spirit and have kept for yourself some of the money you received for the land? . . . You have not lied to men but to God" (Acts 5:3). Ananias and Sapphira also forfeited their lives because of their deception. God *always* knows the truth.

Throughout history humankind has underestimated God. The unspoken assumption goes something like this: "If other people cannot see me do this, then God will not see it either." How seriously mistaken! Listen to the Psalmist: "If I say, 'Surely the darkness will hide me and the light become night around me,' even the darkness will not be dark to you; the night will shine like the day, for darkness is as light to you" (Ps. 39:11,12).

Those two deacons followed their minister, and what they discovered left them stunned. They had no choice but to go to Pastor Williams and tell him what they had seen when they had followed him.

"What are your secrets?"

So then, our God sees and *rewards* accordingly; when we advertise our righteous deeds, we have already received payment in full (Matt. 6:2). Even good deeds (like giving) can be done for false motives. Hypocrisy is not only dangerous, but antithetical to the attitude Jesus desires for the children of the Kingdom.

Jesus Christ modeled a lifestyle pleasing to God; he had little concern for what others thought; he lived to please his Father. Serving humanity was vital to Jesus, while earning praise mattered little to him: "I do not accept the praise of men (Jn. 5:41)." Jesus asked, "How can you believe if you accept praise from one another, yet make no effort to obtain the praise that comes from the only God?" (Jn. 5:44).

Here is *a central biblical truth* of Scripture; listen well because it is one of the greatest principles in all the Bible: *As disciples of*

Christ, we must confess our misdeeds and conceal our good deeds. To do so runs contrary to human nature. Like the Pharisees of old, we modern day believers are tempted to hide our evil and flaunt the good we do, an explicit violation of the ethic of the Kingdom of God. We must not live to *impress others* but to *please* our *Heavenly Father.* As sons and daughters of the King, we must make no effort to cultivate our own reputation. If we solicit acclaim, we take the glory that belongs to God alone. Loving service to others, accomplished without fanfare or self-promotion, is the central ethic of the Kingdom of God.

To be Christlike means following his example. I am reminded of the Scottish lady described by Paul Vincent Carroll in his short story entitled "She Went By Gently."[36] This woman and her husband were awakened in the middle of the night by someone rapping at their door: "Please, come and help us." A woman, an *unmarried* woman, who lived four miles up the mountainside, was about to give birth to a child. The Scottish lady's husband, whom Mr. Carroll calls "himself," "stirred and put his beard irascibly outside the blankets." His wife said, "I'll go." He said, "You'll go none. A slut like that, that gets her child outside of priest and law. . . . I'd let her suffer. A good bellyful o' sufferin' would keep her from doin' it again." The wife said, "I'll go." On a cold winter's night, as snow fell, she made her way four miles up the mountainside to help deliver the baby. Then she hurried home to prepare breakfast for "himself." This compassionate Scottish woman lived her life before the eyes of God; she served others without concern for her own reputation.

Or consider the chaplain—a motel chaplain—described in the newspaper. He goes, night after night, without pay, to a motel to counsel the lonely, the lost, the depressed, the alcoholic, the poor. He counsels in the restaurant of the hotel, explaining, "It isn't appropriate for me to go to the rooms." He offers this ministry freely and cheerfully in Jesus' name. How unlike the religious leaders of Jesus' day who rendered service in order "to be honored by men" (Matt. 6:2).

Such does our Lord seek to serve him: quiet souls, gentle souls who pursue no personal gain. *A willingness to conceal our good deeds and confess our misdeeds demonstrates that we are children of the King.* Writes Charles Wagner,

> There is a secret and inexpressible joy in possessing at the heart of one's being, an interior world known only to God, whence, nevertheless come impulses, enthusiasms, the daily renewal of courage, and the most powerful motives for activity among our fellow men.[37]

Thank God for quiet servants who seek *only* his glory.

Those two deacons went to their minister: "Pastor Williams, we have a confession to make. Wednesday afternoon when you left the church, we followed you. We should not have done so, but rumors were being spread everywhere."

Those deacons saw Pastor Williams drive to a mobile home court; there he spent almost an hour with a severely handicapped boy, playing catch with a beach ball. Then he loaded the young man into his car and took him to an amusement park. For almost an hour he held the boy's hand as he rode a merry-go-round over and over. The minister explained to his deacons, "I should have told you where I was going." "But," he continued, "I got to thinking. Most of what I do is done in the spotlight. Someone is always saying to me, 'You did a wonderful job. You are an outstanding servant of Christ.' I began to question my motives, to fear that I was seeking the praise of men. I just needed to render some service, where only God knew what I was doing."

"What are your secrets?"

****

A Wayward Minister

How often in life we encounter our stories "a piece at a time"; life commonly *happens* to us "in segments." We frequently find ourselves waiting, sometimes with great anxiety, for the end of any given incident. So, when we hear a story in segments, like the narrative of Pastor Williams, we do not regard it as unusual or unnatural; life is like that.

Disequilibrium is fundamental in narrative sermons. I upset the equilibrium in this sermon with my portrait of a *potentially* wayward minister, thereby creating both interest *and* confusion. Within the "question, quest, and discovery," ambiguity is *purposefully cultivated.* I say of this minister, "The only potential source of trouble was *Wednesday afternoon*"; this sentence provides a kind of ominous *foreshadowing* of things to come. Is Pastor Williams good or evil? Perhaps both? What deep secret does he hide? When the deacons followed their preacher and witnessed his behavior, "they were stunned." Narrative sermons will not work without the presence of both struggle *and* subsequent ambiguity; these are the doorway to reality. In the previous chapter, while discussing the "vehicles of encounter," we noted the importance of "getting inside the flow of thought of a person and identifying with her or his struggle."[38] Life pulsates with never ending cycles: danger and safety; conflict and resolution; confusion and subsequent order; constriction and release. We human beings are *always* fighting our way through some bottleneck or another. Explains Lowry: "The reason why it is good advice to 'talk about people' in sermons is that the introduction of people produces ambiguity—as any storyteller knows."[39]

In the above sermon, I had what David Buttrick calls a "secondary intention."[40] By this, Buttrick refers to an "extra agenda . . . like subplots in a drama. . . ."[41] My secondary intention was to address a prevailing cultural situation involving ministers. This sermon was preached a few years back when so-called "televangelists" were struggling with financial scandals and moral shortcomings. A climate of suspicion prevailed, not just of televangelists, but for ministers in general. Critics were concluding, "See, I told you so; preachers are nothing but phonies!" Night after night the national news cited the ugly details of sexual indiscretions among these high profile ministers. Even faithful church folk, troubled by the allegations, were asking: "Do all ministers lead double lives? Do they practice what they preach? What about *my* minister?" I allowed this suspicion of ministers to surface (in the person of Pastor Williams) in order to make a point with my segmented story: *There are a lot of faithful ministers in our society who daily live out the claims of Christ.* Had I concluded the story by making Pastor Williams into an adulterer, I would have contradicted the central biblical truth and confirmed the cultural misperception of ministers. Not only did my story leave Pastor Williams with his morals intact, it gave him both character and credibility. In so doing, I *narratively* defended ministers. Hopefully, this positive ministerial image conveyed some assurance to my listeners: most ministers can be trusted to live what they preach.

Timing and the Sermon

We noted earlier that *timing* is crucial in plotted sermons. I am not a parachutist and have no aspirations in that direction; however, I have known some persons who engage in this "sport." These individuals tell me that *timing*, knowing when to pull the ripcord, is of utmost importance. According to my friends, pulling the ripcord too quickly diminishes much of the fun. By "fun," they refer to the free fall; they get a high out of plunging from the sky at hundreds of miles an hour! On the other hand, if the chutist waits too long to pull the cord, it can be dangerous, even deadly; it takes a certain amount of time for the parachute to slow one's downward momentum. Pulling the ripcord causes the parachutist to experience both *relief* and *disappointment*; she is relieved because the chute has opened, but disappointed because the thrilling ride is almost over. So a formula emerges: *not too soon and certainly not too late.*

In a segmented narrative sermon, the story often intentionally creates ambiguous feelings, putting the listeners in a "free fall" situation. Is Pastor Williams an adulterer sneaking off from his ministry for a clandestine affair? Until resolution comes, listeners experience a kind of *free fall.* But those who listen do not have their hands on the ripcord; they must wait for the preacher (me, in this instance) to open the parachute. Tension builds; what if the ripcord is not pulled? Some congregants may even have concern that the cord will be pulled *too quickly*, ending the "thrill of falling"; *creative anticipation* would prematurely dissipate. The preacher must wait for the right moment to pull the cord: *not too soon and not too late.* Too soon and the suspense is over; too late and listeners become frustrated with story and sermon; they may respond by simply "tuning-out." So, *at just the right moment*, I pull the ripcord, letting them gently down to earth! In the above sermon, I pulled the ripcord *twice*; once when I reached the *logical climax* (the didactic material), and again when I reached the *emotional climax* (the story).

The Dual Climax

In Chapter 4 we described the *denouement* of a story as including both the *climax* and the *falling action*. A climax, we noted, is sometimes called a *crisis*. We defined a climax as "the point at which the central character wins or loses" or "the peak moment in a series of events . . . after which the events can go only in one direction."[42] The remainder of the story we labeled the falling action. In discussing literature, Charlotte Lee distinguishes between what she designates a "logical climax" and an "emotional climax," though in many instances these coincide.[43] The logical climax is "the culmination of the logical content" that occurs when the main point is made "with such clarity that . . . the conclusion is inevitable."[44]

The *emotional* climax arrives when the emotional impact is most keenly felt and may be either "gentle" *or* "dramatic."[45] As I indicated, the above sermon contains *both* climaxes. The logical comes when I announce the central biblical truth toward which the didactic material has moved: *"As disciples of Christ, we must confess our misdeeds and conceal our good deeds."* The segmented story about Pastor Williams cannot reach its emotional climax without this overarching biblical truth; likewise, the Pastor Williams narrative drives home the biblical truth. The denouement of the story reinforces, at an *experiential level*, the truth of the logical climax. Also, note that even the didactic material of the first track utilizes smaller individual biblical narratives like the examples of Achan, Ananais and Sapphira, and Joseph. Smaller present-day narratives (the Scottish lady and the hotel chaplain) are also included after the logical climax and before the emotional climax of the segmented narrative.

These two climaxes must work together to deliver the same message. If the two tracks of a segmented sermon take listeners in different directions, the sermon will flop. We are concerned with the impact of the *entire sermon*—which *most often* will consist of a "complete, unified experience . . . a point of fulfillment."[46] Why do I say "most often"? *Must the segmented narrative always reach a point of fulfillment?* At the risk of contradicting myself, I will answer that on *rare occasions* the story might remain unresolved. When this happens, I call it "suspending the narrative." *In the above sermon, for example, Pastor William's secret might never be revealed, thus allowing listeners to live with the ambiguity of his unfinished story.* In this particular sermon, however, that approach would not have accomplished my purpose. Although we do learn from "unfinished stories," multiple objections might be raised to leaving a story hanging. Marsh Cassady maintains that, "since the audience has suffered with the [main character], they want to rejoice with him. It would be insensitive to end the story at this point; it would be cheating the audience members."[47] Cassady, however, is discussing primarily *stand-alone stories*; we are looking at *two-track sermons.* Segmented sermons, like the one above, might bring the didactic material to a satisfying conclusion, while leaving the contemporary story unresolved. The central biblical truth could lead to a logical climax with *no* emotional climax to the story. We will look more carefully at "suspending the narrative" in a later chapter. Generally speaking, however, the audience has a right to know how the story ends; *most often*, narrative sermons need to finish the story if the sermon is to accomplish its mission.

We have two more narrative sermon designs to examine: "sequencing the narratives" and "suspending the narrative." Our next chapter tackles the first of these two.

CHAPTER 10

SEQUENCING THE NARRATIVES

"Still, I was fond of that singular doctor, and he was never one to hold back when the matter of professional jargon arose. On the day when he brought the subject up, he gave me a stern lecture on my increasingly opaque way of talking with my patients, and he ended with a plea for 'more stories, less theory.' He urged that I err on the side of each person's particularity. . . ."

Robert Coles in The Call of Stories [1]

Thus far we have examined four distinctive narrative sermon designs. Each of the four is plotted around "a question, a quest, and a discovery"; each relies on *creative anticipation* to sustain interest and convey meaning.

1) *Simulating the Movement of the Biblical Text*: The shape of the narrative text (such as a parable) becomes the shape of the sermon.

2) *Sustaining the Narrative*: The preacher simply tells a story (biblical or contemporary); the story *is* the sermon.

3) *Supplementing the Narrative*: A narrative (biblical or otherwise) is told, but is not left to stand on its own. The preacher supplements the story with material spoken directly to the listeners.

4) *Segmenting the Narrative*: A primary narrative is interrupted by a sub-narrative told in "segments" or "pieces." As an alternative, expositional and didactic materials replace the primary narrative; this material is then interrupted by a story related in segments. Whichever approach is taken, the two tracks converge at the end of the sermon to produce resolution.

Two designs remain to be considered in this chapter and the next: "Sequencing the Narratives" and "Suspending the Narrative."

Sequencing the Narratives

"Sequencing the narratives" makes use of multiple narratives (at least two) stacked one upon the other. These stories, though different happenings, raise *the same living question* and provide essentially the same *resolution* (*discovery*). We might picture a child's toy that has a plastic peg extending eight to ten inches upward; objects of *varying shapes* are stacked on the peg. Though the objects differ in size and shape, each has an opening that precisely fits the contour of the peg. In a sequential narratives sermon, the stories might be quite distinct in details; yet, they provide *approximately* the *same problem* and *answer*. The trick is to locate stories that are analogous, so as to evoke essentially the same "question, quest and discovery." If these narratives are not sufficiently analogous, listeners will be unable to make the transfer from one story to another, resulting in aborted communication.

Our sermon example for this design comes from Matthew 11:1-19, the report of John the Baptist's prison cell question to Jesus.

Originally I wrote my sermon for a group of ministers, many of whom were experiencing difficult times; I believed this passage would address their need. Consider a bit of background on the passage: John the Baptist had denounced Herod Antipas for taking his brother's wife (Herodias). In her anger, Herodias had John imprisoned in a fortress called Machereus;[2] his life hung in the balance.[3] Dejected and discouraged, the Baptist sent his disciples to ask of Jesus: "Are you the one who was to come, or should we expect someone else?"[4] Biblical interpreters debate the meaning behind John's inquiry: Was he truly questioning Jesus as God's Messiah?[5] Personally, I think that John the Baptist experienced both confusion and doubt: "Have I lived and preached in vain? Must I pay this price for announcing the Lord's coming and declaring the truth to Herod? Is Jesus *really* Israel's Messiah and God's Son?" Perhaps Jesus was not satisfying John's messianic expectations; after all, Jesus was exerting no effort toward the militaristic establishment of an earthly kingdom.[6]

Eslinger advises, "Typically, the contemporary situation offers an issue or image which is then expanded and related to the biblical witness."[7] While searching for an image or metaphor that might portray the circumstances of John the Baptist, a picture in the newspaper captured my attention. An old man (Willie Griffin) sat on a mountain of used bricks, tool in hand, patiently cleaning each brick; he alone was responsible for this work. A good day, the article reported, amounted to fifteen hundred bricks cleaned and a salary of $30.00. I wondered, "How does Mr. Griffin keep himself motivated? Does he ever become overwhelmed with the magnitude of his task?" I could not shake the *image* of this old man seated in the middle of his rockpile; eventually it provided the governing metaphor for my "sequential narratives sermon." John the Baptist was "on the rockpile," as were several of the preachers whom I would address. Connecting this image of Willie Griffin to the biblical account of the imprisonment of the Baptist, I developed a sequential narratives sermon entitled, as you might guess, "Life On The Rockpile."

Appropriating this text and image generated a third narrative. I recalled a specific occasion in my own ministry when I felt overwhelmed and discouraged; I sat on my own "mountain of bricks." I do not suppose anyone in ministry can avoid spending some time on the rockpile. Ministers must contend with a variety of troublesome obstacles: indifference; criticism; lack of commitment; worldliness—we could fill a page. Most ministers have periods of serious questioning: "Is it worth it? Am I called to ministry? Must I suffer in this manner when I have given so much of myself to the Lord?" My living question became: *"What do we do as ministers when we find ourselves 'on the rockpile?'"* This question led to a quest— to a *High Quest*. Like John the Baptist, my listeners needed a word of assurance from the Lord: "Go back and report to John what you hear and see: The blind receive sight, the lame walk, those who have leprosy are cured, the deaf hear, the dead are raised, and the good news is preached to the poor."[8] *If Jesus is truly who he claims to be*, then we can overcome the down times and emerge with a stronger faith. So then I structured the sermon around three narratives: 1) John the Baptist's imprisonment; 2) my personal ministerial "rockpile"; and 3) the metaphor of Willie Griffin. These three raise *approximately* the same question and lead to *approximately* the same Answer. The Willie Griffin story, of course, provides its question and answer *metaphorically*.

Vehicles of Encounter

In chapter eight, I referred to "vehicles of encounter" or "evoking devices." Among others, I named metaphor and personal testimony, both of which occur below in my sequential narratives sermon. Metaphor and personal testimony are forms of *analogy*, wherein *one idea or experience is compared with another*, usually with the purpose of disclosing similarities. My sermon employs the metaphor of Willie Griffin as a *controlling image*. I *metaphorically* relate Griffin's situation to our ministerial experience, and in the process, shed light on our circumstances.

Analogy may be defined as "a resemblance in some particulars between things otherwise unlike: similarity."[9] According to Otis Walter and Robert Scott, analogy constitutes more than example.[10] Indeed, it is "*indispensable to human thought because it permits us to use the experiences of others.* Without analogical thinking, no one could profit from the success or failure of another . . . it is both necessary and useful."[11] We, of course, take for granted that most biblical stories and examples are, in some way, analogous to particular contemporary situations. These textual accounts constitute an illustrative *map* for life's journey; from them we obtain the wisdom to overcome life's obstacles. The difficulty comes in discerning which of our experiences line up with specific biblical examples; the correlation is never perfect. In his final days, the Baptist must have drawn strength from the words of Christ: "The blind receive sight, the lame walk, . . . the dead are raised, and the good news is preached to the poor."[12] Though the Scriptures do not explicitly inform us, I believe John the Baptist was fortified and encouraged by Jesus' answer. I think the Lord was declaring to John: "*Yes, I am God's Messiah! My words and works demonstrate this fact.*" My ministerial calling, though not precisely like John's, also establishes *me* in the business of announcing the King and the Kingdom. I know that my time of ministerial discouragement does not begin to compare with John's prison experience; because he declared truth, he forfeited his life.[13] But, *like the Baptist*, I too found great encouragement in the words of Jesus.

As previously mentioned, the metaphor of Willie Griffin supplies a *controlling image* in my sermon. Figures of speech, like metaphors, similes, and analogs, serve both to illuminate and clarify. Karl Albrecht indicates that metaphors are a form of "verbal mapping" " . . . in which the maker of the map offers to substitute a selected idea or process as a model for describing the process at hand."[14] We regularly sprinkle our conversations with metaphors and analogs, often without realizing it.[15] Of these "figures of speech" or "vehicles of encounter," Henry Mitchell comments: "they enhance understanding of old ideas and free up new ideas, while also having great affective impact, by emotional identification and experiential encounter."[16] Sermons that deal only in abstractions leave listeners confused and frustrated; concrete images, like metaphors, cut through pulpit fog bringing illumination and insight. For my sermon ("Life on the Rockpile"), I clipped the picture of Willie Griffin from the paper and had it enlarged and laminated. When speaking to this group of preachers, I displayed the picture and asked, "In your ministry, do you ever feel like this?" From my audience, I got chuckles and nods as if to acknowledge, "That's exactly how I feel; how did you know?"

Metaphors, similes, and analogs assist the listeners but *also* impose *expectations* on them. The visualness, the concreteness of these devices make it easier to listen (in one sense, *the ear becomes an eye*). But figures of speech (and vehicles of encounter) require listeners to take the time to "let the literal situation sink in."[17] Then, explains Ryken, "we must make a transfer of meaning(s) to the topic or experience . . . [to which the metaphor refers]."[18] If analogies are to achieve their purpose, the listener must spend time pondering or meditating on them; the absence of such reflection renders the analogy meaningless. When I have finished the sermon, I will not mind if my story and metaphor *disappear* from the consciousness of my listeners—*so long as the words of Jesus connect with their own situations.* Let us not forget that the true test of a sermon's effectiveness is *what happens in the listeners.* The sermon succeeds when my listeners have *remembered* their own stories, *created* their own metaphors, and *preached* their own sermons. Greenhaw writes,

> The ultimate measure of effective preaching is not just that the something said of the sermon is *heard* by the congregation but that the something said can and is *said* by the congregation.[19]

I will amplify on Greenhaw's interpretation a bit later.

I also use *personal testimony* in my sequential narratives sermon; I tell my own story of a season on the "ministerial rockpile." Mitchell claims that such testimony is one of the most powerful vehicles of encounter;[20] it "offers visual clarity and vividness of detail and feeling, and audiences easily identify with it."[21] But personal testimony is subject to misuse through *manipulation*; this is particularly true in reporting one's "conversion story." We have stressed the importance of the preacher's *experience of the text*, which we labeled "appropriation"; therein, God speaks *to us* before he speaks *through us*. Although the sharing of one's personal appropriations is essential to effective narrative communication, we must heed the warnings given by Mitchell: 1) personal material must be used sparingly, and 2) "personal examples, even when used infrequently, should never lend glory to the speaker."[22] Troeger echoes these precautions, "This is not self-display but the use of the self to identify the deep common core we share with other human beings."[23] The Apostle Paul declared, "For we do not preach ourselves, but Jesus Christ as Lord, and ourselves as your servants for Jesus' sake."[24]

In relating the story of my own "ministerial rockpile," I am saying to my listeners, "I know precisely what you are going through; my experience is analogous to yours." If I succeed in convincing my ministerial friends that my problem parallels theirs, then I can suggest that the solution which worked for me will also aid them. I overcame my difficult time through hearing anew the same message that Jesus gave to John the Baptist: "The blind receive sight, the lame walk, . . . the dead are raised, and the good news is preached to the poor." While reflecting on Jesus' words to the Baptist, I myself received a fresh vision of Jesus Christ as *my Messiah and Savior.* Therefore, in my sermon I am declaring, *"Jesus is who he claims to be; with confidence in him we can make it through our difficult times."* This fact or concept serves as the resolution of my living question as given above: *"What do we do as ministers when we find ourselves 'on the rockpile'?"* I want my listeners to *experience* confidence in Jesus, to *apply* his reality to their own rockpiles.

Three Incomplete Stories

A sequential narratives sermon is plotted using two or more analogous stories, each of which contains *approximately* the same problem and solution; my sermon example has three. But notice that these are *not sustained,* i.e., they are *not* told from beginning to end without interruption. After each narrative reaches its climax, it is *suspended to be completed at a later point in the sermon.* In using this approach, I am attempting to *sustain the tension* and to generate *creative anticipation.* I will comment on this technique following the sermon, "Life On The Rockpile."

****

Life on the Rockpile
(Matthew 11:2-6)

I invite you to think back on your life and recall some of the jobs you have had. Perhaps you mowed grass or pumped gas; maybe you were a baby-sitter or a house cleaner. Can you remember your most difficult job for which you received the lowest pay?

As a teenager, I did much farm labor; I can recall several hard, hot, and smelly jobs! The one I disliked the most was stacking bales of hay in the barn. An auger carried the bales up to the loft through a window; almost as quickly as a bale came in you had to stack it and be ready for the next. With tin barn roofs and very little ventilation, temperatures in the hay loft would often exceed one hundred degrees. Dust and chaff drifted in with the bales and poured over your head and down your shirt; it makes me itch to think about it! None of the bales could be left in the field overnight because they would absorb moisture. So our work days often lasted ten to eleven hours. The going pay for this uncomfortable, sticky job was $1.00 per hour; that is what I metaphorically call "hard work, low pay, life on the rockpile."
Willie Griffin

Recently I read an article in the paper about another job that also qualifies as "hard work, low pay, life on the rockpile."[25] An unusual picture accompanied this article; an old man sat alone in the middle of mountains and mountains of bricks. In one hand he held a tool and in the other a brick. The text read: "Before most Knoxvillians have finished their first coffees and punched timecards at work, Willie Griffin has cleaned and stacked more than 200 bricks."

As I read on, I discovered that this old man makes $2.00 for every hundred bricks he cleans and stacks. On a good day, Willie would clean 1500 bricks ($30). The image of Willie Griffin on his brick pile stuck in my mind. I thought, "Why would a man continue such labor? Couldn't he find work more rewarding or less demanding?" Mr. Griffin's job described perfectly the image of "hard work, low pay, life on the rockpile!"

John the Baptist

As we engage our text, John the Baptist has his own personal rockpile; he is a prisoner in a cold, dark, prison cell. Josephus states that John was imprisoned in a fortress called Machereus that sat on a mountain east of the Dead Sea.[26] The Baptist paid the price for preaching his firmly held and publicly spoken convictions. As long as John preached a "religious message," the political leaders did not bother with him. However, when the Baptist began to publicly criticize Herod Antipas for unlawfully taking his brother's wife (Herodias), John had gone too far. At the instigation of Herodias, he was thrown into prison with his very life in the balance (Mark 6:17-19).

Though a man not easily intimidated or discouraged, John the Baptist, like his Old Testament predecessor Elijah, went through a period of despondency. I believe that a combination of factors contributed to John's mood. He was a man of the outdoors; he probably slept under the stars, wrapped in his camel's hair mantle. The prison walls must have galled John as only a man of free spirits could be troubled. Most likely, prison food tasted like garbage compared to his normal robust diet of "locust and wild honey." John the Baptist would have much preferred the scorn and apathy of the political and religious leaders to confinement.

As he lay in his prison cell, questions filled John's mind: "Was Jesus really who he claimed to be? Had John lived his life in vain? Why didn't Jesus begin to set up a military kingdom?" John had adamantly believed that Jesus was the Messiah. Of Jesus, the Baptist said, "I am not fit to untie the thong of his sandals" (Luke 3:16). That confidence in Jesus as God's Messiah had been the sustaining power for preaching in the face of open antagonism; but something did not seem right. Jesus was not following the timetable that John's impetuous nature demanded; John's messianic expectations were disappointed. The Baptist experienced confusion—perhaps even *doubt*. "Could it be," thought John, "that I have given my life for someone who really is not the Messiah? Was I mistaken in saying of Jesus, 'After me comes a Man who has a higher rank than I, for he existed before me'?" (Jn. 1:30).

John the Baptist sat on his own mountain of bricks: "hard work, low pay, life on the rockpile!" He had reached the bottom of his courage and confidence. He simply had to know that his imprisonment was not in vain. If Jesus were indeed the Messiah, then John could face imprisonment or even death. So the Baptist sent his disciples to Jesus with this straight-forward question: "Are you the Coming One, or shall we look for someone else?"

My Time on the Ministerial Rockpile

Does any minister escape spending time "on the rockpile"? We preachers get down occasionally, do we not? Like Elijah under the Juniper tree or John the Baptist in his prison cell, we become despondent. With Elijah we cry out: "I have been very zealous for the Lord, the God of hosts. . . . and I alone am left, and they seek my life, to take it away" (I Kings 19:10). When we find ourselves on the rockpile, we need some special assurance from Jesus: "Are you *really* the Coming One?" Any amount of suffering and discouragement can be faced, any rockpile endured, so long as we have *confidence* in Jesus as God's Son and our Messiah. The entire ministerial house rises and falls on this foundational truth.

I remember a "rockpile" in my own ministry. In the church I pastored, the attendance was down and the bickering was up. Every new idea I suggested met the same tired refrain, "We tried that before and it did not work!" Just when it seemed things could not get worse, a lady parishioner made a personal attack. The church leaders had decided, after many complaints, that she was not qualified to teach Sunday School; they asked her to relinquish her position and take some training. Though I fully concurred, it was not my unilateral decision. As you know, in these kinds of situations the minister often becomes a lightning rod; the lightning struck me. I can still hear her voice echoing through the church hallways: "I hate you! I hate you! I hate you!" Oh, the *joy* of "life on the rockpile!"

"I spoke directly to the Lord: "Father, are you sure that you want me in the ministry? Am I really advancing the cause of *your* Kingdom? Could I not serve you as a carpenter or a salesman?" Self-pity filled my soul: "Lord, I am the only one who cares about your church. The others are just playing games while I do the dirty work. The people hate me; I just don't think I can take it anymore." Life, and particularly life in the ministry, seemed terribly unfair. In my despondency and self-pity, God seemed so remote. Like Job in the Old Testament, I felt estranged from my Creator: "Behold, I go forward but he is not there; and backward, but I cannot perceive him; when he acts on the left, I cannot behold him; he turns on the right, I cannot see him" (Job 23:8, 9).

Willie Griffin

I recalled the newspaper account of Willie Griffin. What keeps him on that mountain of bricks for such low pay? Why does he not just throw up his hands and quit? As I looked again at the picture and reread the article, I discovered my answer: "Holding the brick in his outstretched hand, he said, 'Man that made this brick is dead . . . buildings burned . . . but somebody'll buy this old brick, build a new house with it . . . and someday, somebody like me will clean it again." How marvelous! This old man, a brick cleaner, is a theologian! Somehow, through all the hard work and the low pay, he is able to catch a glimpse of the *eternal significance* of his "calling." Willie Griffin acknowledges that the work he does extends beyond his own limited life span: "Preachers throw you in the ground saying ashes to ashes and dust to dust, but a brick made of ashes and dust just goes on and on." That vision and perspective transformed Griffin's attitude and kept him on the job.

John the Baptist

John the Baptist was searching for the significance of his life and ministry. Was he, John, the forerunner of the Messiah? The Baptist put the question to Jesus, "Are you the Coming One. . . ?" Jesus seemed more than willing to give John the assurance he sought: "Go and report to John the things which you hear and see: the blind receive sight and the lame walk, the lepers are cleansed and the deaf hear, and the dead are raised up, and the poor have the Gospel preached to them" (Matt. 11:4, 5). These were *messianic actions*, confirming Jesus as Israel's long awaited Messiah. I think Jesus was saying: "Yes, John, I am the Messiah. All the works I do and the words I speak make that abundantly clear. John the Baptist, I assure you that your sufferings are not in vain; your work and witness have eternal significance. I know that presently life seems unfair, but just trust me even unto death and you shall receive your reward." The Scriptures do not actually tell us how John received the words of Jesus, but I think it likely that a spiritual renewal occurred in the life of John the Baptist. He caught a fresh vision of Jesus as the Eternal Son of God; John's life had not been lived in vain. For the Baptist, *life on the rockpile suddenly became life on the Rock!*

After the Lord had answered John's question, he continued to reflect on the life of the Baptist: "I tell you the truth; Among those born of woman there has not risen anyone greater than John the Baptist . . ." (Matt. 11:11). We do not know whether these words ever reached the ears of the Baptist; it is my guess that *every word* spoken by Jesus was reported to John by his disciples. We do know from the Biblical record that, through the scheming of Herodias,

John eventually lost his life (Mark 6:17-29). I believe he faced death with the fullest confidence that he had served as God's "messenger" sent to "prepare the way of the Lord" (Matt. 11:10).

My Time on the Ministerial Rockpile

That dark period in my own ministry, when I felt so discouraged and separated from God, did not last. It was a rockpile, to be sure, but a fresh vision of Jesus broke through. The words spoken to John the Baptist were spoken into my heart: "the blind receive sight and the lame walk, the lepers are cleansed and the deaf hear, and the dead are raised up, and the poor have the Gospel preached to them" (Matt. 11:4, 5). My "calling" in ministry, like that of John the Baptist, has *eternal significance*. This world will pass away, but the "bricks" I help clean (men, women, and children) will live forever. Even when people are angry or disappointed with me in my ministry, God is still operative in my life and work.

Sometimes life and ministry can be summed up in a simple statement: "Hard work, low pay—life on the rockpile." We cannot avoid times of frustration and discouragement. But we must never forget that Jesus is our Rock, the foundation of life and ministry. The spiritual and emotional pressures of the ministry are simply too great to bear without this assurance. If we confidently build our lives and ministries upon Jesus the Rock, then, even through the ups and downs, we can faithfully carry-out our duties as ministers of the gospel. Concerning the ministry, Phillips Brooks wrote, "The true salvation from the sordidness and narrowness of professional life comes only with a profound faith that God sent us to be the thing that we are, to do the work we are doing."[27] With this assurance, whatever it takes, *we can do it!*

My colleagues in ministry, like me, you will spend your seasons on the rockpile. The next time you find yourself in a spiritual funk, search out a quiet room away from everyone. Then pour out your heart to the Lord; let him know exactly what you are going through and how you feel: "Right now, Lord, ministry seems so hard. I feel like my life has no constructive purpose. Am I *really* doing your will on this earth? Confirm in me that Jesus *truly* is your Son and my Savior. Let me know again your refreshing presence in my life and your purpose in my world. In Jesus name, amen." Having offered your fervent prayer, listen; listen carefully. Can you hear the words of Jesus: "The blind receive sight and the lame walk, the lepers are cleansed and the deaf hear, the dead are raised up, and the poor have the gospel preached to them" (Matt. 11:5)? When these words of Christ envelop you, your discouragement will give way to dedication; *Christ Jesus will happen to you again.* Inner confirmation will come: "Yes! He is the Son of God and our Messiah!" Such assurance will keep you faithfully doing God's work until at last you see him "face to face." Your life on the rockpile will become life on the Rock!

****

Holding The Tension

I noted earlier that in the initial telling the three sequenced narratives are *unfinished*; the old man is left on his brick pile, John the Baptist is left despondent in his prison cell, and I am left struggling in my ministry. Before I release the tension, I want my listeners to experience the frustration and ambiguity of these three separate, yet analogous stories. In a sequential narratives sermon, the plot of each narrative establishes maximum disequilibrium or irresolution before resolution (or Resolution) can arrive. I do not mind if my listeners ask themselves, "What's going on? Why does he leave all three of these folks (Willie, John the Baptist, and himself) on the rockpile? Isn't he going to resolve those stories?" As I said in an earlier chapter, it does no harm to allow listeners to wait for resolution; question and quest often take a circuitous and painful route *to discovery.* I am sure you have heard the old axiom, "You have to get a person lost before you can get him saved." In other words, unless an individual admits his hopeless state, he will sense no need for God's grace. A similar axiom exists in narrative communication: "Unless a person feels the pain, the frustration, the ambiguity, he or she will not *fully experience* the release (the Discovery)." In "Life on the Rockpile," I wanted my ministerial colleagues to sit for a while on the mountain of bricks, allowing the hot sweat to pour from their brow, as they pondered the difficulty of ministry.

Note that even when resolution comes, the old man *remains* on his rockpile, John the Baptist *remains* in his prison cell, and I *remain* in the difficult situations of my ministry. The gospel does not always deliver us from the pain and ambiguity; rather, *it teaches us through Christ to find meaning in that suffering.* That meaning centers in the reality of Jesus, *who is God's Messiah and our Savior.* The gospel teaches us that living in the service of the King and the Kingdom, though not easy, is not in vain.

The Limits of Analogy

Analogy provides an indispensable tool for narrative communication. Listeners move from something concrete and relatively simple (hot, sweaty life on a rockpile) to something less concrete and more complex (how to survive in periods of ministerial discouragement). Wilder tells us that stories "maintain their sway over the imagination by a combination of surprise (novelty) and familiarity (recognition)."[28] The same could be said of figures of speech like simile, metaphor, and analogs. *The listener* transports truths learned in more familiar settings (Willie Griffin, John the Baptist, and my ministerial experience) to their personal lives and ministries. Note the surprise: "You mean these stories speak to *my situation?* Jesus declares himself to me just as he did to John the Baptist?" We must not minimize *the role of the listener* in transporting and/or translating the metaphor into his or her experience. What the text and sermon are "saying" must be "said" into the lives of listeners *by them.*[29] Momentarily, I will demonstrate more fully what I mean by "saying" and "said."

Given the essential role of the listener in this kind of preaching, we might ask: "Do metaphors or other figures of speech ever limit or retard communication?" Definitely. In "Life On The Rockpile," my analogies move in this fashion: from Willie Griffin working with a mountain of bricks, *to* John the Baptist in his prison cell, *then* to a difficult time in my ministry, and finally, to a difficult time in *their* ministries. In preaching this sermon, I assume that my listeners will make these analogous moves with me, *but that may not be the case.* For example, a minister in my audience might contend: "How does he dare to compare ministry to the dirty, menial task of cleaning bricks; even at its worst, ministry is nothing like that!" Another listener might not think that my painful situation in ministry deserves comparison with the imprisonment of John the Baptist's. A third listener might believe that when John sent his disciples to Jesus with a question, he was not despondent or doubting, but simply curious. Make no mistake, these resistant forms of mental gymnastics are common in our auditors. If the listener, for whatever reason, cannot make the transfer from story to analogy, the *controlling image* may become a *destroying image.* Given the infinite variety of the human species, I know of no guarantee that analogies will always work positively. Some metaphors in themselves are inappropriate, leading to unwarranted conclusions.[30] Unquestionably, we must choose analogies carefully, and be certain we do not draw from them inferences that are unrelated.

The "Saying" and the "Said"

Narrative sermons invite listeners *to share an experience.* If this participation occurs, the speaker will have *evoked* the listeners' stories and served as a catalyst for the generating of their *own metaphors.* As earlier indicated, Richard Eslinger and others refer to this model of preaching as "the expressive-experiential model" of communication.[31] Asserts Eslinger, "Central to the hermeneutics of this model is the conviction that there exists some kind of 'shared interior experience' that is normative, unique, and irreducible."[32] In my sequential narratives sermon, I wanted my listeners to *think and feel, to remember,* and *to re-experience* the weight of their own rockpiles. All three narratives were designed to raise these thoughts and emotions. If my listeners felt the weight of their own rockpiles, then they *more than likely* sensed the *release* of a new hearing of the gospel. My personal example of a "rockpile experience" served as a bridge between the narratives of John the Baptist and Willie Griffin. Hopefully, in hearing my self-revealing testimony, the conscious and/or unconscious thoughts of my listeners advanced like this: "If a fresh vision of Jesus as God's Messiah allowed him to overcome his rockpile, perhaps it will do the same for me." When my listeners have remembered their own stories, created their own metaphors, and preached their own sermon, they will have appropriated this gospel truth. *My story then will disappear* and *theirs alone remain*—precisely our goal.

I have stressed throughout this volume the *role of the listener* in transporting and/or translating the sermon into his or her experience. What the text and sermon are "saying" must be "said" into the lives of listeners *by the listeners.*[33] Understanding this concept will help us appreciate more fully the nature of narrative communication. To demonstrate my point, I want to slightly modify an poignant example given by David Greenhaw.[34] Let us assume that Jim has been dating Jane for several months. Jim decides that he loves Jane and wishes to communicate that love to her. He spends a good bit of time deciding precisely what to say and how to say it. His declaration to her sounds like this, "Jane, you are a very special person, unique among women on this earth. Your eyes sparkle like the stars at night. You have filled my heart with a joy that I have never known before. I love you." Jim's words constitute a "saying." Once Jane has internalized Jim's message, and become convinced that he truly loves her, *his actual words are no longer important.* Her inner knowledge of Jim's love represents for Jane a "said." Explains Greenhaw, "Having gotten us to the 'said' the 'saying' becomes 'irrelevant.'"[35] In fact, Jane may well compose *her own words* or metaphors to express Jim's love; her "figurative mediations" might reflect her inner knowledge of his love, *even better than his.*

In the above sermon, my three narratives, sequenced one upon another, constituted the "saying." My use of metaphor (Willie Griffin) was a form of "figurative mediation" designed to help my listeners grasp the biblical concept: "When we affirm that Jesus is God's Messiah, our times on the rockpile become 'life on the Rock.'" Will my listeners always remember *my story* or *my metaphor*? I hope not; my "saying" will die that their "said" might live on. The "said" occurs when my listeners take this powerful biblical concept and *translate it* into their own story or metaphor. The Prologue of this volume (concerning Douglas Chadwick) offers precisely the same point: *The sermons people preach to themselves are the ones that lead to genuine inner transformation.* I close by again referring to Greenhaw, "The congregation's ability to put a concept in motion, to return it to a figurative mediation, is the measure of the effectiveness of preaching."[36] To his observation I say, "Amen."

CHAPTER 11

SUSPENDING THE NARRATIVE

"The story is a bridge between the divine and the human, the conscious and the unconscious, the physical and spiritual, the soma and the psyche. Stories heard through the ears become a bridge to the heart. Stories touched by the spirit become 'enzymes' in the body. . . ."
Elaine Ward in The Art of Storytelling[1]

The Brothers Grimm recorded a short tale entitled "The Golden Key."[2] According to this story, a young man ventures outside in the cold of winter to search for wood. In the process, he happens upon a mysterious golden key. What could it possibly fit? Soon he discovers a large iron box; cautiously he inserts the key; it fits the lock! Slowly and with growing excitement he twists the key. What wondrous riches will it hold? The story ends with these words, "Then he turned it once round, and now we must wait until he has quite unlocked it, and lifted the lid up, and then we

shall learn what wonderful treasures were in the chest!"[3] *That's it!*
Should a story end *before we see the treasure?* Won't listeners be
frustrated? Can anything positive accrue in telling a story to its
climax and then *quitting the narrative?*

We come now to the final narrative sermon design: "suspending the narrative." Skillful stories frequently catch us off-guard—
they create "effective surprise." Reasons Bruce Salmon, "[Listen-
ers] may find that the unexpected is the most acceptable conclusion, even though they did not anticipate it."[4] What could be
more surprising than a story left unresolved? Of course, such a
story might also leave listeners *upset* or at least *unfulfilled.* Nevertheless, unfinished stories are a natural component of the human
experience. Why should they not, on occasions, be a part of the
sermon? However, let the reader be cautioned; unresolved narratives must be handled with care. As Salmon indicates,

> Those stories that leave the listener 'hanging' pro-
> duce an undeterminate meaning. Occasionally we
> might enjoy an open-ended story where the final
> outcome is somewhat in doubt. More often we
> receive pleasure when the conflict is resolved.[5]

It is my assumption that *suspended stories* have their place in narrative preaching, *so long as the preacher has carefully thought through
the application of this sermonic technique.*

Suspending the Narrative

Lowry advocates a category of narrative sermon designs which
he identifies as "suspending the story."[6] However, his use of that
phrase differs from mine. Lowry foresees a condition in which the
preacher is addressing a particular biblical story and "the biblical
story line runs into trouble."[7] As Lowry describes this predica-
ment, a biblical story such as a parable takes an unusual turn that
rather leaves the sermon in a cul-de-sac. Lowry suggests, "But *if* in

fact there seems no way to negotiate the 'trouble' and still remain within the biblical text, then the preacher will move away from the text . . . to a contemporary situation in order to 'find a way out.'"[8] "Suspension" then for Lowry simply signifies leaving the story *temporarily* in order to deal with some particular problem or obstacle that has surfaced within the text.[9] On the other hand, when I speak of "suspending the narrative," I am referring to a narrative sermon design in which one or more stories *remains unfinished*. The story is not momentarily set aside in order to deal with some difficulty; rather, the sermon *ends without resolving the central conflict in one more of the sermonic narratives.* Upon the completion of the sermon, *the listener carries* with her or him the ambiguity of this unresolved plot.

I recognize that this approach seems to violate the very nature of narrative as I have described it. Did we not say that for a story to have an adequate plot it must have a beginning, middle, and an end? In chapter four I referred to the "climax" and "falling action" of a story as the *denouement;* I wrote: "this final denouement or 'coming together' must occur."[10] I have also quoted R. V. Cassill: "The principle that must be respected is that every story must have some resolution, some denouement. . . ."[11] Nevertheless, I am now suggesting that one or more narratives within a given sermon might be more influential *without resolution*. This suspension does not mean that the sermon has a "question and quest," but no "*discovery.*" Rather, it intends the sermon be so designed that *the listener fashions his or her own discovery*. In other words, the nature of the sermon *compels the listener* to create an appropriate denouement.

David Buttrick relates the story of a family accustomed to having many visitors in the home; the children never knew who would show up at the breakfast table.[12] The children, being of the mischievous bent, decided to trick their visitors. They purchased a thrilling murder mystery and arranged it invitingly on the bedside table in the guestroom. Intrigued guests would read the story, eager to learn who committed the murder. However, when finally arriving at the end of the mystery, they would discover that *the last chapter had been removed.* "Imagine," prompts Buttrick, "red-eyed guest trudging to breakfast table utterly frustrated: 'How did it end?'"[13] Granted, these visitors would suffer frustration, but I can also see *some advantage* for the victimized reader. She might, for example, amuse herself during leisure hours by analyzing clues and pondering the question, "Who committed this murder?" It is even conceivable that the reader could design a *denouement* which is decidedly superior to the missing chapter. Or she might initiate a search in bookstores to locate this particular book: "I just have to find out how this thing ended!" The point is, the missing chapter *stirred the reader to activity. Every* mystery novel could not end before identifying the murderer—but, *on a rare occasion. . . .*

I have indicated that one criticism leveled at deductive preaching—and I think it legitimate—is that it leaves little for the listener to do. In effect it says, "Here's my conclusion; take it or leave it." The preacher spends all week arriving at a biblical truth and then expects auditors to accept that truth when announced from the pulpit. As we have noted, effective communication does not operate in that manner. Listeners want, and need, time to chew and digest their own ideas; seldom does "preacherly imposition" succeed with today's audience. Contemporary listeners like to deliberate for themselves—to determine their own conclusions. Obviously this cannot occur in every sermon; some texts and/or subjects demand a more direct approach. But experience has taught me that listeners appreciate those occasions when the preacher *allows them* to finish the story and to draw their own conclusions accordingly.

Most often in narrative communication, the preacher will resolve the ambiguity. The question and quest will lead to a satisfying denouement; the tension or disequilibrium in any given story will be settled. However, the "suspended narrative sermon" provides a unique alternative. Our sermon example in this chapter ("A Defining Moment") comes from Genesis 39:1-20. This text records the attempted seduction of Joseph by Potiphar's wife. Alongside the story of Joseph, I tell the narrative of a contemporary man named "John." John is a Christian and a deacon in his church; he is also happily married. Nevertheless, when his attractive secretary *makes herself available*, he experiences a moment of indecision. John is trapped between "yes" and "no"; the sermon begins by highlighting his ambivalence and *ends with the same scene*. Of course, the sermon leaves no doubt as to the *right* moral choice. But *knowledge* of what is right does not necessarily guarantee *right behavior*. The ambiguity of John's struggle serves to demonstrate the danger faced in sexual temptation. We humans sometimes act against God's will when confronting these temptations—with catastrophic personal, social, and spiritual consequences. My living question, which grows out of John's ambivalence, leaves the audience to ponder: "What choice would I make if faced with an explicit opportunity to commit sexual sin?"

Background of the Joseph Narrative

Let us briefly consider some background of the Joseph narrative. As we join the story in Genesis 37, significant tension has developed between Joseph and his brothers. A good bit of this tension arose from the fact that Jacob favored his youngest son:[14] "Now Israel loved Joseph more than any other of his sons, because he had been born to him in his old age."[15] Jacob demonstrated this favoritism by giving Joseph "a richly ornamented robe."[16] The hatred which Joseph's bothers felt for him was exacerbated by both this robe and two self-glorifying dreams which he reported.[17] Some disagreement exists among interpreters as to whether Joseph's dreams are revelatory or "merely the product of his own inflated ego."[18] His brothers clearly believed the latter. Future events seem to indicate that God was indeed communicating with Joseph. The brothers, according to J. Gerald Janzen, were economically threatened by Joseph's dreams: "The brothers take Joseph's dream report as his upstart claim on the inheritance, through a boast of greater virility and economic power. . . ."[19] For a combination of reasons, the brothers' hatred of Joseph congealed into a specific plot to take his life.[20] Reuben persuaded the brothers to fake Joseph's death so as to convince their father he had been killed by wild animals.[21] At Judah's suggestion, Joseph was sold into slavery to the Ishmaelites for twenty pieces of silver and then transported to Egypt.[22] Subsequently, Joseph became an attendant in the house of Potiphar, an official of Pharaoh.[23] It was in Potiphar's home that Joseph faced a difficult sexual temptation. Repeatedly, and with what Robert Alter calls "naked directness,"[24] Potiphar's wife attempted to seduce Joseph; her words left no doubt as to her desires: "Come to bed with me!"[25]

To be sure this must have been a powerful temptation to the young and handsome Joseph. Though he had made youthful mistakes, Joseph responded to Potiphar's wife with conviction: "How then could I do such a wicked thing and sin against God"?[26] In describing the dialogue between Joseph and Potiphar's wife, Robert Alter refers to the bluntness of her proposition as compared to the "long-winded statement of morally aghast refusal"[27] from Joseph. Alter continues,

> The brevity of the sexual proposition on the part of Potiphar's wife is a brilliant stylization—for as Thomas Mann was to observe at great length, she *must* have said more than that!—of the naked lust that impels her, and perhaps also of the peremptory tone she feels she can assume toward her Hebrew slave.[28]

For Joseph this proposition provided a significant test of character; it constituted what I am calling a "defining moment." Embarrassed and scorned by Joseph's refusal, the woman lied to her husband thereby placing culpability on Joseph.[29] Potiphar responded by imprisoning him.[30] Interpreters over the years have deemed this a light punishment for the charged offense. It has been conjectured that Potiphar knew his wife's assertions were unreasonable, and for this reason he spared Joseph's life. Of course, Joseph stood under Yahweh's protection, and this could explain the light sentence.

Interpreters often portray Joseph as an arrogant, self-centered character. J. Gerald Janzen, among others, contends that Joseph has gotten a bad rap.[31] Certainly, God is the foremost Hero of the Joseph story; these narratives reveal "what God did with an *unlikely* candidate for success."[32] But Joseph also had positive qualities which commend him.[33] He must not be faulted for reporting his dreams to his father and his brothers; to keep such a vision to oneself would have been considered wrong in the ancient world.[34] Joseph's example in resisting Potiphar's wife is a supreme paradigm of moral uprightness; confronted with an explicit opportunity to commit sexual sin, he makes the right choice. Von Rad underscores the fact that Joseph, in this particular episode, bears a striking resemblance to the ideal young man as described in wisdom literature.[35] In Old Testament wisdom literature, a "wise man" is characterized as one who fears God, who is loyal and dependable, and who enjoys favor and good repute in the sight of God and man.[36] Writes Von Rad, "In Joseph a picture is sketched of a youth and man of best education and upbringing, of faith and experience in worldly affairs, such as the teachers of wisdom had instructed their youths to be."[37] Wisdom literature frequently warns unsuspecting young men of prostitutes and adulteresses: "Can a man scoop fire into his lap without his clothes being burned? Can a man walk on hot coals without his feet being scorched?"[38]

Preaching Old Testament Narrative

Before we look at a sermon that suspends the narrative, I want to examine one more hermeneutical issue that relates to the use of Old Testament narrative in preaching.

Throughout this volume I have referred to the writings of Gordon Fee and Douglas Stewart; I highly recommend their book *How To Read the Bible For All Its Worth.* However, I think they miss the mark in some of their observations on the interpretation of Old Testament narrative. They disallow the use of some Old Testament narrative for contemporary preaching. For example, they contend,

> Joseph's lifestyle, personal qualities, or actions do not tell us anything from which general moral principles may be derived. If you think you have found any, you are finding what *you* want to find in the text; you are *not* interpreting the text.[39]

I disagree. In this particular text, Joseph faced sexual temptation head-on and resisted it in the name of his God. So long as we portray Joseph in a reasonable and balanced manner, why should he not be used as an example of what God expects from us in a similar circumstance? To do so, in my judgment, exalts the God Joseph honored by his steadfast refusal to be seduced. I might add that the New Testament clearly affirms this kind of virtuous behavior.

At the same time, I fully recognize the difficulty in allowing Old Testament narrative to communicate in the contemporary world. We must make the leap from that world to ours with humility. The responsible use of Old Testament narrative demands more than a simple transfer between worlds. We must always keep the broad picture in mind, taking care not to chop the narrative into snippets from which we draw superficial morals. The narrator of Genesis, for example, wants to demonstrate that, in Joseph, God was at work to fulfill his covenant promises to Abraham. Joseph was a link in God's chain of persons through whom Abraham's descendants would become a "great nation."[40] In these narratives, we discern God's providential work through Joseph: "the Lord gave him success in everything he did."[41] Joseph is also a type of "savior figure." Records Gordon Wenham: "Through Joseph's efforts, not only was his own family saved from starvation, but also the Egyptians and many neighboring peoples were delivered. So also in this respect the promise to Abraham was partially fulfilled."[42] But even as we note the broad picture, we cannot ignore individual episodes; these speak forcefully to the contemporary world. As Craddock reminds us, "love is still love, hate is still hate, grief is grief, fear is fear, joy is joy, and forgiveness is forgiveness."[43] I might add that "temptation is still temptation." In a world where moral compromise runs rampant, we need to preach Joseph's example.

With these introductory words, we turn to our final narrative sermon design— "suspending the narrative."

****

A Defining Moment
(Genesis 39: 6a-20)

Today I want to examine those unique moments in our lives that I call "defining moments." At such times we make monumental choices; we choose between "right and wrong" and even "life and death." In our text, Joseph faces one of these "defining moments" as Potiphar's wife attempts to seduce him. Before we turn our attention to Joseph's great temptation, let us look briefly at a man named John; he too encounters a defining moment.

Peek over John's shoulder and read a note he has just received from his secretary, Debra:

> Dear John, I understand that your wife and children are out of town for a few days. I thought this evening around 7:00 might be a good time for a visit to my apartment. I have prepared a chicken casserole that I think you will enjoy. It could prove to be *a very entertaining evening*. Hope to see you then. Love, Debra.

When John receives Debra's note, he feels *both* sick *and* excited. At first he starts to trash the note and pretend it never came, but something inside of him refuses to do so. John has a decision to make; for him this is a *defining moment.*

Temptation comes in many different and powerful forms. The explicit invitation to sin sexually is, in some ways, one of the most potent of temptations. Numerous "good" men and women of reputable standing have been caught in this web and subsequently devoured by the *black spider* of undisciplined passion. *Will John be one of those?*

Before we learn a little more about John, let us turn our attention to Joseph.

The Patriarch Joseph faced his own "defining moment." Our story begins when Joseph is a young man of seventeen. He is tending the flocks of his father Jacob. We are told: "Now Jacob loved Joseph more than any of his other sons, because he had been born to him in his old age" (Gen. 37:3). Jacob demonstrated his partiality by giving him a "richly ornamented robe" (Gen. 37:3). When Joseph's brothers saw their father's favoritism, "they hated him [Joseph] and could not speak a kind word to him" (Gen. 37:4).

The hostility between Joseph and his brothers was strengthened by his unusual dreams which he freely reported. In one, sheaves of wheat (the brothers) bowed down before the sheaf representing Joseph. In another dream, the sun, moon, and stars bowed down before Joseph. The brothers were enraged: "Do you intend to reign over us? Will you actually rule us?" (Gen. 37:8).

As our story continues, the brothers have gone to Shechem to care for the flocks. Jacob said to Joseph: "As you know, your brothers are grazing the flocks near Shechem. . . . Go and see if all is well with your brothers and with the flocks and bring word back to me" (Gen. 37:12,13).

When Joseph located his brothers, they were grazing the sheep near the city of Dothan. They watched him draw near: "Here comes that dreamer! . . . Come now, let's kill him and throw him into one of these cisterns and say that a ferocious animal devoured him. Then we will see what comes of his dreams" (Gen. 37:19,20). Reuben persuaded the brothers not to kill Joseph, but to place him in a cistern; Reuben intended to rescue the young man and restore him to his father. Joseph was stripped of his coat, which was then dipped in goat's blood, to be taken back to Jacob with word of his death. At Judah's suggestion, Joseph was sold into slavery for twenty pieces of silver to Ishmaelites who carried him into Egypt. The loss of his favorite son was a terrible blow to Jacob. He tore his clothes and cried out "in mourning I will go down to the grave of my son" (Gen. 37:35).

The biblical narrator makes it clear that God was protecting Joseph and allowing him to prosper. In Egypt he became an overseer of the house of Potiphar—an official of the Pharaoh. Potiphar put great confidence in his Hebrew slave: "and he entrusted to his care everything he owned" (Gen. 39:4). Potiphar's wife was a beautiful woman of questionable character. When she saw that Joseph was well-built and handsome, she twice attempted to seduce him. The first of her propositions came with shocking bluntness, almost like a command: "Come to bed with me!" (Gen. 39:7). Joseph steadfastly refused her advances and declared his fidelity to Potiphar *and to his God*: "How than could I do such a wicked thing and sin against God?" (Gen. 39:9). As one commentator writes, "[from Joseph's perspective] a wrong against the husband would be a direct sin against God . . . the ethos is completely bound to God."[44] Among the Hebrews, sexual sin was considered a serious transgression, in some circumstances requiring even the death penalty (Deut. 22:22). Joseph recognized the grave nature of this sin and determined in his heart to resist it fully.

Her second attempt to seduce Joseph took a more active form. One day, when the household servants were out of the house, Potiphar's wife caught Joseph by his cloak and demanded that he "come to bed" with her (Gen. 39:12). This was not an easy temptation for Joseph to endure; he was a young man with all the cravings of late adolescence. In one sense, he was the property of this household; slavery demanded absolute obedience to one's master. Again Joseph spurned her advances; he ran from the house, leaving his cloak in her hand. Suddenly this woman's passion transformed itself into uncontrollable rage. By the time her husband arrived, she had turned her anger into wicked deceit: "That Hebrew slave you brought us came to me to make sport of me. But as soon as I screamed for help, he left his cloak beside me and ran out of the house" (Gen. 39:17,18). When Potiphar heard her story, "he burned with anger" and forthrightly had Joseph imprisoned (Gen. 39:19,20). In choosing the *right* over the *expedient*, Joseph lost his favored position—and he could have lost his life. Because of the providence and protection of God, Joseph was spared from this fate. Indeed, he even prospered while a prisoner (Gen. 40:1-23). Nevertheless, I believe that Joseph would have willingly suffered death before sinning against his God.

Joseph encountered a "defining moment" and came away from it with his character intact. He would not sin against God, regardless of the cost. Can the same be said about John from our earlier example? Recall the note that we read earlier.

> Dear John, I understand that your wife and children are out of town for a few days. I thought this evening around 7:00 might be a good time for a visit to my apartment. I have prepared a chicken casserole that I think you would enjoy. It could prove to be *a very entertaining evening*. Hope to see you then. Love, Debra.

I told you that when John first received his secretary's note, he felt *both* sick and excited. His first impulse was to trash the note. But some inner force prevented him; in the deep places of his soul he fought the battle. Unlike Joseph, John does not have the strength of faith and character to make an immediate decision. He dwells in the land of ambivalence, torn between right and wrong. He knows that this is a "defining moment," but still he hesitates.

John is employed as a bookkeeper for a small plumbing company. He is a conscientious man who works hard and enjoys his job. John is a Christian man, active in his church, where he serves as a deacon. He deeply loves his wife, Susan, and has never considered being unfaithful to her during their thirteen years of marriage. But never before has he had such an explicit *and* convenient opportunity. Debra is both beautiful and available; she wants nothing more than a one night stand.

This is a tormenting moment for John. The demons of hell pull him in one direction while the angels of heaven stretch him the other way. Deep down he has some sense of the awful price he and his family will pay if he says yes to Debra. John has witnessed examples of both men and women who have had their lives and families destroyed by moral compromise. He has heard his minister quote from Proverbs: "With persuasive words she led him astray; she seduced him with her smooth talk. All at once he followed her—like an ox going to slaughter, like a deer stepping into a noose till an arrow pierces his liver, like a bird darting into a snare, little knowing it will cost him his life" (Proverbs 7:21-23). Yes indeed, this is a "defining moment."

Have you ever been so tempted? Only once in my lifetime has anyone attempted to seduce me. It might surprise you that a minister would be the target of a sexual proposition; but in a culture like ours, I doubt that anyone is exempt. The details of my experience are not important; it happened "in a far away place and a far away time." I thank God that I took my stand with Joseph; I could not sin against my wonderful wife—*or my gracious God*. I have never regretted for a single moment that "I did not choose the pleasures of sin for a season" (Heb. 11:25). Had I said "yes" to this proposition, I would have lived *forever* with regret. Who can place a price on one's moral integrity?

We all face defining moments, do we not? Opportunity and desire come together like ingredients for a bomb. The temptation we confront may not be sexual; Satan shapes the temptation to fit the individual. Nevertheless, these moments are powerful and seductive; our future and the future of those we love often hang in the balance. What we stand to lose is a million times more valuable than what we would gain. When we say "yes" to "the pleasures of sin for a season," we are simultaneously saying "no" to the God who loves us even beyond our comprehension. This is not to say that sexual sins lie outside the pale of God's forgiveness; but even forgiven sins leave their mark on body and soul. Often the scars stay with us for a lifetime. The best answer always is to say what Joseph said, "How than could I do such a wicked thing and sin against God?" (Gen. 39:9). The best action is the one Joseph took: "Let me out of here!" I am not sure who first made this statement, but it is powerfully true: "Saying 'yes' to God means saying 'no' to anything that offends his holiness." The Apostle Paul expressed it in a slightly different manner: "The body is not meant for sexual immorality, but for the Lord, and the Lord for the body. . . . Flee from sexual immorality" (I Cor. 6:13,18).

We know what Joseph did when a wicked woman attempted to seduce him. His character stands like an eternal signpost in the sands of history.

Having received Debra's note, John feels *both* sick and excited. Beyond question, this is for him a "defining moment."

May I ask: "What if you were in John's shoes? *What choice would you make if this were your 'defining moment'?*" Amen.

****

Characters Making Choices

Daniel Taylor advises, "The key to good plot is characters making choices. Choices instill values—right and wrong, good and evil, true and false, wise and foolish—into an otherwise sterile sequence of events."[45] Joseph encounters a powerful temptation and chose wisely. What choice did John make? In our imaginations John lives on in an eternal tortured limbo, suspended between "yes" and "no." Will my listeners feel uncomfortable with this unfinished story? It is to be hoped that moral ambivalence makes us uncomfortable— for both John and ourselves. In reflecting on the temptation of Adam and Eve, John Collins writes,

> The advantage of the narrative symbol is that we can give expression to this sense of temptation without claiming to [fully] understand it. . . . No discourse on the abstraction 'temptation' has anything like the evocative power of the illusive snake, mysteriously fascinating and fraught with danger.[46]

I want my listeners to *experience* the evil power of an illicit sexual temptation. More than that, I want them to fully sense the *serpent-like danger* to body and soul when we waver, as did John, in the face of an explicit sexual proposition. I want *John's ambivalence* to bury itself deep within the psyches of my listeners so that their response in a similar situation will always reflect the example of Joseph. As James declared, "Resist the devil, and he will flee from you."[47]

Notice that I mentioned in my sermon an occasion when a woman attempted to seduce me. This particular experience came to my awareness as I appropriated the Joseph narrative. Even though it happened many years ago and in a different location, I was not comfortable reporting more details. I simply wanted my listeners to recognize that no one is exempt from an attempted seduction—including preachers. More importantly, I purposed to say, "I too was faced with a moral decision and with God's help I made the right choice." I am not submitting myself as a paragon of virtue, morally superior to others. Rather, I am affirming the need, in any given temptation to know that others before have found the spiritual resources to choose rightly. The fact is, we write our own stories and we shape our own destinies according to our choices. Again I quote Taylor:

> We are characters making choices over time—and living with the consequences—and that is the essence of story both in literature and in life. The

more we are conscious of our role as characters making choices that have consequences, and the more we purposefully choose the stories by which we live, the healthier we will be as individuals and as a society.[48]

"Time-Delay Charges"

I see narrative sermons as planting "time-delay charges." This phrase comes from Robert Delnay who reminds us that much of Jesus' teaching and preaching did not become fully clear until many months or even years later.[49] Delnay calls these messages "time-delay charges" because they "go-off," so to speak, only as the disciples think back on his words. Consider Jesus' statement in "the parable of the tenants": "Then the owner of the vineyard said, 'What shall I do? I will send my son, whom I love; perhaps they will respect him.'"[50] Many who heard this parable had no concept of incarnation, i.e., God becoming flesh in the person of his Son. Jesus' predictions of his death and resurrection also fall into this category. After his crucifixion, for example, believers remembered his words: "But I, when I am lifted up from the earth, will draw all men to myself."[51] Following his resurrection the disciples no doubt recalled: "Destroy this temple, and I will raise it again in three days."[52] Jesus spoke, as did the prophets, with one eye on the future. His disciples did not always understand; but someday they *would understand.* Events that were future at the time Jesus spoke had to transpire before his meaning took root in his listeners. In a sense, the Lord was teaching his followers to "creatively anticipate." I wonder how many times Jesus thought to himself: *"Someday they will understand."*

Repeatedly, I have stressed the need for our stories to evoke the stories of our listeners. When they tell their *own* stories and preach their *own* sermons, we know that our sermons have connected. What if a given sermon does not resonate with anything they have experienced? Unquestionably that will happen; we cannot be certain that, in every instance, our auditors will have a reservoir of personal narratives to draw upon. Sometimes our sermons anticipate the future experiences of our listeners, the time they *will understand*. We preachers deal with problems "peremptorily"—before they arise. As Delnay advises, "We need to attach time-delay fuses to our admonitions, so that what they barely understand now they will remember when the need arises."[53] Someday, individuals who have heard my sermon are going to face a powerful temptation of their own; when that happens, hopefully, they will have discovered an answer of *their own*. The time-delay charge will go-off: "Wow! I feel most uncomfortable. This must be for me a 'defining moment'; I think I shall, with haste, remove myself from this situation!" If my listeners reach this point, the *quest* will not have been in vain.

One more thought before we wrap up this chapter. Should I have spoken more about "grace" in the above sermon? God's grace must be made available to those have who have already fallen into a sexual sin. Both grace *and* law are essential elements for the preaching of the gospel; *both must have their day in the pulpit*. However, I decided not to say much about grace in this particular sermon; some might fault me for that omission. While I recognize the value of asserting frequently the willingness of God to forgive, every sermon cannot express everything. I decided to wait for another Sunday to communicate more about grace. The best remedy for sexual sin is *avoidance*; if that fails, let there come an extended *Word of grace*.

CHAPTER 12

"HAPPILY EVERAFTER"

"As the sermon drew to a close, and the mist of his emotion began to disperse, individual faces of his audience again focused in the preacher's vision. Mr. Drew's head was down. . . . No one in the abbey church of Glaston that morning would have suspected that the well-known successful man of business was weeping. Who could have imagined another reason for the laying down of his round, good-humored, and contented face on his hymnbook than pure drowsiness? Yet there was a human soul crying out after its birth-right. Oh! to be clean as a mountain river! clean as the air above the clouds or on the seas!"[1]

George McDonald in The Curate's Awakening

A new world order is emerging; whether it takes twenty years or one hundred years, *a postmodern world is coming.* The world shaped by that historical period called the Enlightenment (the "modern world") is collapsing because it was constructed on the shifting sands of "human reason." Western civilization as we know it cannot survive; even now an "intellectual revolution [is] occurring in both academia and in popular culture."[2] Enlightenment thinkers, believing that good societies could be built and sustained without the Christian God or the Christian gospel, reasoned in this manner: "We want humankind to be good, compassionate, and giving; we want a future filled with promise and hope; but we do not need God or a 'divine pattern' to make it happen; all we need is 'enlightened human reason.'" Robert Jensen argues that any sense of coherence, hope or optimism that existed in the post-enlightenment period was a legacy of Judeo-Christian religion.[3] The modern world, reasons Jensen, had to collapse because it "lived on a moral and intellectual capital that it has not renewed."[4] The gospel provided much of the "moral and intellectual capital" to which Jensen refers; that hope, created by God's action in Christ, is the ultimate form of *creative anticipation.*

A prevailing *skepticism* toward God, church, and the Bible characterizes the new world order; it defines reality apart from any reference to the Transcendent One. What will popular culture be like in the postmodern world? Jensen asserts that many who inhabit contemporary culture do "not apprehend or inhabit a narratable world."[5] People *without a story* are *dangerous* because they exist in a universe *without hope*—or at least with *counterfeit* forms of hope, like material prosperity. Many young adults, for example, live for the moment; from their perspective, it is the only time they have. I am reminded of a college student who was asked why he abused drugs; he responded, "If there is no view, why not frost the windows?"

In this twenty-first century, humankind will hunger and thirst for a coherent Narrative that offers meaning and substance to life. In so describing the coming world order, I am not suggesting that we throw up our hands and surrender to a Story-less future. I am convinced that the sovereign God controls the flow of human history. But *only in the gospel* do I have any sense of confidence in tomorrow; Christ alone furnishes *hope* for a postmodern world. In

Chapter 1, I quoted Robert Jensen: "if the church does not find her hearers . . . inhabiting a narratable world, then the church must herself be that world."[6] As Stanley Hauerwas expresses it, "Jesus is the story that forms the church."[7] I am persuaded that *all faith* finds its origin in the event we call *incarnation*; *all love* finds its origin in a place called *Calvary*; *all hope* finds its origin in his *empty tomb*. Jesus alone puts the "Happily" in our "Everafter"; *our world has no other Story.*

These observations lay the groundwork for *three* vital questions I want to answer as we close. The first has been the focus of this book: "What sort of *sermon* will it take to communicate in a postmodern world?" In summing-up the message of this volume, I will only touch briefly on the other two questions: "What sort of *preacher* will it take to communicate the gospel in a postmodern world?" and "What sort of *church* will it take to transmit the gospel into a postmodern world?"

What Sort Of Sermon?

To communicate with the contemporary world, we must be willing to shape the sermon so that it will receive a hearing. Narrative sermons fit the evolving postmodern consciousness; they respect the listener and honor the current way of understanding our world. We have noted that rationalistic and propositional sermons strike the listeners as inconsistent with the world they inhabit, thus blocking the release of the Living Word. On the other hand, narrative modes of communication allow the church to be that "narratable world" to which Jensen refers.

Earlier we described the narrative sermon as "an ordered form of moving time."[8] Narrative communication is consistent with human "temporality"—the flow of the river, or the fluid nature of human existence. Daniel Taylor, among others, distinguishes between the Greek words *chronos* and *kairos.*[9] *Chronos* refers simply to clock time: "It is succession without progression, or even meaningful cause and effect." *Kairos* on the other hand is "right time"[10]—

even "God's time."[11] In the ancient world, the preaching of the gospel of Christ lanced the wounds of hopelessness and transformed *chronos* into *kairos*. The Christian Story brought hope and purpose; it was an "antidote to a fatalism that made one the passive victim of time and chance."[12] The preaching of the gospel can fulfill a similar role in the new world order.

In the prologue of this book, we listened in as a hypothetical minister, Douglas Chadwick, recorded his "Monday Memoirs." Recall how Chadwick evaluated his sermons. He was fairly confident the sermon had connected when an auditor would say to him, "Preacher, your sermon made me think of an experience in my own life; let me tell you about it." I have called this inner response by listeners the "second sermon" and indicated that it is *more important than the first.* It reveals that the message has *evoked* "something deep within the listener that causes him or her to process the gospel personally."[13] The "outer sermon," the one proclaimed from the pulpit, serves to trigger this "inner sermon." David Greenhaw cautions, "Transformation will take place only when the congregation takes up the interpretive work themselves, when they speak the gospel into their own lives."[14] That moment arrives in a narrative sermon when it *all comes together.* The climax has been reached; suddenly, often unexpectedly the quest and question lead to a forceful *denouement.* The quest transforms itself into a *High Quest;* auditors experience a "moment of epiphany." "Aha! Now I understand! God has spoken his Word into my heart."

Henry Mitchell gives an example.[15] Suppose that a sermon has been proclaimed on the subject of "The Christian Hope." The effectiveness of that sermon cannot be measured by the fact that listeners can *define* the biblical concept of "hope," or even quote Scriptures on the topic. We are not preparing them to compose an essay on "biblical hope"—though comprehension is not unimportant. We desire that our listeners relate the biblical meaning of hope with the topography of their *own experience.* Greenhaw refers to this process as the "circularity of religious hermeneutics."[16] The preacher appropriates a biblical word of hope, allowing it to link with some personal narrative—either real or imagined. Then that *incarnated experience of hope* is translated into "figurative mediations" (stories, metaphors, analogs, etc.) which we release into the community of believers. The preacher's words are then transmuted by listeners into *their own figurative mediations.* In this manner *they internalize the gospel;* God's Story joins with their story. They too *experience confidence* in the God who alone supplies hope; at a soul level they *feel hopeful.* The real "aha!" for the sermon comes, avows Greenhaw, with "the congregation's ability to put a concept in motion, to return it to figurative mediation, [this] is the measure of effectiveness in preaching."[17]

I repeat: "logical argumentation" and "creative anticipation" must *both* be mobilized in communicating the gospel. I am not rejecting deductive or discursive sermons. Some in our culture still function within a "rational world paradigm;" they think and speak in syllogistic logic. But their numbers are shrinking. Sooner or later, as Robert Stephen Reid indicates, we will have to acknowledge that "increasingly the prevailing skepticism of our culture will demand the courage to face its implications."[18] I am not suggesting that preachers compromise the Truth. But to reach men and women in the twenty-first century, we must *reshape the vehicle* that transports Truth. In positing the need for story-preaching, I am not repudiating logic or argument; rather, I am endorsing the *logic of plot.* As I hope my sermon examples make evident, we are moving "from argument to art, from syllogism to symbol—from awesome oratory to experiential encounter [with the Living God]."[19] In my discernment, that defines the intent of preaching.

We must bear in mind that the sermon represents *but one* of God's instruments for the affecting of his will, even as the preacher is *but one* of his servants. The sermon sits in the context of *a worship experience* that includes music, prayer, Scripture, and often the Lord's supper. *All of these* work simultaneously, with the support of the Holy Spirit, to transform persons into the image of Christ. Furthermore, listeners are molded not by a single worship service or a given sermon but by hundreds, even thousands, throughout a lifetime. If a given sermon fails to accomplish its mission, there will come another Sunday—another sermon. Maturing into the "people of God" is an ongoing procedure not unlike a farmer raising a crop; even as we are busy about the business of planting, cultivating, and watering the seed, we know that "only God . . . makes things grow."[20] Affirms Donald Smith, "Every step leading to the harvest is part of a long continuing process by which generation after generation learns of him, responds, and then tells the next generation."[21] We preachers offer God our humble efforts, faulting and halting as they may sometimes be, trusting that God will have his way "to the praise of his glory."[22]

What Sort Of Preacher?

What sort of preacher will be needed to announce the "good news" in a postmodern world? In our most recent Christmas letter to friends and family, my wife and I wrote: "We are so glad we chose to define our lives by The Story." For all of us, that astonishing Story weaves itself into the fabric of our being; from it we secure our *identity*. Early on, I defined preaching as "the integrating of your story, their story, and God's Story in such a way that souls are saved, wounds are healed, and Christ is exalted."[23] We only have a message to preach when the gospel has recreated us, only when Jesus has captured our hearts and minds. Yielding to the Lordship of Christ, we mature into children of the Kingdom— a people living under the symbol of the cross; like Paul, we know nothing "except Jesus Christ and him crucified."[24] This Story becomes for us *the house we dwell in*, an *alternate realm* to the one around us. As heralds of the Living Word, we devote our lives to calling others to join us in this "Household Of Faith." In this old, old Story, then, we have discovered a new, new identity; this God-created Narrative imparts ultimate meaning to all our stories. We preachers become the conduit as personal empowerment is transmitted *through us* to our auditors; they likewise acquire *a Christian identity*.

The Apostle Paul declared, "for all have sinned and fall short of the glory of God, and are justified freely by his grace through the redemption that came by Christ Jesus."[25] We live on a globe scarred by sin and death; yet, our Creator reclaims us through the blood of his Eternal Son. Through this amazing Narrative, we perceive the twin realities of "sin and grace"; without the Story, sin *controls* us and grace *escapes* us. John Macquarrie expresses it well:

> The Bible tells us the story of how God in the beginning destined the human race to be the bearers on earth of his own image, and of how again and again he has summoned them out of their failures to resume their march toward the kingdom of God.[26]

This is the only Universal Story in the universe told by the only Universal Storyteller. From it and by it we are filled with profound confidence ("hope") grounded in the risen Christ; this hope extends even beyond the grave. As Stanley Hauerwas writes: "No longer does the threat of death force us into desperate measures to insure our safety or significance."[27]

The new world order will necessitate preachers who are *saints, scholars, dreamers, and storytellers.* First and foremost, the preacher must be a *saint.* I wrote earlier:

> Saints are a people set apart; they are overwhelmed by the reality of God's grace; they are unashamedly in love with God; their hearts burn with a desire to do his will. Spirit-filled preaching flows from Spirit-filled people; personal conviction is a prelude to powerful preaching.[28]

What does it mean to be a *saint?* Put in simplest terms, the Bible summons us *to be like Jesus.* From our spiritual birth to our physical death, we attempt to emulate Christ so that we may affirm with Paul, " . . . and I no longer live, but Christ lives in me."[29] In our new birth, we identify with Jesus; then we spend the rest of our mortal existence growing more like him: " . . . until Christ be formed in you."[30] If someone were to ask, "Preacher, what do you want out of life?" We can truthfully respond: "I want to be formed, conformed, and transformed into the image of Jesus Christ." This desire to be like Jesus must become the *consuming passion* of our temporal reality.

With respect to the sermon, the saint *prays* it into existence; the *scholar* thinks it into existence; the *dreamer* imagines the sermon into existence. Then the *storyteller* (with a pinch of "prophet" and two pinches of "poet") proclaims the sermon. Can one person fulfill all these roles? Are we not asking a great deal? No one ever claimed that the preaching task would be effortless; nor did anyone dictate we do it *alone;* God is with us from the beginning of our pilgrimage to its culmination. When feeling inadequate, I have turned often to the words God spoke to a hesitant and timorous Jeremiah:

> Get yourself ready! Stand up and say to them whatever I command you. Do not be terrified by them, or I will terrify you before them. Today I have made you a fortified city, an iron pillar and a bronze wall to stand against the whole land—against the kings of Judah, its officials, its priests and the people of the land. They will fight against you but will not overcome you, for I am with you and will rescue you," declares the Lord.[31]

As we resolutely hurl the Word against the darkness, let us not forget the assurance of our Lord: "I am with you always, to the very end of the age."[32] Above all else, that message should keep us *hopeful.*

What Sort Of Church?

It seems appropriate that a book on preaching should end with a reflection on the church. The Story supplies us not only with an individual identity but also with a *corporate identity*; *together* we are the "Body of Christ." Furthermore, *preaching and the church* are inextricably interwoven. Describing the church, Paul counseled: "speaking the truth in love, we will in all things grow up into him who is the Head, that is, Christ."[33] We cannot "grow into him who is Head" apart from the Christian community and the proclaimed Word. For believers, identity is not an individual matter; we belong to a Kingdom—to the *ekklesia* or "the called-out ones." We cannot become like Christ apart from the mediating work of God's church; we need each other. Emphasizes Richard Foster, "Christlikeness is not merely the work of the individual; rather, it grows out of the matrix of a loving fellowship."[34] As members of the Body of Christ, we sustain and support each other in love. But we must not stop there; our concern must reach beyond the walls of the church building to a hungry, hurting, and hopeless world. Our Lord felt a burden for *those on the outside:* "he had compassion on them, because they were harassed and helpless, like sheep without a shepherd."[35] By sharing this compassion, the church defines herself and fulfills her mission.

The Church Father, Origen, often claimed that Jesus Himself is the "*autobasileia—the kingdom in person.*"[36] We are therefore a *Kingdom Community*—"a people created by the Story." Stanley Hauerwas describes the church as a community of *character*, as "the organized form of Jesus' story."[37] Jesus molds us together into a dynamic *community* of faith, fellowship, worship, service, and proclamation. Wrote the Apostle Paul: "There is one body and one Spirit—just as you were called to one hope when you were called—one Lord, one faith, one baptism; one God and Father of us all, who is over all and through all and in all."[38] We who call ourselves Christians have the same Father; the same blood pulses through our spiritual veins—the blood of the Lamb; we eat at the same table—the Lord's Table. The same Story profoundly unites us; indeed, we worship together in a "community of sacred stories"— all of which draw life from this one Universal Narrative. As this Story and these stories shape our identities, we continue to articulate them to generation after generation; Shea calls this a "network of passing on."[39] "In this way," he explains, "we not only receive a tradition, we enrich it and pass it on."[40] Thus, the ever-burning torch of the gospel continues to give light and hope to a world caught in pervading darkness.

Already we have witnessed enough of the postmodern world to view it as a place of monstrous evil *and* of unparalleled opportunity. As our society continues to turn its back on the Christian Story, we may encounter what Stephen Crites calls "the chaotic night of nihilism."[41] But our cosmic struggle against evil and the Evil One will not defeat us; God will have the last Word: "The kingdom of this world [will] become the kingdom of our Lord and of his Christ, and he will reign for ever and ever."[42] The Church of Jesus Christ stands as an island of stability in a sea of relativity. The gospel is the supernatural glue that holds us together as individuals, communities, and as a culture. Without that glue, we are a fragmented people, groping in the darkness for identity, meaning, and purpose. In Tolkien's trilogy, "*The Lord of the Rings*," the hobbit Frodo and his companions must brave a treacherous journey to Mordor. Repeatedly they encounter demonic forces determined to annihilate them. At one stage of their journey they are especially worn-down, almost to the point of despair. But in that desperate moment, the hobbits come to a remarkable place called "Rivendell"— the "Last Homely Home east of the Sea."[43] Tolkien describes this haven of rest and renewal as "a perfect house whether you like food or sleep or storytelling or singing, or just sitting and thinking best, or a pleasant mixture of them all. Merely to be there was a cure for weariness, fear, and sadness."[44] Our journey into the future is forbidding; the forces of evil appear ominous. But let us not forget *the church*—our haven of rest and renewal— for it is "the Last Homely Home this side of the [Jordan]."

Christ's Church is a *hoping* and a *waiting* community. From the very inception of his preaching, Jesus gave hope to the hopeless with assertions like this: "Blessed are those who mourn . . . *they will* be comforted."[45] Did Mary, on that first Easter morning, contemplate such reassuring words as she came to the tomb only to find the stone rolled away? Inquired the angelic messenger: "Why do you look for the living among the dead?"[46] Then were spoken the seven words that forever transformed the universe: "He is not here; he is risen!"[47] Insisted Paul, "And if Christ has not been raised, your faith is futile; you are still in your sins. Then those who have fallen asleep in Christ are lost. If only for this life we have hope in Christ, we are to be pitied more than all men."[48] If womb to tomb is the sum of it, the word for this day and every day is *gloom*! However Paul would have none of that: "But Christ has indeed been raised from the dead, the firstfruits of those who have fallen asleep."[49] Hope, life-giving hope! Let us drink it in like persons stumbling upon a fresh-water spring after days wandering in the desert. Declares Jurgen Moltman,

> We are called to hope! Let us go forth from our anxieties and learn to hope from the Bible. Let us reach out beyond our limitations in order to find a future in a new beginning. Let us take no more account of barriers, but only the one who broke the barriers down. He is risen. Christ is risen indeed. He is our future. [50]

Above all else, the church of the postmodern era must be a *community of hope*. According to Desmond Tutu of South Africa, to be a part of this body is to believe that,

> Goodness is stronger than evil,
> Love is stronger than hate,
> Light is stronger than darkness,
> Life is stronger than death.

Victory is ours
Through Him who loved us.[51]

As the people of God, we hope; but we also *wait*; we are a people stranded between the "already" and the "not yet." Writes Buttrick, " . . . we live in the momentum of a denouement when the prose of everyday is shot though with a poetry of consummation. The hermeneutic of Christian preaching is social and eschatological."[52] God's people have their own unique mode of waiting for the *eschaton*; it is not like standing in line at the bank or grocery store. Rather, our expectancy resembles a child on the night before Christmas, or a young couple the day before their wedding; we tremble with confident expectation. In one sense, "to be on your way is to be home";[53] eternal life *has already begun* for those of us who have claimed Jesus as Lord. Yet, we *hopefully* wait; we *creatively anticipate* the day when "every knee should bow, in heaven and on earth and under the earth, and every tongue confess that Jesus Christ is Lord, to the glory of God the Father."[54] It will happen: "For the Lord himself will come down from heaven, with a loud command, with the voice of an archangel and with the trumpet call of God, and the dead in Christ will rise first."[55] Each day we stand poised, our ears cocked for the distant sound of the trumpet and the flutter of angel's wings, awaiting our Returning Lord. In his classic book on the life of Christ, Malcolm Muggeridge recorded: "The world is always ending, Jesus is always coming, we are forever in transit—on our way to a destination which, like Augustine's City of God, is beyond our reach but within our comprehension."[56] To the forces of darkness that threaten to overwhelm us we declare: "Bring on the darkness and we will bring on the Son!" Until then, we live and pray and preach as a *people of hope*. With Paul we triumphantly shout: "But thanks be to God! He gives us the victory through our Lord Jesus Christ."[57]

ENDNOTES

Prologue: Looking Back On Sunday's Sermon

1. *The Creative Years*, (New York: The Seabury Press, 1959) p. 128,129.

2. Ibid.

3. Eph. 5:21.

4. All Scripture quotations, unless otherwise noted, will be taken from *The Holy Bible, New International Version* (North American Edition), copyright 1973, 1978, 1984 by the International Bible Society.

5. Phil. 2:7.

6. Phil. 2:8.

7. Eph. 5:25.

8. These comments were made in 1976 at the "Continental Congress on the Family" held in St. Louis, Missouri.

9. This, of course, is an assumption. But, as shall be demonstrated throughout this volume, it is an assumption grounded in the nature of human nature.

10. David M. Greenhaw says it well: "Transformation will take place only when the congregation takes up the interpretive work themselves, when they speak the gospel into their own lives." See *Intersections: Postcritical Studies in Preaching*, edited by Richard L. Eslinger (Grand Rapids, Michigan: William B. Eerdmans Publishing Company, 1994), p. 121.

11. Sometimes, of course, the sermon triggers their reflection, but they don't tell their story to the preacher. They may share their reflection with a mate, a child, or a friend; or they may simply ruminate within themselves. So long as the sermon serves as the catalyst, it has achieved its objective. The preacher's sermon, if successful, evokes something deep within the listener that causes him or her to process the Gospel through his or her life. I call this "the second sermon."

Chapter 1 – Creative Anticipation

1. Robert Coles, *The Call of Stories* (Boston: Houghton Mifflin Company, 1989), pp. 35,36.

2. Quoted by Leland Ryken in *How to Read the Bible As Literature* (Grand Rapids, Michigan: Academie Books, 1984), p. 42.

3. Amos Wilder, *The Bible And The Literary Critic* (Minneapolis: Fortress Press, 1991), p. 134.

4. Ibid.

5. Ibid.

6. Ibid.

7. Ibid.

8. Ibid. , p. 144.

9. Richard Ward, *Speaking from the Heart* (Nashville: Abingdon, 1992), p.60.

10. Amos Wilder: ". . . the imagination has its seductions and the heart its idols" (*Literary Critic*, p.147).

11. Some authors make a distinction between "story" and "narrative." For my purposes, I'm making no such distinction.

12. Pat Conroy, *The Prince of Tides* (New York: Bantam Books, 1986), p. 167.

13. I do not regret this emphasis; I think it laid a good foundation for my preaching and teaching responsibilities.

14. This image is common in homiletical literature, but I am uncertain of the origin.

15. "The Narrative Quality of Experience as a Bridge to Preaching," *Preaching* (September-October, 1990), p. 18. This article is a reprint from *Journeys Toward Narrative Preaching* (Pilgrim Press, 1990).

16. Donald M. Wardlaw makes this observation concerning James Broadus. See *Preaching Biblically*, ed. by Donald Wardlaw (Philadelphia: The Westminster Press, 1983), pp. 14,15.

17. *A Captive Voice: The Liberation of Preaching* (Louisville, KY: Westminster/ John Knox Press, 1994), p. 83.

18. Thomas Long in *Preaching Biblically*, ed. by Donald Wardlaw (Philadelphia: The Westminster Press, 1983), p. 87.

19. Eugene Lowry, *How To Preach A Parable* (Nashville: Abingdon, 1989), p.25.

20. Ibid.

21. Even as I acknowledge the viability of sermons that have narrative form but

no story or stories, I must say that I believe any sermon could be improved with the use of narrative.

22. For a more detailed discussion of the uses of "narrative," see John S. McClure, "Narrative and Preaching: Sorting It All Out", *Journal for Preachers* 15, 1 (Advent 1991), pp. 24-25.

23. 1 Cor. 1:21.

24. 1 Cor. 1:24.

25. Morris J. Niedenthal, Charles L. Rice, and Edmund A. Steimle, *Preaching the Story* (Philadelphia: Fortress Press, 1980), p. 133, 134

26. For an excellent analysis of the postmodern world, see: *Postmodern Theology: Christian Faith in a Pluralist World* (San Francisco: HarperSanFrancisco, 1989), pp. ix-xvi.

27. *A Relevant Word: Communicating the Gospel to Seekers* (Valley Forge: Judson Press, 1995), p. 34.

28. Robert Stephen Reid, "Postmodernism And the Function of the New Homiletic in Post-Christendom Congregations," *Homiletic* XX, 2 (Winter 1995), p. 5. (Hereafter, PNH)

29. "How the World Lost Its Story," *First Things* 36 (October 1993), p. 21. (Hereafter, HWS)

30. Ibid., p. 22.

31. Writes Steimle, "The biblical story, like any story, has a beginning, a middle (and that's where we are right now), and an end. But the end of the story is safely in God's hands" (*Preaching the Story*, p. 138).

32. Fee and Stuart claim that understanding this tension between the "already" and the "not yet" is the primary hermeneutical key to understanding much of the New Testament. See Gordon Fee and Douglas Stuart, *How To Read the Bible For All Its Worth* (Grand Rapids, Michigan: Academie Books, 1982), pp. 120, 121. Quote on p. 133.

33. *Preaching the Story*, p. 120.

34. John 14:16-18; Eph. 1:13,14.

35. Acts 1:11.

36. 2 Tim. 4:8.

37. Eph. 6:16.

38. *Speaking from the Heart*, p. 59.

39. I am not here justifying sin: "Shall we go on sinning so that grace may increase? By no means!" (Rom. 6:1). Nor am I suggesting that gross sins like adultery are common in minister's lives. Rather, I am simply reflecting the ups and downs of our spiritual pilgrimage.

40. This distinction comes from Richard Jensen in his book, *Telling the Story* (Minneapolis: Augsburg Publishing House, 1980), pp. 131, 132. Jensen draws on the work of John Dominic Crossan who says that "metaphors of illustration" are dispensable; once people have gotten the point they gradu-

ate from "illustration to information." On the other hand, metaphors of participation differ "for they are indispensable!"

41. Merril Abbey, *Living Doctrine in a Vital Pulpit*, (Nashville: Abingdon Press, 1964), p.54.

42. "Risking Education," *The Teaching Professor* (January, 1992), p. 1.

43. Mark Twain, *The Adventures of Tom Sawyer* (Chicago: The Spencer Press, Inc., 1953), p. 40.

44. Quoted by Batsell Barrett Baxter, editor, *The Heart of the Yale Lectures* (New York: The Macmillan Company, 1954), pp. 145,146.

Chapter 2 – Releasing the Word

1. Barbara Michaels, *Greygallows* (New York: Berkley Books, 1972), pp. 154,156.

2. 1 Cor. 9:22b.

3. "Accommodation to Secular Norms in Preaching," *Homiletic* XIX, No. 2 (Winter 1994), p. 3.

4. Donald K. Smith, *Creating Understanding: A Handbook For Communication Across Cultural Landscapes* (Grand Rapids, Michigan: Zondervan Publishing House, 1992), p. 47.

5. Horton Davies is here quoting Inge. See *Varieties of English Preaching 1900-1960* (Enlewood Cliffs, New Jersey: Printice-Hall, Inc., 1963), p. 81.

6. Martin F. Camroux reflects on Fosdick's metaphor in "Liberalism Preached: Harry Emerson Fosdick," *The Expository Times* 106, no. 2 (November 1994), pp. 44-47.

7. *Lectures on Preaching* (New York: W. P. Dutton and Company, 1877), p. 5.

8. Ibid.

9. "The Heart of Art," *Eternity* (March 1985), p. 24.

10. *Preaching and the Literary Forms of the Bible* (Philadelphia: Fortress Press, 1989), p. 33.

11. Richard Lischer, "The Limits of Story," *Interpretation* 38, no. 1 (January 1984). (Hereafter, TLS).

12. Ibid., p. 26.

13. Ibid., pp. 35,36.

14. Ibid., p. 30. Lischer writes: "Some theologians and preachers have adopted these assessments and promptly redefined their respective disciplines as modes of storytelling, without, however, giving due attention to the ways in which story falsifies those vast and deep non-narrative domains of human life."

15. Ralph and Gregg Lewis have an excellent chapter on "inductive-deduc-

tive" sermons. See *Inductive_Preaching: Helping People Listen* (Westchester, Illinois: Crossway Books: 1983), pp. 102-120.

16. *Integrative Preaching* (Nashville: Abingdon Press, 1981), p. 27.

17. Fred Craddock, *Overhearing the Gospel* (Nashville: Abingdon, 1978), p. 9.

18. Ibid. Craddock bases his book around these words by the Danish theologian, Soren Kieregaard: "There is no lack of information in a Christian land; something else is lacking, and this is something which one man cannot communicate to the other (p. 9)."

19. Ibid., p.122.

20. Ibid.

21. Matt 23:15.

22. Cadoux is quoted by William Barclay, *And Jesus Said: A Handbook on the Parables of Jesus* (Philadelphia: The Westminster Press, 1970), p. 14.

23. 2 Sam. 12:1-13.

24. 2 Sam. 12:5.

25. 2 Samuel 12:7

26. *Overhearing*, p. 125.

27. The best description and analysis I have seen of this type problem comes from J. Randall Nichols in *Building the Word* (San Francisco: Harper & Row Publishers, 1980), pp. 58-75. Nichols imagines a hypothetical preacher whom he calls, Dr. Wordbinder: ". . . in the pulpit he becomes a theological throwback. His sermons are long, rambling, and obese with theological jargon. His style is alternately aggressive and whining; his illustrations reinforce the most banal pietism of oversimplification" (p. 60).

28. Helmut Thielicke, *The Trouble With The Church*, (New York: Harper & Row, Publishers, 1965), pp. 3-19.

29. Ibid., p.16.

30. Ibid., p. 3.

31. Richard Jensen, *Thinking In Story*, (Lima, Ohio: C. S. S. Publishing Co., Inc., 1993), p.110.

32. *Integrative Preaching*, p. 20.

33. Heb. 4:12.

34. James Daane, *Preaching With Confidence* (Grand Rapids, Michigan: Eerdmans Publishing Company, 1980), p. 29.

35. Eugene Peterson, *Working the Angels* (Grand Rapids, Michigan: William B. Eerdmans Publishing Company, 1987), p. 78.

36. Ibid.

37. Fran Ferder, *Words Made Flesh* (Notre Dame, Indiana: Ave Maria Press, 1986) p. 112.

38. Ibid.

39. At the same time, Dan McCartney and Charles Clayton remind us of the hermeneutical danger in making too much of the word *dabar*. See *Let the Reader Understand: A Guide To Interpreting And Applying The Bible* (Wheaton, Illinois: BridgePoint Books, 1994), p. 115.

40. Gen. 27:1-46.

41. Ferder, *Words Made Flesh*, p. 112.

42. This high view of words in the tradition of the Jews carried over into their religion. Amos Wilder writes, "The primitive man does not first see an object and then give it a name. Rather in naming it he calls it into being. Hence the enormous role in such societies of the oracle, the spell, the curse, the blessing." See *Early Christian Rhetoric* (Cambridge, Massachusetts: Harvard University Press, 1976), p. 6.

43. Isa. 55:10,11.

44. Rom. 6:5.

45. Rom. 6:6.

46. Buttrick writes: "Thus, Christian preaching can transform narrative identity. By locating our storied lives within the framework of beginning and end, Christian preaching poses the possibility of faith. We sense that our life stories may be related to the purposes of God that span human history; we may be living in some sort of God-with-us story." *Homiletic: Moves And Structures* (Philadelphia: Fortress Press, 1987), p. 13.

47. *Creative Preaching: Finding the Words* (Nashville: Abingdon, 1980), pp. 37,38.

48. Ibid., p. 38.

49. Henry Mitchell, *Celebration and Experience in Preaching* (Nashville: Abingdon, 1990), p. 36.

Chapter 3 – Narrative and "Inner Appropriation"

1. Thomas Moore, *Care of the Soul* (New York: Harper Collins Publishers, 1992), p. 35.

2. "In Pursuit of Character," *Christianity Today*, 11 December 1995, p. 34. (Hereafter, POC.)

3. "The Narrative Quality of Experience," *Journal of the American Academy of Religion* 39, no. 3 (September 1971), p. 291. (Hereafter, NQE.)

4. Ibid., p. 294.

5. *Storytelling Imagination and Faith* (Mystic, Connecticut: Twenty-Third Publications, 1984), p. 33.

6. *A Room Called Remember* (San Francisco: Harper & Row, Publishers, 1984), p. 166.

7. Ibid.

8. *The Wounded Healer* (Garden City, New York: Image Books, 1979), p. 38.

9. Ibid.

10. *Preaching Biblically*, p.103.

11. *The Bible in the Pulpit* (Nashville: Abingdon, 1978), p.62.

12. "An Address Delivered Before the Senior Class in Divinity College, Cambridge, Sunday Evening, July 15, 1838," in *Complete Works of Ralph Waldo Emerson*, 12 vols. (Boston: Houghton Mifflin Co., 1903-4), 1:127-151.

13. Chevis Horne, *Crisis in the Pulpit* (Grand Rapids, Michigan: Baker Book House, 1975), p. 39.

14. *Preaching the Story*, p. 23.

15. Rice, *Preaching Biblically*, p. 104.

16. *A Room Called Remember*, p. 53.

17. John Shea, "Storytelling and Religious Identity," *Chicago Studies* 21, no. 1, (Spring 1982) pp. 23-43. (Hereafter, SRI.)

18. Ibid., p. 27.

19. Ibid.

20. Donald English, *An Evangelical Theology of Preaching* (Nashville: Abingdon Press, 1996), p. 17.

21. Ibid., 17,18.

22. SRI., p. 27.

23. *Care of the Soul*, p. 13.

24. SRI, p. 28.

25. *The Wounded Healer*, p. 39.

26. *Celebration and Experience*, p. 40.

27. *The Bible, p. 62.*

28. *Preaching Biblically*, p. 103.

29. SRI, p. 27.

30. Ibid. John Shea says it in this manner: "We re-experience in diminished form the feelings and insights of the event [itself]."

31. J. Howard Grant, *Creativity in Preaching* (Grand Rapids, Michigan: Zondervan Publishing House, 1987), p. 12.

32. *Imagining a Sermon* (Nashville: Abingdon Press, 1990), p. 97.

33. *The Waiting Father* (New York: Harper & Row, Publishers, 1957), pp. 61-70.

34. Matt. 13:31,32.

35. *The Waiting Father*, p. 62.

36. Matt. 28:18.

37. *The Waiting Father*, p. 62

38. Ibid.

39. Hebrews 2:17.

40. Walter Wangerin, Jr., "Flying in the Night Wind," *Christianity Today*, 9 April 1990, pp. 23-26. This material is a recasting of Wangerin's chapter in *The Classics We've Read, The Difference They've Made*, edited by Philip Yancey (New York: McCraken Press, 1993).

41. Ibid., p. 24.

42. Ibid., p. 23.

43. Ibid.

44. *Imagining a Sermon*, p. 89.

45. *Doing Time In The Pulpit: The Relationship Between Narrative And Preaching* (Nashville: Abingdon Press, 1985), p. 19.

46. Buttrick, *A Captive Voice*, pp. 82, 83.

47. "Catching Hope," *The Living Pulpit* (January to March 1992), p. 9.

Chapter 4 – The Nuances of Narrative

1. This statement was quoted by David Weber at a meeting of the Speech Communication Association held in San Antonio, Texas (fall, 1995). I could not locate the volume from which the quote came.

2. For an excellent discussion of the distinction between the "right brain" and the "left brain" see: Betty Edwards, *Drawing on the Artist Within: An inspirational guide to increasing your creative powers* (New York: Simon & Schuster, 1986).

3. *Thinking In Story: Preaching In A Post-literate Age (Lima, Ohio: C.S.S. Publishing Co., Inc., 1993)*, p.109.

4. Ibid., p.29.

5. While it's true that there are millions of "readers" in western culture, there are also millions who disdain books and opt for television and movies for their interaction with the world. I think this will be all the more true as we move into a postmodern world.

6. *Thinking In Story.*, p. 114.

7. *The Classics We've Read, The Difference They've Made*, edited by Philip Yancey (New York: McCraken Press, 1993), pp. 97,98.

8. Ibid., p. 98.

9. Ibid., p. 97.

10. Marsh Cassady, *Creating Stories For Storytelling* (San Jose, California: Resource Publications, Inc., 1991), p. 58.

11. *Bible as Literature*, p. 40.

12. Ibid., p. 39ff.

13. Tremper Longman III, *Literary Approaches To Biblical Interpretation* (Grand Rapids: Academie Books, 1987), p. 93.

14. *Creating Stories For Storytelling*, pp. 26-50.

15. *Writing Fiction,* (Englewood Cliffs, New Jersey: Printice-Hall, Inc., 1975), p. 29.

16. Writers like Charles Dickens, Jane Austin, or Anthony Trollope employed much character description, which often carried on for many pages. Modern authors, for the most part, are much less interested in extensive detail. They want simply to create impressions and let the reader's imagination do the rest.

17. *Bible as Literature*, p. 44.

18. *The Literary Critic*, p. 144.

19. Ibid.

20. Ibid.

21. *Bible as Literature*, p. 34.

22. *Storytelling & The Art of Imagination* (Rockport, Massachusetts: Element, 1992), pp. 38-67.

23. Mellon has some creative exercises for experimenting with different settings, though they are more suited for storytelling than preaching. For example, "Create an imaginary mountain that you would truly like to visit. What is its dominant color? Who and/or what inhabits this place? How do you get there? What treasure is held there? Cast this mountain into a story. In front of the mountain, imagine two or three giants or other guards who must be outwitted or understood in order to make safe passage to the heights and depths of your mountain possible (*Storytelling*, p. 41)."

24. I find Wilder's observation at this point very interesting: "Even in fables and fictions . . . we can recognize a common impulse. Human nature is prompted to probe, to extrapolate on all its horizons, backward and forward without and within. This also serves orientation. This also is a kind of charting of the way. Is it too far fetched to think of the internalized memory which guides the flight patterns of migratory birds? If indeed much of this story is imaginative and fabulous, we should not reproach it for departing from

actuality and realism. We should rather recognize that daily life is itself mysterious and dynamic" (*The Literary Critic*, p. 138).

25. *Storytelling Imagination and Faith* (Mystic, Connecticut: Twenty-Third Publications, 1986), p. 58.

26. Stanley Hauerwas analyzes *Watership Down* as a "A Story-Formed Community." See *A Community of Character: Toward A Constructive Christian Social Ethic* (Notre Dame: University of Notre Dame Press, 1981), pp. 9-35.

27. *Creating Stories*, pp. 55, 56.

28. Ibid., p. 56.

29. As retold by Lillian Hammer Ross in *Highlights For Children*, March 1989, p. 7.

30. *The Literary Critic*, p. 138.

31. *Storytelling*, p. 58.

32. *Doing Time*, p. 59.

33. *Literary Approaches*, p. 87.

34. Ibid.

35. Longman observes that most narrative in Scripture is told from a third-person perspective (*Literary Approaches*, p. 86).

36. *Literary Approaches*, p. 86.

37. Ibid., pp. 85,86.

38. Longman quotes Rhoads and Michie: "When the narrator is omniscient and invisible, readers tend to be unaware of the narrator's biases, values, and conceptual view of the world." Rhodes and Michie, *Mark as Story*, p. 36, as quoted by Longman in *Literary Approaches*, p. 86.

39. (Brea, California: Educational Ministries, Inc., 1990.), pp. 29,30. Ward credits this story to Theophane the Monk, *Tales of a Magic Monastery* (Crossroad, New York, 1989).

40. *Telling Your Own Stories* (Little Rock, Arkansas: August House Publishers, Inc., 1993), p. 20.

41. Ibid.

42. Ibid.

43. Lowry, *Doing Time*, p. 38.

44. *Telling the Story*, pp. 131,132.

45. This is a paraphrase of Walter Wangerin. See Chapter 3, p. 64.

46. *on Knowing: essays for the left hand* (Cambridge, Massachusetts: Harvard University Press, 1962), p. 18.

47. *Ibid.*

48. *Storytelling in Preaching*, p. 42.

Chapter 5 – The Question, The Quest, and The Discovery

1. George Eliot, *Amos Barton* (Stamford, CT: Longmeadow Press, 1990), p. 800.

2. Robert Reid, Jeffery Bullock, David Fleer, "Preaching As the Creation of An Experience: The not-so-Rational Revolution of the New Homiletic," *The Journal of Communication and Religion* 18, 1 (March 1995), p. 6. (Hereafter, PCE.)

3. SRI, p. 38.

4. *Manual On Preaching: A New Process of Sermon Development* (Valley, PA: Judson Press, 1977), p. 73.

5. SRI, p. 38.

6. Taylor is using the language of Kyle Haselden at this point. See *Preaching Biblically: Creating Sermons in the Shape of Scripture*, edited by Donald Wardlaw (Philadelphia: The John Press, 1983), p.141,142.

7. Ibid., p.142.

8. *Design For Preaching* (Philadelphia: Fortress Press, 1958), p. 5.

9. Ibid., p. 4.

10. Ibid.

11. *Preaching: The Art of Connecting People* (Waco, Texas: Word Books Publisher, 1985), p. 93,94.

12. Ibid.

13. Ibid.

14. Ibid.

15. Ibid.

16. *Manual On Preaching*, p. 51,52.

17. *Preach A Parable*, p. 35.

18. *Helping People Listen*, p. 83.

19. *Brain Power* (Englewood Cliffs, New Jersey: Prentice-Hall, Inc., 1980), p. 153.

20. Ibid.

21. *The Homiletical Plot: The Sermon As Narrative Art Form* (Atlanta: John Knox Press, 1975), p. 38.

22. *Preaching the Creative Gospel Creatively* (St. Louis: Concordia Publishing House, 1983), p. 52.

23. Ibid., p. 51.

24. *Thinking in Story*, p. 111.

25. Ibid.

26. *Preach A Parable*, p.33.

27. I'm not suggesting that the preacher is *never* an explainer; that would be foolish. But in the beginning stages of preparing a narrative sermon the preacher is primarily an *investigator*.

28. "The Rediscovery of Biblical Narrative," *Chicago Studies*, 21, no. 1, (Spring 1982), p. 57. (Hereafter, RBN.)

29. 1 Thess. 4:13 (KJV).

30. 1 Cor 13:12.

31. *Preaching*, p. 99.

32. *Telling the Story*, pp. 130,131.

33. Ibid., pp. 131,132.

34. *The Literary Critic*, p. 134.

35. Eph. 6:12.

36. *The Homiletical Plot*, p. 42.

37. *Preaching Biblically*, p. 88.

38. Rev. 5:5.

39. *The Classics We've Read*, p. 43.

40. This isn't to say that narrative sermons are simply art. They partake of characteristics of art but, in my judgment, they go beyond that. They communicate not only Goodness, Beauty and Truth, but also the Source of these virtues; they are, in every sense, a High Quest.

41. *The Green Journey* (New York: Ballantine, 1986), p. 106.

42. Ibid.

43. Ibid.

44. Ibid.

45. *The Homiletical Plot*, p. 48.

46. Ibid.

47. Acts 9:4.

48. *Preaching Biblically*, p. 88.

49. 1 Cor. 2:4,5.

50. *Thinking In Story*, p. 113.

51. 2 Samuel 12:1-14.

52. *A Song of Accents* (Nashville: Abingdon Press, 1968), p. 66.

Chapter 6 – Text and Sermon

1. Bob Benson, *"See you at the house"* (Nashville: Generoux Nelson, 1989), p. 104.

2. McCartney and Clayton define a "determinate meaning" as "a knowable true meaning outside of ourselves . . ., a universally valid standard of meaning toward which we must strive." See Dan McCartney and Charles Clayton, *Let the Reader Understand: A Guide To Interpreting And Applying The Bible* (Wheaton, Illinois: Victor Books, 1994), p. 31.

3. Ibid., p. 138.

4. Ibid.

5. *Preaching Biblically*, pp. 160,161.

6. *The Bible in the Pulpit*, p. 58.

7. *Finally Comes The Poet: Daring Speech For Proclamation*, (Minneapolis: Fortress Press, 1989), p. 2.

8. *Overhearing the Gospel*, p. 26.

9. Ibid.

10. Quoted by Ernest Kurtz and Katherine Ketcham in *The Spirituality of Imperfection: Storytelling and the Journey to Wholeness*, (New York: Bantam Books, 1992), p. 142.

11. Ibid.

12. James Earl Massey, *Designing the Sermon: Order and Movement in Preaching* (Nashville: Abingdon Press, 1980), p. 45.

13. Ibid.

14. "What We Mean When We Say It's True," *Christianity Today,* 23 October 1995, pp. 18,19.

15. *Let the Reader Understand*, p. 273.

16. *The Bible in the Pulpit*, p. 55.

17. Ibid., p. 53ff.

18. Ibid., pp. 61,62.

19. Ibid., p. 57.

20. Ibid., p. 59.

21. Ibid., p. 63.

22. Ibid.

23. Ibid. Writes Keck, "The vicarious listener knows what these responses are likely to be when he has genuine solidarity with the people, on the one hand, and when he is in sufficient touch with his humanity to be able to extrapolate from his own response, on the other."

24. Ibid., p. 61.

25. Discussed by Eugene Lowry in, "The Revolution of Sermonic Shape," *Listening to the Word* (Nashville: Abingdon Press, 1993), p. 108.

26. *The Bible in the Pulpit*, p. 63.

27. *For All Its Worth*, p. 13.

28. *The Bible in the Pulpit*, p. 67.

29. Ibid., p. 63.

30. Walter Brueggemann writes, "When we embrace ideology uncritically, it is assumed that the Bible squares easily with capitalist ideology, or narcissistic psychology, or revolutionary politics, or conformist morality, or romantic liberalism." See, *Finally Comes The Poet,* p. 2.

31. 2 Timothy 4:2.

32. *Finally Comes The Poet*, p. 4.

33. Ibid.

34. Jer. 20:9.

35. *Literary Approaches*, p. 76.

36. *The Modern Preacher and the Ancient Text* (Grand Rapids: Inter-Varsity Press, 1988), p. 21-23.

37. Ibid.

38. *Literary Approaches*, p. 78.

39. Ibid., p. 81.

40. *Preaching Biblically*, p. 32.

41. Fred B. Craddock, *As One Without Authority* (Nashville: Abingdon, third edition, 1979; first edition, 1971), p. 163.

42. Writes Craddock: "Why should the multitude of forms and moods within biblical literature. . . be brought together in one unvarying mold, and that copied from Greek rhetoricians of centuries ago?" See *As One Without Authority*, p. 143).

43. *The Modern Preacher*, p.18.

44. Ibid., p. 19.

45. *Literary Forms*, p. 127.

46. *How to Preach a Parable*, p. 38.

47. Ibid.

48. Lowry, *Listening to the Word*, p.107.

49. *And Jesus Said: A Handbook on the Parables of Jesus* (Philadelphia: The Westminster Press, 1970), p. 15.

50. *Bible As Literature*, 140.

51. *Walking Shadow* (New York: Berkley Books, 1994), p. 13.

52. *How to Preach a Parable*, p. 21.

53. *And Jesus Said*, p. 16.

54. Luke 18:9.

55. I am aware of the fact that Christians have not always been fair and objective in their critique of first century Judaism, including our assessment of the religious leaders. In Matthew 23:23-24, we have these words of Jesus: "Woe to you, teachers of the law and Pharisees, you hypocrites! You give a tenth of your spices—mint, dill and cummin. But you have neglected matters of the law—justice, mercy and faithfulness. You should have practiced the latter, without neglecting the former. You blind guides! You strain out a gnat but swallow a camel." Obviously, there were some religious leaders who were accurately characterized by Jesus' words. However, the condemnation must not be viewed as universal; Judaism during this period had not deteriorated entirely into a religion of trivia and abuse. See, for example, a study of early Judaistic literature by E. P. Sanders. I quote: "The possibility cannot be completely excluded that there were Jews accurately hit by the polemic of Matt. 23, who attended only to trivia and neglected the weightier matters. Human nature being what it is, one supposes that there were some such. One must say, however, that the surviving Jewish literature does not reveal them." See E.P. Sanders, *Paul and Palestinian Judaism: A Comparison of Patterns of Religion* (Philadelphia: Fortress Press, 1977), p. 426ff

56. *Literary Approaches*, p.97.

57. Ray Summers, *Commentary on Luke* (Waco, Texas: Word Books, 1972), p. 208.

58. *How To Be A Christian Without Being Religious*, edited by Fritz Ridenour (Glendale, California: Regal Books, 1962), "Introduction."

59. *Commentary on Luke*, p. 208.

60. *Bible As Literature*, p. 144.

61. Ibid., p. 145.

Chapter 7 – Sustaining the Narrative

1. Workman is quoting a presumed "Preacher Test." See *Fireflies In A Fruit Jar* (Little Rock, Arkansas: August House Publishers, 1988), p. 89.

2. *How To Preach a Parable*, p. 25.

3. *Listening to the Word*, p.107.

4. *Storytelling in Preaching: A Guide To the Theory and Practice* (Nashville: Broadman Press, 1988), p. 43.

5. *The Modern Preacher*, p. 19.

6. *Literary Forms*, p.127.

7. Ibid.

8. Richard Eslinger makes this comment in summarizing the homiletical thought of David Buttrick. See *A New Hearing: Living Options in Homiletic Method* (Nashville: Abingdon Press,1987), p. 144.

9. Ibid., p. 143.

10. The version of this story which I first encountered was in *The Spirituality of Imperfection* by Ernest Kurtz and Katherine Ketcham (New York: Bantam Books, 1992), p. 119. They give a brief history of the story (p. 266) and credit Nikos Kazantzakis with one version. See *The Greek Passion* (New York: Paulist Press, 1988), p. 229.

11. *Telling Your Own Stories*, p. 16.

12. Matt. 25:40,45.

13. SRI, p. 41.

14. *Thinking in Story*, p. 115.

15. Ibid.

16. Ibid.

17. SRI, p. 41.

18. John 3:8.

19. Amy McRary, *The Knoxville News-Sentinel* (Knoxville, TN: August 24, 1995).

20. Ibid.

Chapter 8 – Supplementing the Narrative

1. Garrison Keillor, *Lake Wobegon Days* (New York: Penguin Books, 1985), p. 63,64.

2. TLS, p. 31.

3. *Preaching*, p. 196.

4. *Celebration & Experience,* p. 39.

5. Ibid., p. 38.

6. Ibid., p. 46.

7. Ibid.

8. Gen. 22:2.

9. Gen. 12:2.

10. *Bible As Literature*, p. 42.

11. "Words From God's Heart," *Christianity Today*, 23 October 1995, p. 26.

12. While using the language of H.G. Gadamer (*Truth and Method*), I am not recommending Gadamer's hermeneutical theories. I use "fusing the horizons" as these words are defined by Dan McCartney and Charles Clayton: "the meaning of a text for today is a matter of taking the author's linguistic and historical situation (his or her 'horizon'), and then seeing that the interpretive result from the standpoint of the present 'horizon of understanding' . . . ." *Let the Reader Understand*, p. 280.

13. Gen. 22:1.

14. Gen. 12:2.

15. Gen. 16:1.

16. *Preaching Biblical Text: Expositions by Jewish and Christian Scholars,* edited by Fredrick C. Holmgren and Herman E. Schaalman (Grand Rapids, Michigan: William B. Eerdmans Publishing Company), p. 39.

17. Gen. 16:6.

18. Gen. 16:8.

19. Gen. 16:9.

20. Gen. 16:15.

21. Gen. 17:15-27.

22. Gen. 17:17.

23. Ibid.

24. Gen. 17:19.

25. Gen. 21:10.

26. Gen. 21:11.

27. God told Abraham to give-in to Sarah's wishes (21:11,12). Was this because God intended to protect Hagar and Ishmael? Some biblical scholars suggest that God agreed only as a test for Abraham—to see if he would remonstrate with Sarah over this treatment of Ishmael and his mother. Though Abraham was distressed (21:11), he did not stand-up to Sarah or refuse her wishes.

28. Gen. 21:10-14.

29. Gen. 21:15-21.

30. Ryken, *The Bible As Literature*, p. 49.

31. Gen. 12:13; 20:2.

32. Gen 18:23,24.

33. *Preaching Biblical Text*, p. 40.

34. *Literary Approaches*, p. 91.

35. *Preaching Biblical Text*, p. 44.

36. Genesis 22:12.

37. Heb. 11:19.

38. Rom. 4:3.

39. Rom. 4:16.

40. *Homiletic*, p. 19.

41. Genesis 22:14.

42. Daniel March, *Night Scenes In The Bible* (Philadelphia: Zeigler, McCurdy & CO., 1869), p. 47.

43. Ibid., p.49. Similar language is used by March.

44. Ibid., p. 57.

45. Ibid.

46. *The Classics We've Read*, p. 71.

47. Ibid.

48. *How To Preach A Parable*, p. 74.

49. *Inductive Preaching*, p. 81.

50. Ibid., pp. 79-92.

51. *Preaching Biblical Text*, p. 41.

52. *How to Read the Bible*, p. 81.

53. *Celebration & Experience*, p. 31.

54. Ibid.

55. *Literary Approaches*, p. 95.

Chapter 9 – Segmenting the Narrative

1. *Lake Wobegon Days*, p. 62.

2. *Homiletical Plot*, p. 42.

3. Ibid.

4. This information is recorded by David L. Barr, *New Testament Story* (New York: Wadsworth Publishing Company, 1995), p. 7.

5. Ibid.

6. *Mr. Midshipman Easy* (New York: Penguin Books, 1982), p. 223.

7. Ibid.

8. "A Poetics of the Pulpit for Post-Modern Times," *Intersections: Post-Critical Studies in Preaching*, edited by Richard L. Eslinger (Grand Rapids, Michigan: Wm. B. Eerdmans Publishing Company, 1994), p. 47.

9. *A Survey of the New Testament* (Grand Rapids: Zondervan Publishing Company, 1970), p. 85.

10. Matt. 5:17.

11. Matt. 5:21,22.

12. *Eerdmans' Handbook To The Bible*, edited by David and Pat Alexander (Grand Rapids: Eerdmans Publishing Company, 1973), p. 474.

13. Matt. 5:18.

14. Matt. 5:17.

15. *New Testament Foundations: A Guide for Christian Students* (Grand Rapids, Michigan: Wm. B. Eerdmans Publishing Company, 1975), p. 231.

16. Matt. 15:8. The biblical writer is quoting Is. 29:13.

17. Writes Joachim Jeremias, "[We must note] the incompleteness of the Sermon on the Mount. What Jesus teaches in the sayings collected together on the Sermon on the Mount is not a complete regulation of the life of the disciples, and it is not intended to be; rather, what is here taught are symptoms, signs, examples of what it means when the kingdom of God breaks into the world which is still under sin, death, and the devil." See *The Sermon on the Mount*, (London: The Athone Press, 1961), p. 31.

18. Matt. 6:1.

19. Ibid.

20. Matt. 6:4,18.

21. Matt. 5:20.

22. Matt. 5:22.

23. Matt. 5:38.

24. *The Sermon on the Mount* (London: The Athone Press, 1961), p. 31.

25. *The New Group Therapy* (Princeton, New Jersey: D. Van Nostrand Company, Inc., 1964), pp. 66-71.

26. Ibid., p. 66.

27. Rom. 5:20,21.

28. "Preaching the Christian Faith," *Liturgy* 2, no. 3, p. 54.

29. Charlotte I. Lee, *Oral Interpretation* (Boston: Houghton Mifflin Company, 1972), p. 22.

30. William Barclay, *The Gospel of Matthew*, Vol. 1 (Philadelphia: The Westminster Press, 1956), p. 187.

31. Ibid.

32. Ibid.

33. Ibid.

34. Matt. 6:3.

35. *The Sermon On the Mount* (Grand Rapids, Michigan: Zondervan Publishing House, 1972), p. 178.

36. This story appears in anthology of stories selected by Thomas B. Costain and John Beecroft, *More Stories To Remember* (Doubleday & Company, Inc.: Garden City, New York, 1958), pp. 295-300.

37. *The Simple Life* (McClure, Phillips & Co.: New York, 1904), p. 114.

38. *Celebration & Experience,* p. 46.

39. *The Homiletical Plot,* p. 29. Lowry almost equates ambiguity with "interest." He writes, "In my view, interest is the first psychological state of ambiguity. (Advanced states of ambiguity may be fear, dread, and repression.)"

40. *Homiletic,* p. 300.

41. Ibid., p. 299.

42. Charlotte I. Lee, *Oral Readings of the Scripture* (Boston: Houghton Mifflin Company, 1974), p. 90.

43. *Oral Interpretation,* p. 21.

44. Ibid.

45. Ibid., p. 22.

46. Ibid.

47. *Creating Stories For Storytelling*, p. 46.

Chapter 10 – Sequencing the Narratives

1. *The Call of Stories*, p. 27.

2. Josephus, *Antiquities*, XVIII, 5:2.

3. Mark 6:17-19.

4. Matt. 11:2.

5. See this example from an older commentary: "Most assuredly John does not doubt that Jesus is a divine messenger." F. Godet, *Commentary on the Gospel of St. Luke*, (Edinburgh, T. & T. Clark, 1889), p. 344.

6. According to Lenski, John the Baptist was expecting Jesus to exercise immediate judgment on his enemies. John had preached of a Messiah who would come with an ax of judgment and "burn up the chaff with unquenchable fire" (Matt. 3:7-11, KJV). Lenski argues that John was not doubting Jesus as Messiah, but simply asking whether Jesus himself would judge or if someone coming later would perform that act. See R. C. H. Lenski, *The Interpretation of St. Luke's Gospel* (Columbus: The Wartburg Press, 1946), p. 404.

7. *A New Hearing*, p. 26.

8. Matt. 11:4,5.

9. *Websters Collegiate Dictionary*, tenth edition (Springfield, Massachusetts: 1993), p. 41.

10. *Thinking and Speaking: A Guide to Intelligent Oral Communication*, 5th edition (New York: Macmillan Publishing Company, 1984), p. 185.

11. Ibid., p. 186.

12. Matt. 11:5.

13. Mark 6:25-29.

14. *Brain Power*, p. 88.

15. Ibid. Albrecht mentions: " . . . *grasping* an idea, *facing* a problem, and *shooting down* a project."

16. *Celebration and Experience*, p. 45.

17. *The Bible As Literature*, p. 95.

18. Ibid., p. 95.

19. *Intersections: Post-critical Studies*, p. 122.

20. *Celebration and Experience*, p. 44.

21. Ibid.

22. Ibid.

23. *Intersections: Post-critical Studies*, p. 59.

24. 2 Cor. 4:5.

25. Gary Hamilton, "Someday, somebody like me will clean it again," *The Knoxville Journal*, July 19, 1985.

26. *Antiquities*, XVIII, 5:2.

27. Alexander V. G. Allen, *Phillips Brooks: Memories Of His Life With Extracts From His Letters And Note-Books* (New York: E. P. Dutton & Co., Inc. Publishers, 1907), p. 39.

28. *The Bible and the Literary Critic*, p. 139.

29. *Intersections: Post-critical Studies*, p. 116.

30. Karl Albrecht gives this example of a misleading metaphor: A man says, "Look—life is a game. There are winners and losers. If you get more chips than the other guy, you win. If he gets the chips, you lose. Its as simple as that. I play to win." But what, suggests Albrecht if life *is not* like a game? See *Brain Power*, p. 174

31. *Narrative Imagination: Preaching the Worlds That Shape Us* (Minneapolis: Fortress Press, 1995), p. 14.

32. Ibid., p. 14.

33. *Intersections: Post-critical Studies*, p. 116.

34. Ibid.

35. Ibid.

36. Ibid., p. 120.

Chapter 11 – Suspending the Narrative

1. Elaine Ward, *The Art of Storytelling* (Brea, California: Educational Ministries, Inc., 1990), p. 35.

2. Lily Owens, editor, *The Complete Brothers Grimm Fairy Tales,* (New York: Avenue Books, 1981), p. 658.

3. Ibid.

4. *Storytelling in Preaching*, p. 42.

5. Ibid., p. 41.

6. *How to Preach a Parable*, p. 39.

7. Ibid.

8. Ibid.

9. Ibid., p. 39. Lowry describes "suspension" as a "flashback, a flash-for-ward, or a flash-out" in which the preacher momentarily leaves the story and then returns to it once the obstacle has been dealt with."

10. Chapter 4, p. 73.

11. Quoted in Chapter 4, p. 73. From: *Writing Fiction*, p. 29.

12. *Homiletic*, pp. 12,13.

13. Ibid., p. 13.

14. Of course, Benjamin was the youngest of all the sons. Janzen postulates that "the narrator is establishing the character of the relations between grown sons, of whom Joseph is distinctly the youngest." See the *International Theological Commentary: Abraham and All The Families of the Earth, Chapters 12-50*, Frederick Carlson Holmgren and George A. F. Knight, General Editors (Grand Rapids: Wm. B. Eerdmans Publishing Co., 1993), p. 149.

15. Gen. 37:3.

16. Ibid.

17. Gen. 37:5-11.

18. Gordon J. Wenham, *Word Biblical Commentary: Genesis 16-50*, John D. W. Watts, Old Testament editor (Dallas, Texas: Word Books, Publisher, 1994), Vol. 2, p. 351.

19. *International Theological Commentary*, p. 149.

20. Gen. 37:19.

21. Gen. 37:21, 31.

22. Both Ishmaelites and Midianites are mentioned in this text (Gen. 37:28). Some have said that this reflects imperfectly harmonized variants. J. Gerald Janzen suggests an alternative explanation: "But the text as it stands may imply that Judah looked around for the best price, which in the end he got from his richly laden cousins. (A fine irony: Joseph the outcast is sold into Egypt by way of outcast Ishmael)." See the *International Theological Commentary*, p. 150.

23. Genesis 37:36.

24. Robert Alter, *The Art of Biblical Narrative* (New York: Basic Books, Inc., Publishers, 1981), p. 108.

25. Gen. 39:7,12.

26. Gen. 39:9.

Endnotes

27. *The Art of Biblical Narrative*, p. 72.

28. Ibid., p. 73.

29. Gen. 39:14,15.

30. Gen. 39:20.

31. For example, much has been made of the fact that Joseph brought his father (Jacob) a "bad report against his brothers" (Gen. 37:2). J. Gerald Janzen argues that the correct interpretation of this passage indicates that Joseph was an innocent person being unfairly criticized by his brothers. Writes Janzen: "Our first picture of Joseph, then, is of an individual surrounded like Jeremiah or the innocent psalmist by those who wish him evil." See the *International Theological Commentary*, p. 148.

32. *How To Read The Bible*, p. 85.

33. Gerhard Von Rad says that Joseph represents a young man "who is trained . . . by discipline and self-control [and] radiates something edifying, a beneficent goodness." See *Genesis: A Commentary* (Philadelphia: The Westminster Press, 1961), p. 437.

34. Ibid., pp. 351, 352.

35. Ibid., p. 435 ff.

36. Prov. 3:3,4.

37. *Genesis: A Commentary*, p. 435.

38. Prov. 6:27-28; See also: Prov. 2:16; 5:3, 20; 6:24; 22:14.

39. *How to Read the Bible*, p. 86.

40. Gen. 12:2.

41. Gen. 39:3.

42. *Word Biblical Commentary*, p. 358

43. *Preaching*, p. 130.

44. Gerhard Von Rad, *Genesis: A Commentary*, p. 365.

45. POC, p. 35.

46. RBN, p. 51.

47. James 4:7.

48. *POC, p. 34.*

49. *Teach As Jesus Taught: How To Apply Jesus' Teaching Methods* (Chicago: Moody Press, 1987), p. 71.

50. Luke 20:13.

51. John 12:32.

52. John 2:19.

53. *Teach As Jesus Taught*, p. 71.

Chapter 12 – "Happily Everafter"

1. George McDonald, *The Curate's Awakening* (Minneapolis, Minnesota: Bethany House Publishers, 1985), p. 160. This work was originally published as *Thomas Wingfold, Curate* (London: Hurst and Blackett, 1876).

2. PNH, p. 5.

3. Jensen, HWS, p. 20.

4. Ibid.

5. HWS, p. 21.

6. Ibid., p. 22.

7. *A Community of Character*, p. 50.

8. *Doing Time*, p. 38.

9. POC, p. 35.

10. *Doing Time*, p. 32.

11. Ibid., p. 34.

12. POC, p. 35.

13. See footnote nine, "Prologue," p. 6.

14. *Intersections*, p. 121.

15. "Catching Hope," *The Living Pulpit*, Vol. 1, No. 1 (Jan.-March, 1992), pp. 8,9.

16. *Intersections*, p. 118.

17. Ibid., p. 120.

18. PNH, p.11.

19. Henry Mitchell, *The Living Pulpit*, p. 8.

20. 1Cor. 3:7.

21. *Creating Understanding*, p. 48.

22. Eph. 1:14.

23. Chapter 1, p. 27.

24. 1 Cor. 2:2.

25. Rom. 3:23,24.

26. "Hope as Idea and Reality," *The Living Pulpit*, Vol. 1, No. 1 (Jan.-March, 1992), pp.20,21.

27. Hauerwas, *A Community of Character*, pp. 49,50.

28. Chapter 2, p. 47.

29. Gal. 2:20.

30. Gal. 4:19.

31. Jer. 1:17-19 (NEB).

32. Matt. 28:20.

33. Eph. 4:15.

34. "Becoming Like Christ," *Christianity Today*, 5 February 1995, p. 28.

35. Matt. 9:36.

36. See Hauerwas, *A Community of Character*, p. 45.

37. *Ibid.*, p. 50.

38. Eph. 4:4-6.

39. SRI, p. 43.

40. Ibid.

41. NQE, p. 310.

42. Rev. 11:15.

43. J. R. R. Tolkien, *The Fellowship of the Ring* (New York: Ballantine Books, 1965), pp. 296,297.

44. Ibid.

45. Matt. 5:4.

46. Lk. 24:5.

47. Lk. 24:6.

48. I Cor. 15:17-19.

49. I Cor. 15:20.

50. Quoted by Joan Delaplane, "A Future Full of Hope," *The Living Pulpit* 1, no. 1(January to March 1992), p. 16.

51. *Prayers, Praises, and Thanksgivings*, edited by Sandol Stoddard (New York: Dial Books, 1992), p. 76.

52. *Homiletic*, p. 16.

53. This phrase is adapted from a poem written by Joseph Pintauro. See *Prayers, Praises, and Thanksgivings,* edited by Sandol Stoddard (New York: Dial Books, 1992), p. 76.

54. Phil. 2:10,11.

55. I Thess. 4:16.

56. Malcolm Muggeridge, *Jesus: The Man Who Lives* (New York: Harper & Row Publishers, 1975), p. 148.

57. I Cor. 15:57.